WINNER OF THE JULES AND FRANCES LANDRY AWARD FOR 2021

Walter Lynwood Fleming Lectures in Southern History

SOUTHERN JOURNEY

The Migrations of the American South, 1790–2020

EDWARD L. AYERS

Maps by Justin Madron and Nathaniel Ayers

LOUISIANA STATE UNIVERSITY PRESS

BATON ROUGE

Published with the assistance of the V. Ray Cardozier Fund

Published by Louisiana State University Press
www.lsupress.org

Manufactured in Canada
First printing

Designer: Barbara Neely Bourgoyne
Typeface: Whitman
Printer and binder: Friesens Corporation

Cover map by Justin Madron and Nathaniel Ayers

Library of Congress Cataloging-in-Publication Data
Names: Ayers, Edward L., 1953– author.
Title: Southern journey : the migrations of the American South, 1790–2020 /
  Edward L. Ayers ; maps by Justin Madron and Nathaniel Ayers.
Other titles: Walter Lynwood Fleming lectures in southern history.
Description: Baton Rouge : Louisiana State University Press, 2020. |
  Series: Walter Lynwood Fleming lectures in southern history | Includes
  bibliographical references and index.
Identifiers: LCCN 2020015157 | ISBN 978-0-8071-7301-5 (cloth)
Subjects: LCSH: Human geography—Southern States—History. | Southern
  States—Emigration and immigration—History. | Southern
  States—Emigration and immigration—Social aspects.
Classification: LCC F220.A1 A94 2020 | DDC 975—dc23
LC record available at https://lccn.loc.gov/2020015157

To my graduate students, who often showed the way

CONTENTS

HOW TO READ THIS BOOK

We are not surprised when maps show the southeastern corner of the United States standing apart in politics, religion, health, economics, and opinion. The South, after all, has differed in fundamental ways from the rest of the country since the nation's founding. That difference has been fed by constant movement, by restless journeys to, across, and from the South from the eighteenth century to the twenty-first century. The migrations of the South weave throughout American history, with indigenous, enslaved, citizen, and immigrant people moving among one another, their paths tracing patterns both bold and intricate.

Today, new migrations carve channels of their own. For the first time in the nation's history, people are choosing to move southward in large numbers, their arrival creating an American South with an unwritten and unmapped history before it. The migrations do not flow in smooth waves and currents. Instead, the movements surge and recede, rushing around seen and unseen obstacles, pushed and pulled by forces near and distant.

The maps of this book reveal the swirling patterns of the southern past as we have not seen them before. Skilled colleagues at the University of Richmond—Justin Madron and Nathaniel Ayers—have devised ways to make legible and compelling the journeys followed by people who otherwise left few marks on the historical record. The maps show clear and striking patterns, shades of copper in the places where the number of people increased, and gradations of blue where they declined. The brighter the colors, the greater the change.

They also reveal patterns that are too complex to reduce to columns and rows, too shifting and simultaneous to convey in words alone. Understanding the scale, velocity, and consequences of southern migration requires a conversation between maps and narrative, each raising questions and offering answers to the other.

Maps, like stories, require framing, selection, and purpose. We have chosen our methods with two particular goals in mind: to reveal patterns we could not see otherwise among the lives of millions of people, and to produce maps as consistent and clear as possible across more than two hundred years of American history. Toward those ends, we use small geographic units, straightforward numbers, and focused chronology. These high-resolution techniques reveal patterns invisible in methods that rely on state-level maps, artificially aggregated subregions, and formulas divorced from contexts of place and time.

Mapping census data across time presents well-known challenges, the most obvious of which are shifting boundaries. As the nation expanded and developed, states continually created new counties, divided counties, and combined counties. Such changing boundaries make it difficult to compare places from one decade to another. To avoid that problem, we have laid down a grid of small hexagons over the landscape, defining spaces more precisely than county borders and minimizing the effect of variations within each hexagon. The strategy, its details described in the technical appendix, allows us to see complexities and continuities otherwise invisible.

We combine a simple method with the hexagons to limit another common challenge in mapping change over time and space: the "small denominator problem." In counties with small populations, a relatively small change in migration appears as a large rate of change. To avoid that distortion, our maps register the actual number of people of a particular ethnicity who increased or decreased over a given decade. To create a meaningful metric of growth and decline, the maps before the twentieth century focus only on the South because few Black southerners managed to leave the region before then and few immigrants arrived. The maps after the turn of the century broaden their range to include the entire United States, showing southern migrations in national and international context. Where rates of natural increase and decline shaped populations in particularly significant ways—such as in the domestic slave trade—we explain why.

Each map also uses a tight chronological focus, the decade between censuses. People moved, the maps clearly show, in the context of historical events, pressures, and opportunities that varied sharply over time as well as space. Migration immediately reacted to changes near and far, in turn setting the stage for unanticipated changes yet to come. The narrative, working at the same regional scale as the maps and drawing on a rich historical literature, allows us to understand the patterns in ways the maps themselves cannot explain.[1]

The maps of *Southern Journey*, using these strategies, embrace everyone who lived in the South—free and enslaved, rich and poor, male and female, native and immigrant, settler and suburbanite—from the first national census of the late eighteenth century to the sophisticated surveys of the early twenty-first century. Across all those generations, all those migrations, the movement of people beat as the very pulse of southern history.

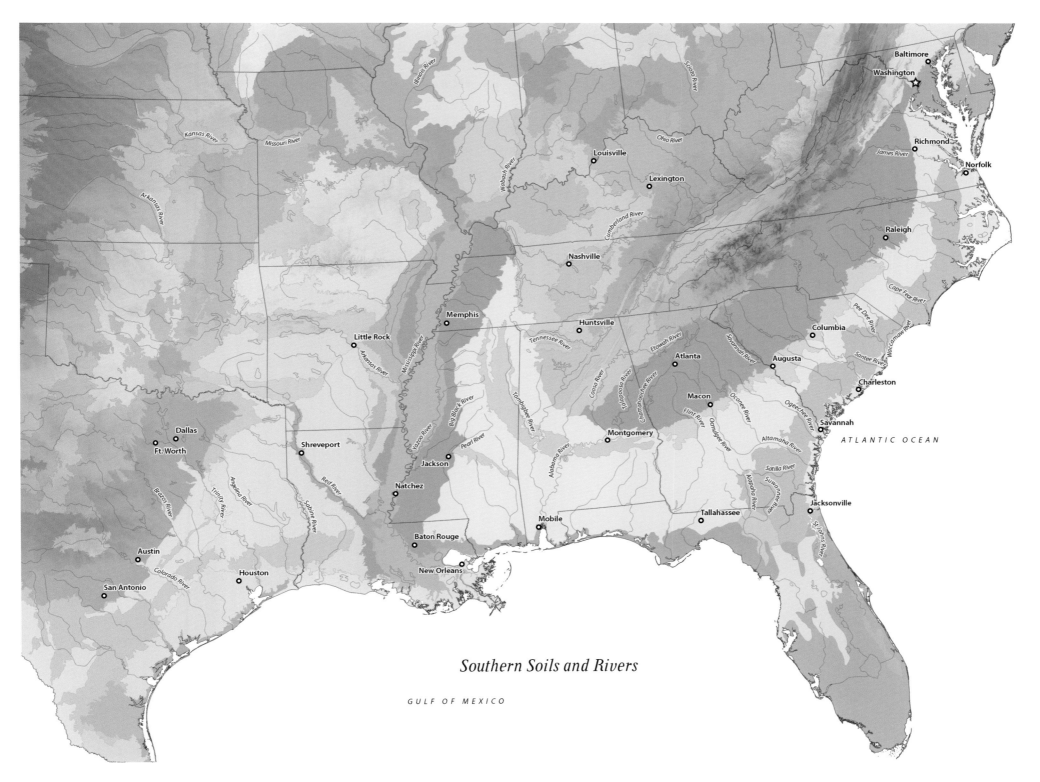

Southern Soils and Rivers

GULF OF MEXICO

The differences among the soils in the southeastern quarter of what became the United States has shaped the patterns of all settlement, displacement, enslavement, and migration, even to the present day.

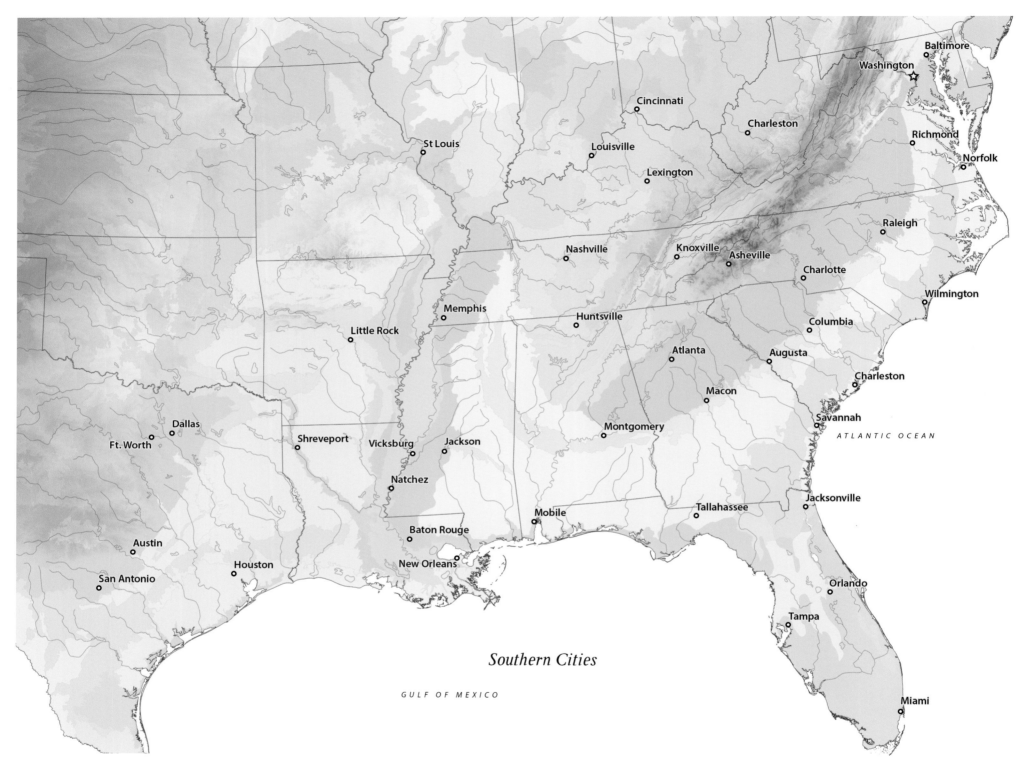

Southern Cities

GULF OF MEXICO

The cities of the South have played important roles in its history, their growth tied closely
to migration within the region at first, then from the rest of the nation and the world.

SOUTHERN JOURNEY

ONE

CREATING THE SOUTH, 1790–1860

The American South expanded with a speed and to a size few could have imagined in 1790. Three migrations created the South over the next seventy years: tens of thousands of indigenous peoples driven from ancestral lands, millions of white farmers filling an enormous expanse, and millions of enslaved people moved to raw, new plantations. The paths of migration began from many sources and flowed in many directions at the same time. Tracing those paths reveals the enormous scale, velocity, and complexity of the few decades in which the American South took the form that would shape it for centuries to come.

Migration created the anomalies that defined the slave South. Slavery concentrated on the richest land and yet spread everywhere in the region. Most white southerners did not own enslaved people, yet the institution went everywhere white settlers went. It benefited nonslaveholders little, and yet the migration of nonslaveholders allowed the slave South to expand as fast as the North. The place of slavery in the territories held little practical consequence for the white majority of southerners, and yet they went to war to defend that expansion. Only migration can explain these puzzles.

THE NEW UNITED STATES

No new technologies of transport or communication pushed rapid settlement in 1790, the year of the first U.S. census. People still dragged crops on sledges or behind heavy and cumbersome wagons pulled by oxen. Ships and boats moved by the same wind and currents that had moved vessels for hundreds of years. Settlers cleared land as they had for centuries, with axes and fire.

After centuries of continual conflict and change, indigenous peoples maintained a presence in every part of the southeast of North America, from the Atlantic Ocean to the Gulf of Mexico to the southern plains. Some had been reduced to small and isolated groups, some bound themselves with other Native peoples and refugees from slavery to form new alliances. Neighboring towns often spoke different languages, incorporating words from one another, from Europeans, and from people born in Africa. They regularly communicated, traded, cooperated, and warred with one another—often across great distances—on well-defined and heavily traveled routes. They sometimes enslaved one another. They found ways to live amid loss, gain, and threat from the growing and relentless white population descending on them from all directions, negotiating for advantage in trade or military alliance.[1]

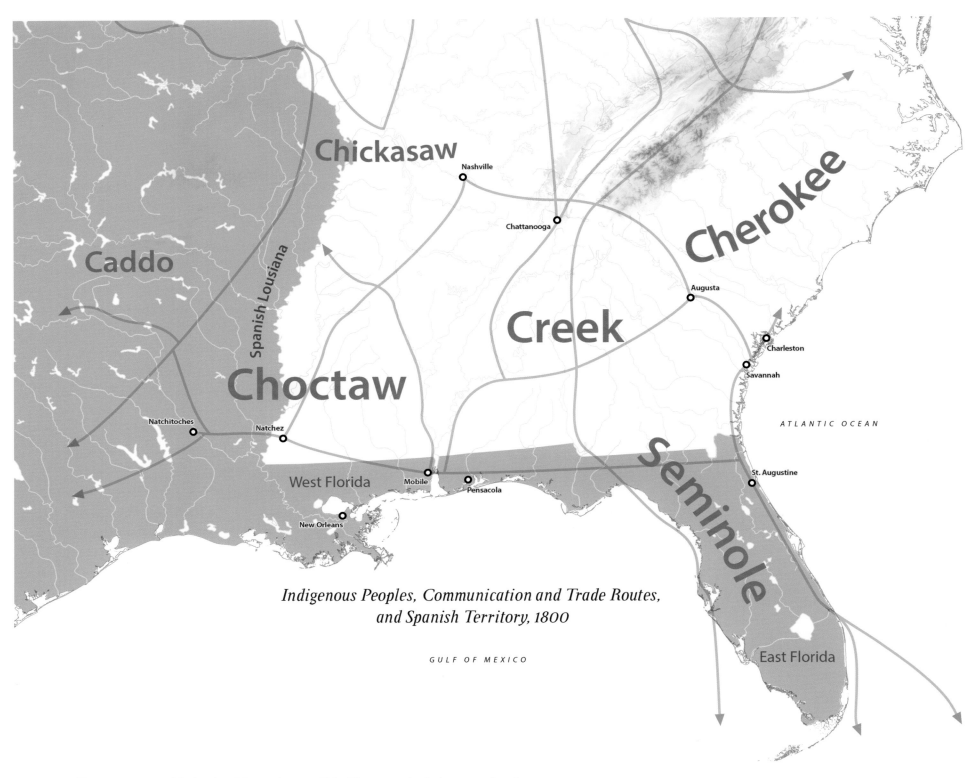

*Indigenous Peoples, Communication and Trade Routes,
and Spanish Territory, 1800*

The great expanse of the interior of the southeastern United States remains in the possession of Native peoples in 1800, surrounded by territory lightly occupied by the Spanish and scattered settlers of various backgrounds. These diverse groups trade and travel among one another and with the Caribbean people to the south and the indigenous peoples to the north.

The tensions and conflicts within and among the indigenous peoples grew more urgent as European empires gave way to American settlers. While some Native men and women embraced ideas of private property and some became Christians, others defiantly sustained older loyalties and ways of life. Mobility and exchange defined the social experience of Natives, but they increasingly defined their sovereignty in terms of territories and boundaries to defend themselves from those who would invade and take their lands. The Cherokee, Creek, Chickasaw, Choctaw, Seminole, and Caddo peoples made clear their determination to keep the lands they occupied. Their populations increased in the first third of the nineteenth century, but white Americans, friendly and otherwise, spoke of the American Indians as an endangered race whose survival depended on removal from competition with white people.[2]

As the United States tried to establish itself on the continent after the American Revolution, slavery became destabilized. Enslaved people had used the war to ally with the British and to escape bondage. Ideas of human liberty emanated from the pulpit and the political stump, leading to slavery's end in several northern states. The Constitution of the United States called for an end to participation in the international slave trade by 1808. Bondage frayed in the Chesapeake Bay region, where tobacco fell into decline and wheat demanded less year-round labor. And yet slavery flourished elsewhere despite the dislocations of the Revolution. More than 100,000 enslaved people labored in the rice fields of South Carolina, and slave traders transported people directly from Africa to fantastically wealthy rice plantations. Charleston grew into a sophisticated port city built around the wealth and tastes of slaveowners.[3]

Slavery also prospered in the new sugar districts of Louisiana, where 30,000 people lived in slavery in 1790, beyond the bounds of the United States. Expatriate planters from Saint Domingue, fleeing a revolution of the enslaved, brought laborers with them to new plantations and found ways to extract sugar from cane despite the short growing season of continental North America. New Orleans grew rich from the cargo on the flatboats that floated down the Ohio and Mississippi Rivers, delivering the bounty of new farms and plantations hacked out of the forests along those waterways and their tributaries. The international slave trade brought people from Africa and the Caribbean to the increasingly voracious plantations of Louisiana. The United States coveted the great port city of New Orleans, resting uneasily in the hands of the Spanish and the French on the edge of land claimed by the Americans.[4]

The vast Gulf of Mexico coastline offered immense expanses of land, forests, and rivers that both beckoned and challenged white settlers. Spain claimed Florida on the eastern coast of the Gulf and Texas on the western end. Native peoples hostile to American settlement occupied much of the land in between. The Creeks and Choctaws, living in towns along the rivers in the rich Alabama territory, tended droves of cattle numbering in the hundreds. They did not welcome white settlers, who stole their livestock and competed for the grazing lands. Enslaved people escaped raw plantations along the ragged frontier of southern Georgia and Alabama to the lightly governed and heterogeneous West Florida, which stretched from Tallahassee to Mobile, finding refuge by establishing their own settlements and in connection with Native, Spanish, and French people.[5]

The lands of the Gulf South held fecundity undreamed of in the wasted and gullied lands of Virginia and the Carolinas. White people in those eastern states looked hungrily upon the region they called the Southwest, where rivers could carry crops to markets cheaply and rapidly. Slaveholders possessed the labor to clear the trees, break the land, build the fences, and put up the shelters that would produce profits impossible on their old farms and plantations. But no one in 1790 knew how, when, and by what means white Americans might move to those lands or what they might grow there if they did.[6]

Pressures for migration mounted in the Atlantic slave South as the white population grew. Plantations in Virginia, farmed for over a century by that time, became less productive with each passing season. Even the Piedmont, the foothills of the Appalachian Mountains, had been planted in tobacco, beginning the enervation of the soil there. Planters turned to wheat, but that crop did not take full advantage of the labor capacity of the hundreds of thousands of enslaved people who lived in the state.[7]

THE 1790S

Some white Virginians, especially those who owned no slaves or who held moral, economic, or racial qualms about the practice, abandoned the Old Dominion for one of the new free states in the Northwest Territories, especially Ohio. White people more fully invested in slavery looked for new places to establish plantations on the other side of the Appalachian Mountains.[8]

Expeditions from Virginia in the 1760s had discovered a route around the mountains at the Cumberland Gap on what would become the border of Tennessee and Kentucky. Through that break in the mountains, long known to Native people, migrants could move north into central Kentucky. As early as 1775 Daniel Boone and other guides began leading settlers into that region to establish permanent homes.[9]

After the Revolution, tens of thousands of men, women, and children from eastern Virginia streamed south through the Shenandoah Valley to the Cumberland Gap. They gathered on the Long Island of the Holston River in Tennessee and then followed what was known, imposingly and accurately, as the Wilderness Road north into Kentucky. The "road" was really a trail in many places, steep and rocky, crossed by fallen trees and blocked by stubborn stumps, hard for heavy wagons pulled by oxen to navigate. Dismayed by the growing procession, Cherokee and Shawnee bands harassed and sometimes killed the settlers descending into their hunting grounds but could not stop their relentless flow.[10]

Finally arriving in central Kentucky after weeks of walking, the white newcomers confronted dense and towering canebrakes, growing up to twenty feet high, covering much of the land. The cane marked rich and well-drained soil, from which a meadow grass called "bluegrass" grew in profusion when the cane fell. The settlers cut and burned the cane to carve farms out of the tangle. Pigs and cattle rooted and lumbered their way into the brakes and woods, disturbing the wild game.

The settlers cleared land to which they had no title—"squatting," as the those who disapproved called it—in hopes that the improvements they made would grant them legal claim when the surveyors and federal officials arrived. Some early settlers succeeded, especially those who traveled with other family members or friends or who had the capital or the slaves to establish themselves quickly. Many others, though, found themselves competing with land speculators who sent lawyers and surveyors in their stead. In such cases, the speculators held the land on which the squatters established farms, increasing the land's value, then sued to evict the settlers. Lawsuits grew as thick as the cane, choking courts and slowing settlement.

Kentucky quickly proved to be a frontier for slavery as well as for free people. Though some early legislators fought to keep the new state free, the number of slaves grew rapidly from the outset and then doubled again in the 1790s. Enslaved people were driven along the Wilderness Road in chained coffles from Tidewater Virginia. About a quarter of white Kentucky households claimed a slave in the 1790s, while other enslaved people worked on farms to which they were hired or loaned out. If they came with owners—often a younger son of a plantation owner in the Tidewater—the enslaved people might have a chance to keep their family together. More often, teenaged boys and girls found themselves taken from their families and sold in the slave markets of Virginia, then marched to the new fields of Kentucky.

The 12,000 enslaved people in Kentucky in 1790 grew to more than 40,000 by 1800, their labor making central Kentucky soon resemble an improved and updated version of Tidewater Virginia. The new capital in Lexington boasted fine mansions and claimed enterprise that Virginians envied. Billing itself as the "the greatest inland city of the western world," Lexington boomed during the first decade of the nineteenth century. More than 90,000 horses grazed on the bluegrass by 1800. Most of the new planters of Kentucky grew hemp, a fiber of many uses, including for making durable slave clothing. Hemp, moreover, demanded work across the year and occupied slaves' labor in a way both profitable and reassuring to their owners that the wheat grown in Virginia had not. To the south and west of Lexington, the Green River area enjoyed access to the Mississippi River and produced a new strain of burley tobacco preferred by discerning smokers. That region prospered even more than Lexington.

Middle Tennessee, to the immediate south, bore a strong resemblance to central Kentucky in its topography and its early history. The area around Nashville on the Cumberland Plateau attracted slaveholding settlers from Virginia and North Carolina. Those coming into Tennessee from the east traveled by boat on the Holston River and then followed relatively easy trails and roads into the rich lands of the middle part of the emerging state. Many stopped along the way in the 1790s, allowing East Tennessee, despite political instability, to grow rapidly. Tennessee became a state in 1795, only three years after Kentucky, and by 1800 claimed more than 80,000 free and 13,500 enslaved residents. Ten years later more than 250,000 free settlers and 44,000 enslaved people had spread across a large part of the state. Its rich western reaches remained in the hands of the Chickasaw, but they would be displaced by 1818.[11]

The admission of Kentucky and Tennessee into the Union before any state to the north except Vermont demonstrated the advantage that slavery offered in rapid settlement. Because indigenous people did not pose an entrenched threat in central Kentucky and Tennessee, the settlers did not have to fight protracted frontier wars. Because settlement lay relatively near large enslaved populations, planters could move a working population to the growing

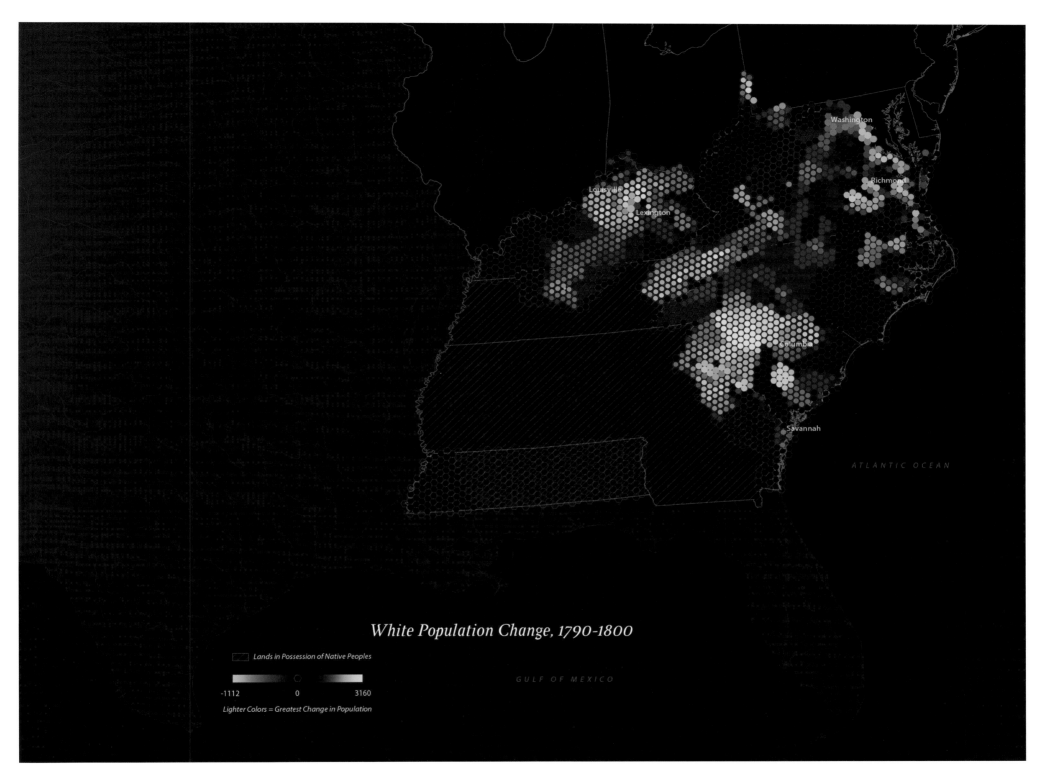

White Population Change, 1790-1800

Lands in Possession of Native Peoples

-1112   0   3160

Lighter Colors = Greatest Change in Population

In the first decade after the United States creates its federal census, white population surges into central Kentucky, eastern Tennessee, and the upcountry of South Carolina and Georgia. White population declines in the older eastern areas of Virginia and South Carolina, even in some newer areas bypassed by more promising lands nearby.

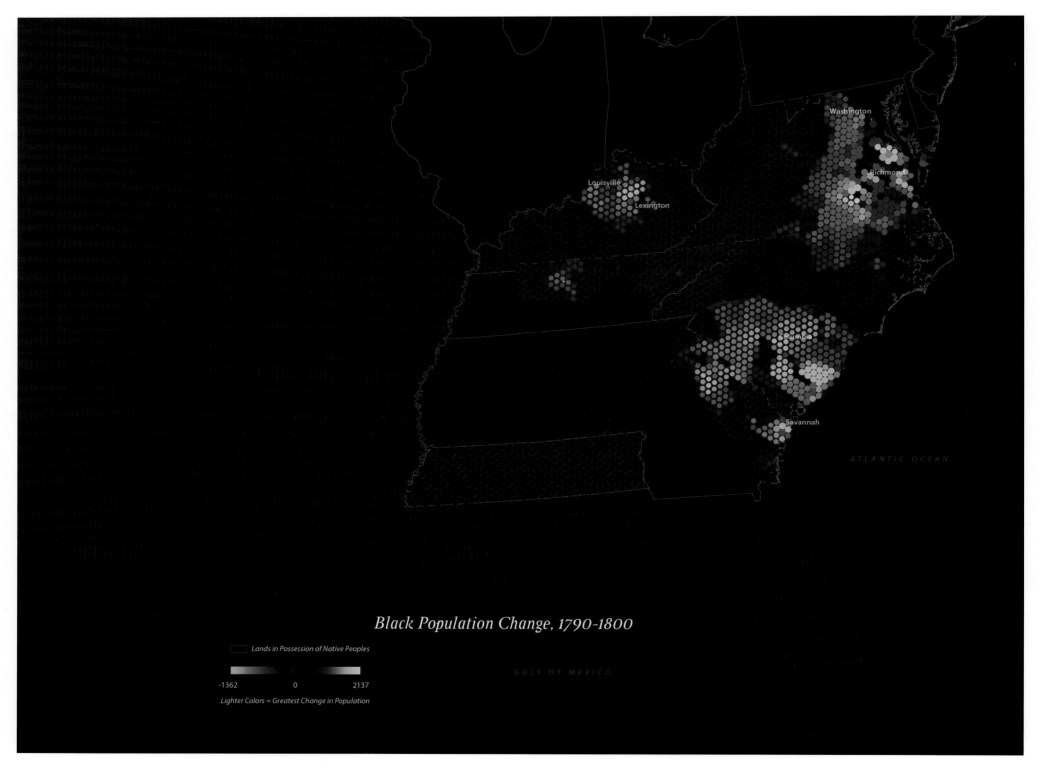

Black Population Change, 1790-1800

Lands in Possession of Native Peoples

-1362   0   2137

Lighter Colors = Greatest Change in Population

The population of enslaved people grows in more targeted areas than the white population. Slavery expands where planters can afford rich lands and where such labor can be made to pay most rapidly: the rich bluegrass region of Kentucky and the cotton-producing areas of upcountry Carolina.

communities at low cost and without long delays. Enslaved people quickly proved their skill with new crops and tasks, especially raising the mules, horses, and oxen that would become and remain the most valuable products of the region. Enslaved men also led immense droves of cattle and hogs from Kentucky and Tennessee to the north and south. Enslaved women worked in the fine houses of the new states, allowing these residences to claim an instant air of gentility.

Slaveless white people also moved to Kentucky and Tennessee even though they could afford neither the beautiful bluegrass land nor enslaved people. They could, however, turn livestock loose in free-range land to feed themselves. White families could also work fresh land claimed, for the moment at least, by no one else. Mountain hollows in eastern Kentucky and Tennessee that offered little prospect for cash crops offered an independence hard to find among eastern lands dominated by large farms and plantations. Settlers to the mountains valued the rich hardwood forests, abundant game, healthy water, uncomplicated land claims, and sheer beauty of the region. They sought above all to avoid debt and obligation.[12]

The paths of white people of different classes crossed and intertwined, branching with ever finer distinctions. These routes of migration traced the contours of elevation, water, soil, and forest with great precision. People moved to their west in the same latitude because they understood the environment they encountered. Migrants knew that trees revealed the kind of soil into which their roots reached. They knew how to find springs that would not stop during dry times. They realized that a good farm needed woodlots, gardens, fields, and hunting lands. They understood that hopes and expectations could not overcome facts of soil and sun. The rewards of good decisions were high, but the punishment of bad decisions came without mercy.

The enslaved people of the emerging South lived as pioneers. For decades, in one place after another, they would clear land, swing axes, dig ditches and wells, cook game over open fires, birth children in freezing or sweltering cabins, and die in malarial swamps. Slavery worked with a terrible logic, deploying bondsmen to places where their labor and their bodies would pay quickly and predictably. If plantations or businesses failed under debt, ill health, drunkenness, or miscalculation, enslaved people soon found themselves sold or moved once again to yet another frontier. While white migrants fanned out in search of diverse opportunities, the forced marches of Black people followed narrow but lengthening channels of white profit.

THE SETTLER-SLAVE SOCIETY

Kentucky and Tennessee embodied a transforming force in the new nineteenth century: "settler" society. In English-speaking colonies and former colonies around the world, white settlers claimed the right to take land from indigenous peoples as a destined path toward civilization. They displaced Native peoples through forced migration or death rather than incorporating them into their new societies.

Settler societies, whether in Australia, New Zealand, South Africa, Canada, or the United States, depended on breakneck growth, instant local government, and the template of the culture of Britain as their plan for rapid settlement. Cheap land, valuable commodities, high profits, and assumed racial and cultural superiority drove and justified the migrations of millions of English-speaking people in every hemisphere during the nineteenth century.[13]

The United States, with its vast internal frontiers, possessed particular advantages as a settler society. Most American settlers to the West in the nineteenth century were native-born. They required no ocean journey halfway around the world to strange new climates, soils, and crops. They used familiar techniques, tools, and livestock on their frontier and obtained convenient financing and trade with friends and family. American settlers after the Revolution controlled their own governments at the local, state, and national levels, shaping critical policies of land acquisition, banking, tariffs, and the means by which the indigenous peoples would be contained, controlled, and driven away.

In all these ways the white migrations of the American South typified those of other settler societies of the early nineteenth century. The South, though, stood apart because some of its white settlers carried enslaved people of a nonindigenous group with them. No other settler society enjoyed such portable labor. The journeys of those slaveholders and the journeys of the enslaved people wound together at every turn.

The American South also differed from the other large slaveholding regions of the hemisphere: Jamaica, Brazil, Cuba, and British Guiana. While white people in those places, as in the South, took land from indigenous peoples and fed on the forced migration of enslaved people, only the Americans created a dominant landed class that routinely ripped itself up by the roots to create new plantations in its own vast and expanding territory. Only they built a sprawling, borderless, efficient domestic slave trade that fueled frantic disruption. The volatile combination of an expansive settler society and an expansive slave society would define the South.[14]

In the same years of the 1790s that white settlers and enslaved pioneers straggled over the Appalachians from a diminished eastern Virginia, the low country of South Carolina and Georgia fostered ever-wealthier plantations. There, 250 white families held nearly 50,000 enslaved people on plantations on islands along the Atlantic coast, where they grew rice in vast quantities. Looking for ways to take fuller advantage of their wealth and their slaves, rice planters experimented with another crop—cotton—from seed imported from Barbados. The planters shifted thousands of enslaved workers from rice to sea-island cotton, a long-staple fiber that produced a luxurious and expensive cloth.

Seeing the profits of low-country planters from cotton, farmers and merchants sought to extend the bounty away from the narrow coastal reaches to the upland territories of the Piedmont of South Carolina and Georgia. People knew of a green-seed, short-fiber cotton that flourished in the upcountry but whose fibers could not be efficiently removed from the seed. Permutations of a cotton gin, developed on a Georgia plantation in the early 1790s by a young visiting tutor named Eli Whitney, spread rapidly and widely. The gin permitted workers to clean about fifty-five pounds of the upcountry cotton in ten hours, ten times the speed of cleaning by hand. Southern mechanics immediately made improvements to the simple machine, avoiding the fees Whitney charged. Planters in upcountry South Carolina and Georgia soon began producing large crops of cotton for the booming market in England's new textile factories.[15]

Planting cotton in new ground, fighting the weeds that imperiled it, pulling the cotton from sharp-edged bolls, and dragging the heavy bags from the fields exhausted even the strongest workers. To meet the labor demanded by the new cash crop, wealthy planters shifted enslaved people from low-country plantations to upcountry farms. The requirements and the possibilities of upcountry cotton drove slavery's expansion at a feverish rate. The distances from the coast to the upcountry were not great, the business relations between planters and merchants were already established, the land was already surveyed, the government in place, and the Native people resided at a comfortable remove or were establishing their own plantations. Young men and women taken to cut timber, clear underbrush, and plow the first rows in a new upcountry outpost might never see their mothers and fathers again. Women bearing children on the frontier would be far from the comforts of loved ones and midwives.

Planters established other frontiers of slavery at the beginning of the nineteenth century, responding to international demand and fueled with international capital. Planters in northern Alabama cleared rich soil along the Tennessee River, which flowed to the Ohio River, then into the Mississippi, and on to the market in New Orleans. Two thousand squatters occupied the land around what would become the town of Huntsville, awaiting the federal land sale of 1809 as soon as the Chickasaw and Cherokee nations ceded the territory. The number of enslaved people grew to 4,200 by 1816 as traders marched "great droves" of slaves from the East, clearing 20,000 acres for cotton within just a few years and feeding 4.5 million pounds of cotton into 150 commercial gins.[16]

The purchase of the Louisiana Territory from France in 1803 brought the slave port of New Orleans into the United States and opened a new slave frontier 150 miles up the Mississippi River. The old French river town of Natchez became an American plantation outpost and the administrative center of the Mississippi Territory of the United States. Farmers floated down the Mississippi on flatboats coming from Kentucky and Tennessee to Natchez, carrying food for plantations, selling their boats for wood, and walking home along the Natchez Trace, a trail that led back to Nashville. Choctaw and Chickasaw people moved farther west to avoid the white settlers claiming lands on bluffs high above the river between Natchez and the new town of Vicksburg.[17]

Many settlers along the Mississippi depended on the natural increase of hogs and cattle. Owners notched the animals' ears to brand them as their property and then let them wander, fattening themselves on the mast on the forest floor. One family's animals mated with those from others, growing everyone's investments. By combining yields from their free-range livestock, cornfields, hunting, and gardens, a new Mississippi household could support itself in just a year or two. Some sold cattle from their growing herds to raise cash and purchase enslaved people.

Planters and American officials saw that the Natchez region, with rich land and immediate access to the Mississippi River, would be ideal for cotton. "I know that cotton is the most profitable production of the US. and that the Mississippi territory is well adapted to it," Thomas Jefferson wrote in 1802. Planters, arriving with enslaved laborers and financial credit to buy land, took advantage of the earlier settlers' clearing and planting. New Orleans immediately became the main site of American cotton consolidation and shipping,

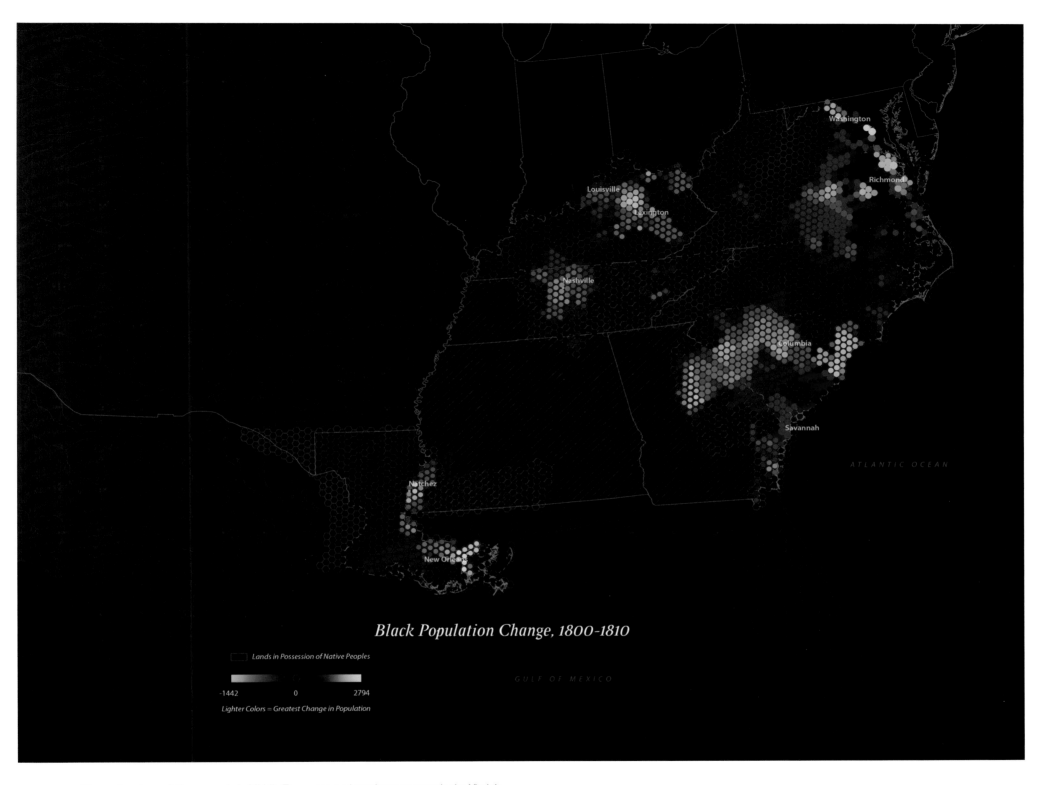

Black Population Change, 1800-1810

Lands in Possession of Native Peoples

-1442   0   2794

Lighter Colors = Greatest Change in Population

The enslaved population expands in Middle Tennessee and continues to grow in the Virginia Piedmont. Far to the west, slavery spreads rapidly along the lower Mississippi River between Natchez and New Orleans, fed by the introduction of cotton and sugarcane.

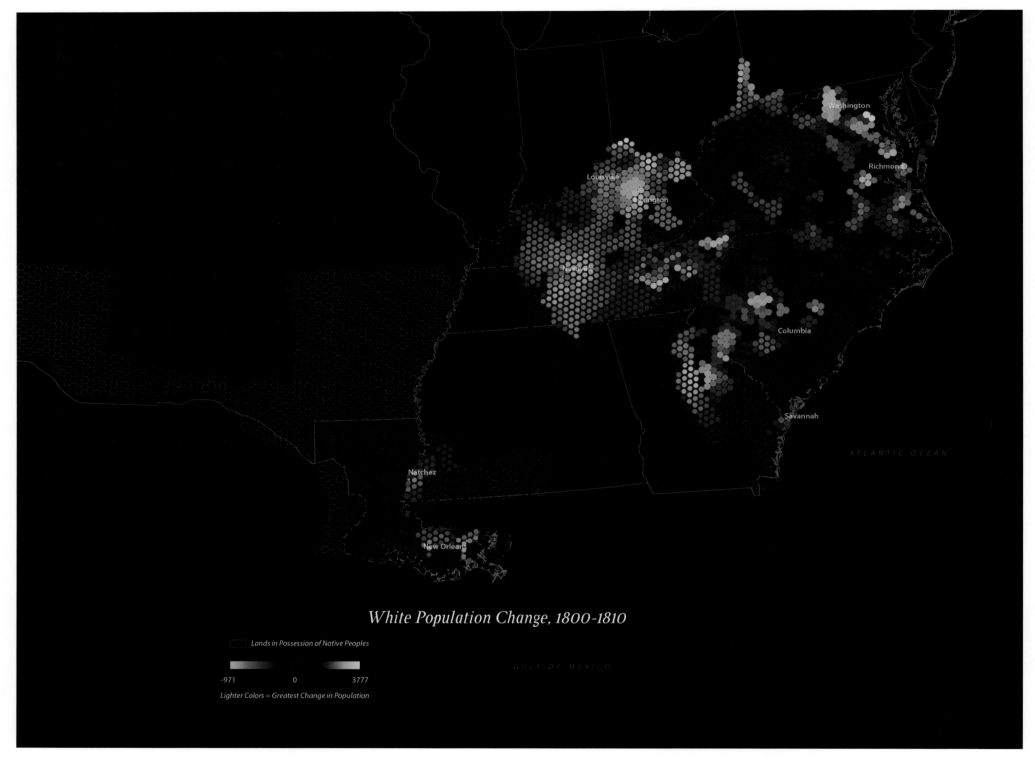

White Population Change, 1800-1810

Lands in Possession of Native Peoples

-971   0   3777

Lighter Colors = Greatest Change in Population

White settlers without slaves pour into central Kentucky and Tennessee to take possession of inexpensive land even as they leave parts of the Carolina and Georgia Piedmont, where slavery is growing rapidly. Some white Americans move to the lower Mississippi Valley. In the meantime, eastern Virginia and North Carolina continually lose white residents.

handling the exchanges between planters along the Mississippi River and buyers in New York and Liverpool. By the time the state of Louisiana entered the Union in 1812, nearly half its population of 76,000 lived in slavery.[18]

By 1810, then, outposts of slavery and plantation agriculture had appeared around the borders of what would soon become the South. The migration of the mixed farming of Virginia into Kentucky and Tennessee; the extension of low-country planter society along the Atlantic coast; the creation of an upcountry cotton society in South Carolina, Georgia, and northern Alabama; the spread of massive sugar plantations along the rivers of Louisiana; the trade networks converging at Natchez; and the river-based cotton farming that stretched east from the river into Mississippi revealed just how adaptable the hybrid settler-slave society could be. The cotton gin was not a deus ex machina of southern history or of slavery, as it often appears, but a cog in a much larger machine of a settler-slave society. Lenders deployed capital with remarkable speed to anywhere land, slavery, and transportation might pay.

CONSOLIDATING THE AMERICAN SOUTHEAST

War broke out with the British across North America in 1812, engulfing the lives of indigenous, white, and Black people in the South. Thousands of enslaved Virginians joined with the British Army and the Royal Navy to help secure their own freedom. Native nations sided with the British to stop the incursions of white settlers into their lands. During the war and afterward, American officials and soldiers punished the enslaved and Native peoples, including some who had allied with the United States.

Major General Andrew Jackson defeated a faction of the Creeks at what the United States called the Battle of Horseshoe Bend in central Alabama, seizing twenty million acres of land, about half of their territory in the South, in an 1814 treaty. Those lands included much of southern Georgia and about two-thirds of what would soon become the state of Alabama.

Jackson then fought Seminoles and escaped slaves who occupied the "Negro Fort" in Spanish-controlled West Florida on the Gulf coast. The United States demanded that Spain either establish control over the indigenous peoples and escaped slaves in Florida or cede the land. Spain, in a weak position, chose to sell its possessions in 1819. Two years later Florida became a territory, and in the early 1820s, the Americans moved the overpowered Seminoles to a reservation in the middle of the Florida peninsula, separated from the coasts to avoid contact with traders from the Caribbean. The land around

Tallahassee quickly emerged as yet another new plantation area devoted to cotton and slavery.[19]

In just a few years after the War of 1812, then, treaties, cooptation, and fraud had opened to white settlers and slaveowners a large part of what would soon become the slave South. The power of several Native nations was now shattered and divided. Foreign threats were gone from Louisiana and Florida. Sites of possible refuge for enslaved people with the British Army, the Seminoles, and the Spanish had been eradicated. Millions of acres entered the public domain and became available to purchasers.

The massive acquisitions of land by the United States fed rather than sated the demand for yet more acreage. Vast territories still lay under the control of the Cherokees and Creeks in Georgia and Alabama, the Chickasaws and the Choctaws in Mississippi and Tennessee, and the Seminoles in Florida. Settlers who had missed earlier chances for land determined that they would not be left behind again. Those who had already profited once from seizing Native lands determined that they would do even better the next time.

Southern settlements, dispersed from the Atlantic Ocean to the Mississippi River and from the Ohio River to the Gulf of Mexico, depended on migration, global markets, national policies, flimsy credit, and enslaved people, whose price rose and fell. The Panic of 1819 revealed the fragility of the expansive new settler-slave society. Intricate webs of credit with which southern planters had built their new plantations snapped when banks began to call in debts on heavily mortgaged land. The price of American cotton dropped 25 percent in a single day, triggering immediate and massive declines of land and crop prices. Migration had superheated the markets for all the ingredients of plantation society.

Migration also triggered a crisis in Missouri. Southern slaveholders had rushed to establish plantations along the Missouri River in the northern part of the territory. Ten thousand enslaved people grew hemp in Missouri by 1820, just as they continued to do in Kentucky. The flexibility of slavery, proven repeatedly over the preceding two decades, took on a new and ominous aspect when it drove into what many northerners believed should remain free territory. After intense struggle in Congress, the Compromise of 1820 declared that slavery would not expand above a line from the southern border of Missouri to the Pacific Ocean. The threat of migration, and to migration, immediately became the defining grievance between the emerging North and the emerging South. It would remain so for the next forty years.

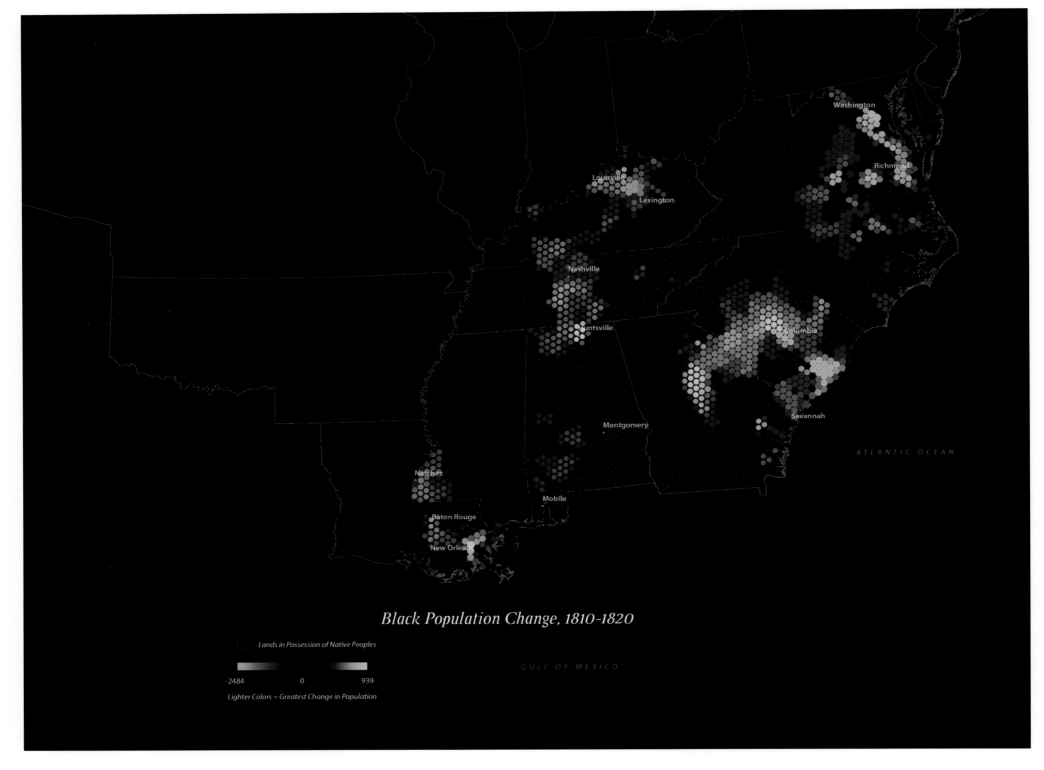

Black Population Change, 1810-1820

Planters and traders move enslaved people into northern Alabama as cotton production spreads into the interior and along the Mississippi River. The enslaved population builds on the eastern boundary of the Cherokees in Georgia. Eastern Virginia exports ever more enslaved people into the new cotton lands.

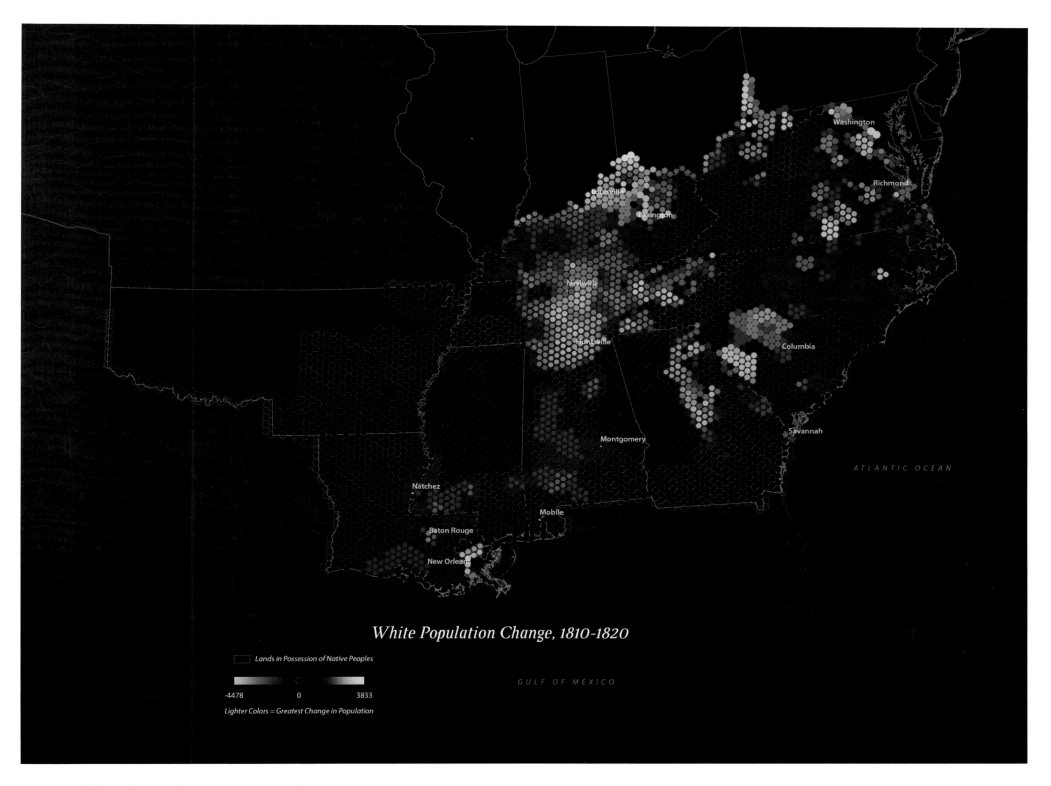

White Population Change, 1810-1820

Lands in Possession of Native Peoples

-4478   0   3833

Lighter Colors = Greatest Change in Population

White settlers, distributed more thinly than enslaved people, spread over lands coming into
white possession from several Native nations. The white exodus from the East depopulates areas
from Virginia to Georgia. Even places in the upcountry, settled by whites only a decade before,
begin losing white residents, who push into new lands in Alabama, Louisiana, Arkansas, and
western Tennessee.

THE 1820S

Most of the enslaved people moved to the new outposts of the South during the first years of the nineteenth century marched to their destinations in chains. Gathered by traders from the older farms, plantations, and villages of the Chesapeake, men and women trudged for weeks, shackled to one another. The traders fed them enough so they would sell, but the migration by foot agonized ill or malnourished people. Many died along the way, while many others tried to escape or rebel. The slave traders deployed whips, guns, horses, dogs, and allies to cut their losses.

Through these brutal means, the enslaved populations of all the new plantation areas grew and dispersed with remarkable speed. The number of slaves in Kentucky quadrupled between 1800 and 1830 to 165,000 and grew in Tennessee more than tenfold to 141,000. South Carolina doubled its numbers of enslaved people to 315,000 by 1830. Georgia, much of its land still occupied by the Cherokees in the 1820s, more than tripled its enslaved labor force to 218,000 people.

The enslaved population continued to grow in the East through reproduction, even though slave traders carried people away every day. Virginia, where the slave trade operated most aggressively, saw slavery grow by more than 100,000 people to 454,000 in bondage. Those in slavery in the South as a whole grew from 736,000 in 1800 to 1.8 million in 1830, an increase of 40 percent. By 1830, more than a million enslaved people already lived in states to the west and south of Virginia and the Carolinas.

Alabama, entering the Union in 1819 as the Creeks were forced to cede ever more land, increased its enslaved population most rapidly during these years. People in Virginia and the Carolinas became obsessed with the new state. "The *Alabama Fever* rages here with great violence and has carried off vast numbers of our citizens," one North Carolinian complained. "I am apprehensive if it continues to spread as it has done, it will almost depopulate the country."[20] Since most of the land in Alabama had never been tilled, planters who could import enslaved men to reduce the forests to fields held a great advantage over those without slaves. Enslaved women and children helped burn brush, clear undergrowth, and plant the first crops in the rough fields. They planted corn, edible by both people and animals, alongside the cotton. Clearing and planting went on side by side for years as plantations expanded along with their labor force.[21]

The cotton frontier expanded among the indigenous peoples as well, even as white people took land through violence, fraud, purchase, or cooptation. Some Cherokee, Choctaw, and Chickasaw men used enslaved Black people as white people did—trading slaves, hiring them out and renting them, and working them on small farms and large plantations. These Native owners navigated the world of property and markets with skill and success, adopting the ideals and strategies of individual aggrandizement that so profited white people.[22]

White squatters settled among the Natives without authorization, whiskey merchants preyed on them, and speculators pushed them to abandon farms altogether. As their debts mounted and their options diminished, Creeks, Cherokees, Choctaws, and Chickasaws sold or ceded ever more land and turned to the U.S. government for food and medicine. After years of abuse, white people argued that the only hope for the Native peoples was to leave the Southeast entirely for lands of their own on the other side of Mississippi River. Some Native leaders agreed with them and moved to the West.[23]

As Alabama's white population surged from 13,000 in 1813 to 127,000 in 1820, new white residents demanded that the territorial government extinguish the claims of Native residents. They also demanded that squatters gain preemption rights, in which improvements to the land on which they lived but did not own entitled them to that land at a low price. Settlers and speculators demanded that the government grade and price land by its quality so that it could enter the market as quickly and efficiently as possible.[24]

The South's expansion accelerated during the 1820s. The number of cotton bales produced on new lands doubled between 1815 and 1820 and then doubled again over the next five years. By 1826, recently occupied areas of Alabama, Louisiana, Mississippi, and Tennessee produced about 40 percent of the nation's cotton crop. Traders and planters dragged and shipped enslaved people to these new cotton lands in ever-growing numbers. In the 1820s, about one enslaved person out of ten in the South was shipped across state lines; in the 1830s, one in seven.

Lands along the Mississippi River in Tennessee, Mississippi, and Louisiana boomed with cotton and sugar plantations. The growth of the enslaved population outstripped the free. Steamboats, driven by heavy engines and mountains of wood, worked up and down the Mississippi River. The boats reduced the cost of shipping from five cents per ton in 1820 to one-half cent by 1830, shortening the travel time from New Orleans to Natchez to less than forty-eight hours.[25]

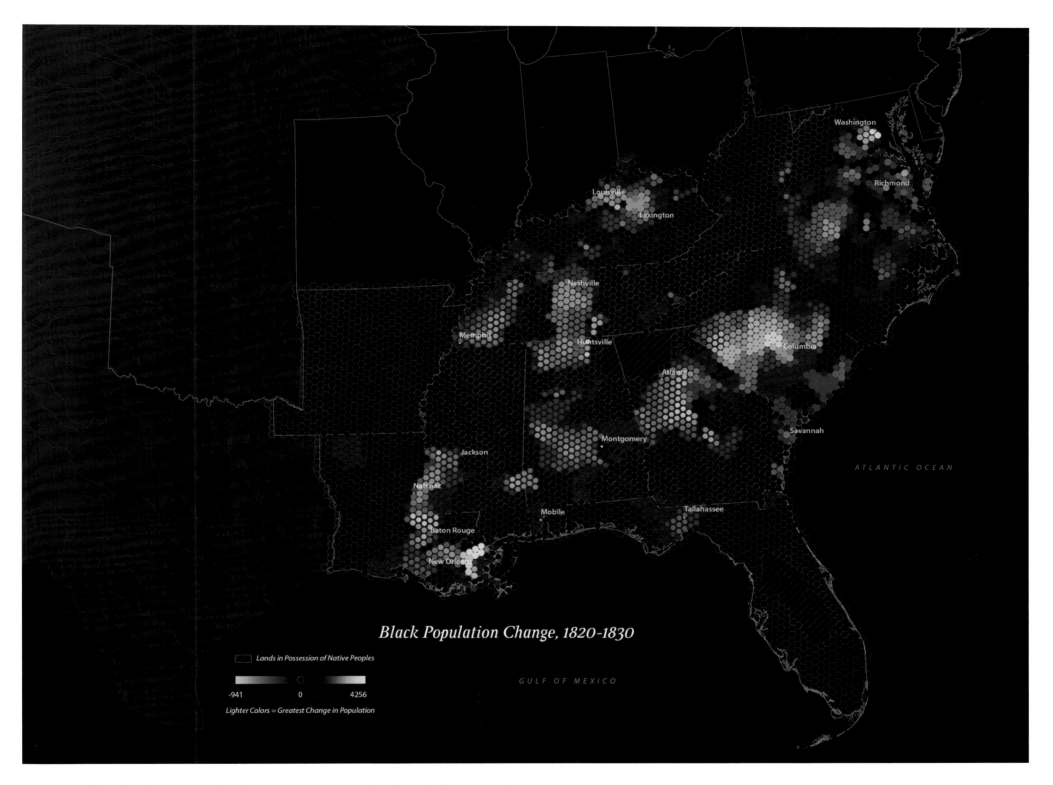

Black Population Change, 1820-1830

▨ Lands in Possession of Native Peoples

-941 0 4256

Lighter Colors = Greatest Change in Population

African American people are brought to many places at once, from Kentucky, Tennessee, and
northern Alabama in the Upper South to the burgeoning Piedmont of South Carolina, Georgia,
and Alabama as well as to the lower Mississippi Valley and Louisiana.

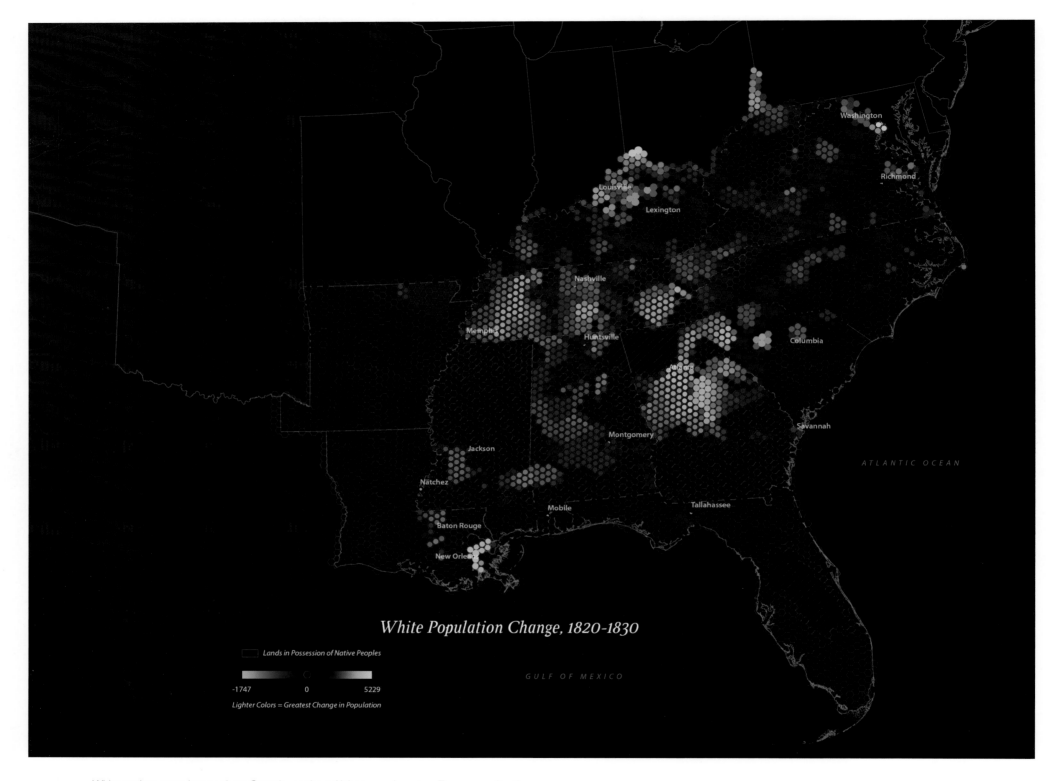

White Population Change, 1820-1830

Lands in Possession of Native Peoples

-1747   0   5229

Lighter Colors = Greatest Change in Population

ATLANTIC OCEAN

GULF OF MEXICO

Washington
Richmond
Louisville
Lexington
Nashville
Memphis
Huntsville
Columbia
Athens
Montgomery
Savannah
Jackson
Natchez
Mobile
Tallahassee
Baton Rouge
New Orleans

White settlers surge into northern Georgia, northern Alabama, and western Tennessee after the
War of 1812 and the treaties that follow. The eastern parts of the South suffer declining white
populations as the fever for cheap land spreads.

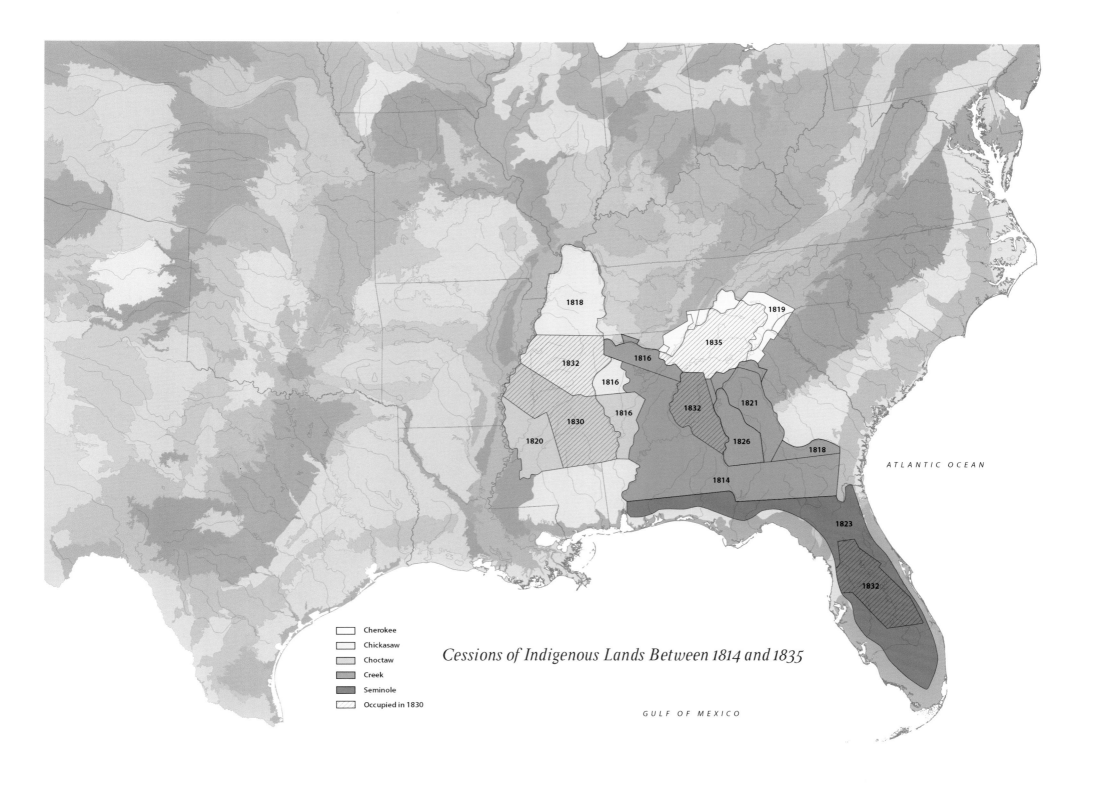

1818

1819

1835

1832

1816

1816

1832

1821

1830

1816

1826

1820

1818

1814

1823

1832

ATLANTIC OCEAN

	Cherokee
	Chickasaw
	Choctaw
	Creek
	Seminole
	Occupied in 1830

Cessions of Indigenous Lands Between 1814 and 1835

GULF OF MEXICO

After white incursions on their lands throughout the early nineteenth century, by 1830 Native peoples had become concentrated in areas that white settlers, slaveholders, and politicians demanded that the federal government remove altogether.

Settlers from the South pushed into the Mexican province of Texas during the 1820s. When Mexico won its independence from Spain in 1821, the new Mexican government encouraged foreign settlers to the area to help populate and stabilize the province. Despite the continuing threat of Comanche raiding parties, tens of thousands of Americans accepted the invitation. Mexican citizens of the region, known as Tejanos, worked with leaders of that immigrant community—especially Sam Houston and Stephen F. Austin, both originally from Virginia—to create a profitable outpost for slavery and cotton beyond the U.S. border. No one doubted the suitability of the rich land for cotton, but the Mexican government and leaders of its other provinces longed to rid their new nation of slavery. The major impediment to American settlement, in fact, was doubt about whether slavery would be safe in Mexico.[26]

Over the course of the 1820s, Tejanos and the earlier American settlers worked to stop Mexican antislavery efforts from reaching Texas. Promises of hundreds, or even thousands, of acres of free land, with bounties of even more for men who brought women and slaves, began to appear in newspapers across the United States in the wake of the Panic of 1819. Thirty-nine families arrived in 1821 and set enslaved people to the work of girdling trees and burning underbrush to create corn and cotton fields. The seeds for the cotton they planted came from Mexico, a variety valued for its resistance to a fungus that had spread among other kinds of cotton. By 1825, a quarter of the American population in Texas was held in slavery.

South Carolina suffered massive emigration from the state during the first two decades of the nineteenth century. Nearly half of all white people born in the state after 1800 left, and the white population of the upcountry would not expand for decades. Carolina migrants left for Piedmont Georgia, Alabama, and Mississippi. In sharp contrast, the Black population of South Carolina increased across the entire state despite constant sales and forced migrations. White South Carolinians, watching the racial demography of their state shift ever more toward a Black majority, became the most aggressive defenders of slavery's expansion.

The balance of power in Georgia shifted as landless settlers pushed into the state's upcountry to take land to grow cotton. Those who sought the territory ceded by the Native peoples in Georgia wanted no impediments to their success. They demanded low prices, easy debt, and strict control over all African American people. Slaves transported to Georgia's new cotton planta-

tions from the old farms, plantations, and villages of Virginia, Maryland, and the low country confronted a place even more rigid, bifurcated, and hopeless than the ones they had known. Georgia politics, like that of all the southern states that followed, became aggressively egalitarian for white men, aggressively opposed to any claims by indigenous people, and aggressively devoted to protections for slavery and the control of those enslaved.[27]

The Native peoples of the American South, despite decades of war, violence, fraud, and pressure, still occupied twenty-five million acres of ancestral lands in 1830. About 60,000 Cherokees, Chickasaws, Choctaws, and Creeks lived between the Appalachian Mountains and the Mississippi River. They would not move willingly. The Cherokees who occupied northern Georgia, western North Carolina, and East Tennessee fought against white settlers and officeholders through legal means, using courts to challenge efforts to displace them. They also often converted to Christianity, turned communal lands into private property, adopted gender roles more like that of European than Native families, cultivated cash crops, and purchased enslaved African Americans.[28]

Every strategy by the Cherokees failed. White settlers in Georgia repeatedly infringed on Cherokee land—in 1806, 1809, 1817, 1828, and 1829. At each step, the Cherokees ceded land, losing nearly seven million acres in those years in addition to the fourteen million they had lost between the American Revolution and 1800. Faced with such relentless pressure, some Cherokees decided they would do better farther west. Some moved to Arkansas, Missouri, and Texas during the 1820s. Most hung on in Georgia through the decade, however, resisting removal with every resource they could find. President Jackson wearied of their resistance. "Build a fire under them," he told white Georgians in 1830. "When it gets hot enough, they'll move." The Georgians would do just that. Settlers did not wait for land issues to be determined by law before they moved in.

Pushed by the continual agitation in the southern states, Jackson demanded and won the Indian Removal Act of 1830. "What good man," he asked rhetorically, "would prefer a country covered with forests and ranged by a few thousand savages to our extensive Republic . . . filled with all the blessings of liberty, civilization, and religion?"[29] Congress, after bitter opposition from the indigenous nations and from missionaries and other white advocates, narrowly empowered the president to negotiate with the Natives for their forced expulsion to the Indian Territory, west of the Arkansas Territory.

THE 1830S

By 1830, two million people lived in the newly settled states in the American South, six hundred thousand of them held in slavery, and yet the South remained thinly populated. The slave trade, growing in reach and velocity with each year, remained haphazard and unreliable. Erratic banking, currency, and land policies fed and then killed speculative fever. White settlers and enslaved people flowing into Texas moved beyond the control of U.S. federal law. Tens of thousands of white settlers had descended on Native lands illegally, even though the indigenous people still occupied and owned them through American laws. The population of the South surged forward, sideways, and even backward, better chances seeming always to lie somewhere else.

Moving and settling had become economic drivers for merchants, lawyers, and agents, the key elements of new counties and towns, the raw material for ambitious politicians. The labor of migration and settlement consumed the energies of enslaved people, on every kind of frontier, in every kind of agriculture. Migrations of both white and Black people flowed in many directions at once, moving in channels created by land cessions from indigenous peoples, by rivers, by the quality of the land, by the availability of capital, by prices for crops, and by the valuations of enslaved people.[30]

Most white southern migrants did not own slaves, moved to areas where plantations were not emerging, and would not acquire slaves in coming years. By and large, they went where land was inexpensive and accessible to people without many resources. The presence of large numbers of slaves, in fact, indicated that planters and speculators had already cornered the market on the best land and driven up the price.

Though most white southerners did not move in order to advance slavery, their migrations had that effect nonetheless. Nonslaveholders helped establish the counties and communities in which slavery could take root and expand. Men without slaves helped police all Black people, creating a white majority that held slavery in place. Widows and unmarried women hired slaves as domestic help, and young single men worked as overseers and foremen on plantations. Slaveholding and nonslaveholding families intermarried, the boundaries between the classes blurred by kinship and church membership.

The migration of the nonslaveholding majority imprinted the political machinery and ideology of the South at the region's birth. As new states emerged, they adopted constitutions and political styles shaped around the needs and

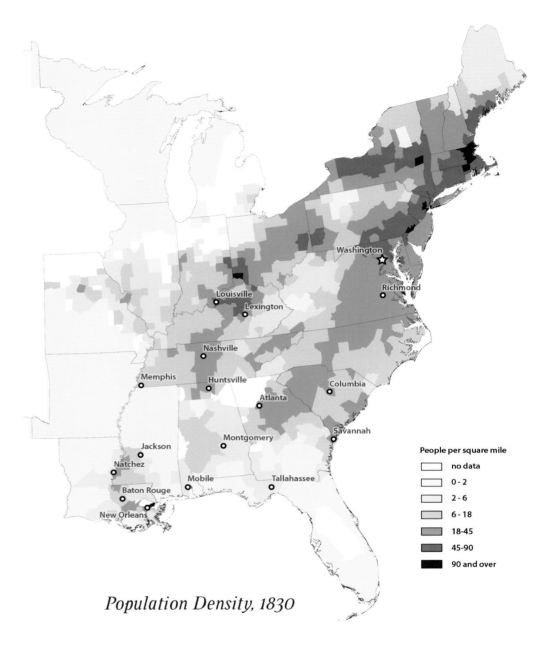

People per square mile

☐	no data
☐	0 - 2
☐	2 - 6
☐	6 - 18
☐	18-45
☐	45-90
☐	90 and over

Population Density, 1830

By 1830, the Piedmont, the bluegrass and Cumberland Basin, the Holston Valley of Tennessee, coastal South Carolina, and a few places along the Mississippi River hold relatively dense populations. Most of the South, however, remains lightly settled. The areas occupied by Native peoples have diminished, but they are still evident.

demands of white men, with or without enslaved people, who declared themselves independent and equal because of their "settlement" of the land taken from Native peoples. The new constitutions written for the new southern states spoke a boldly democratic language for all white men. The demands of those men drove the policies of the state and federal governments, using the power of those authorities to dispossess the indigenous peoples who stood in the way of their future mobility and demanding that their representatives in Washington fight for every inch of territory to the west.

The interstate slave trade almost doubled in the 1830s, rising from 155,000 people during the 1820s to 288,000 in the next decade. While about one-third of those people walked to new plantations behind their owners, two-thirds were driven or shipped farther south by slave traders. At the same time, sales between neighbors, debt sales, and gifts and loans among white family members dislocated twice the number of people as interstate slave sales. Taken together, more than 2 million enslaved people suffered interstate, intrastate, and local sales in the three decades after 1830.[31]

THE SLAVE TRADE, FREE BLACK PEOPLE, AND ESCAPE

The hydra-headed slave trade grew into an immense business. Being sold once was no guarantee a person would not be sold again, even on the way to a new location. The slave trade was perpetual and omnipresent. Those channeled through the market represented half a billion dollars in property, spinning out multiplier effects in related businesses. Banks and commission-taking factorage houses enabled financing. Specialized companies transported, housed, clothed, fed, and medically treated enslaved people during the one, two, or three months required to sell them. Slaves became insured property in transit, investments protected by company-backed policies. Government treasuries benefited as well, for sales had to be notarized and sellers taxed. Millions of dollars circulated through all parts of the southern economy and civic life as a result of this buying and selling of people.[32]

The slave trade never rested. Interstate traders spent late summer buying slaves at courthouse estate sales, at private sales on plantations and farms, and from one another. They housed the people they purchased in pens and jails, where they paid the jailor a fee, keeping them there for weeks or months before shipping them south from late fall into early spring. Enormous slave pens filled cities in the East, such as Richmond, and cities in the West, particularly New Orleans, where planters from across the Southwest came to purchase people shipped from Virginia and the Carolinas. Buyers looked particularly for young men, skilled artisans, or what the sellers called "fancy girls," young women, often of light complexion, to be abused as concubines or prostitutes. An enslaved person had about a 30 percent chance of being sold in his or her lifetime. Seeing a loved one sold was a certainty.

These millions of exchanges marked a massive relocation of the enslaved population of the South. In 1800, two-thirds of the nation's slaves lived in the states of the Atlantic Seaboard, where slavery had grown for a century and a half. By 1840, half of all enslaved people lived in the new states of the Southwest. This human property efficiently followed the money in the South, for those who sold slaves, traded slaves, and purchased slaves proved discriminating businessmen. The market was alert to every opportunity, performing its heartless sifting and sorting by economic fluctuations and geographic differences.

The price for enslaved people rebounded soon after the depression triggered by the Panic of 1837 finally ended in 1843, after which prices mounted steadily for the next fifteen years. As slave prices rose, simply owning enslaved people became one of the best investments a white person could make, whether the owner was male or female, in the country or in town, or in a plantation district or elsewhere. The average value of an enslaved person more than doubled between 1843 and 1860.

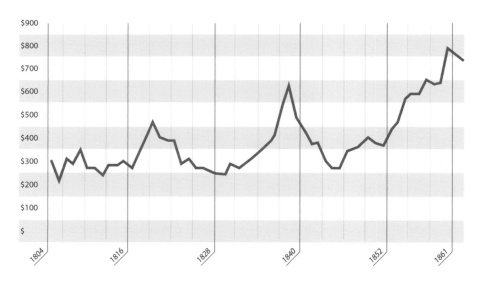

Prices of Enslaved People, 1804–1861

(in contemporary dollars)

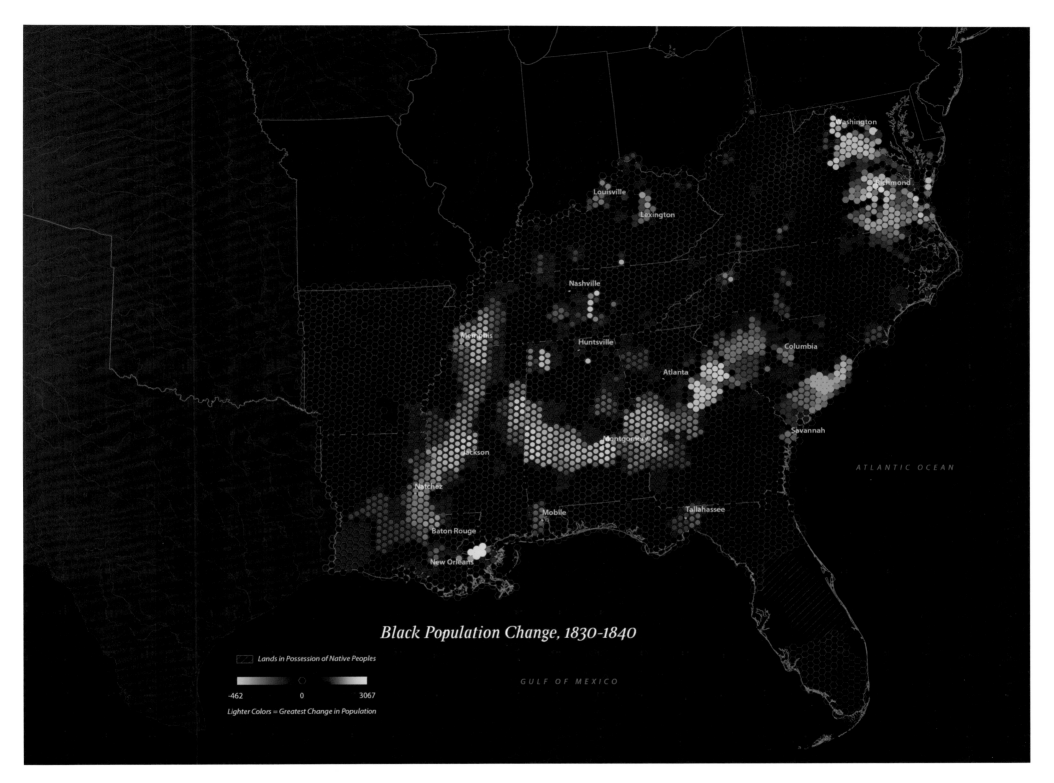

Black Population Change, 1830-1840

Lands in Possession of Native Peoples

-462   0   3067

Lighter Colors = Greatest Change in Population

ATLANTIC OCEAN

GULF OF MEXICO

Washington
Richmond
Louisville
Lexington
Nashville
Memphis
Huntsville
Columbia
Atlanta
Jackson
Montgomery
Savannah
Natchez
Mobile
Tallahassee
Baton Rouge
New Orleans

Opposite page: The prices for enslaved people rise to great heights and then plummet, but beginning in the mid-1840s, fed by the relentless global demand for cotton and the transformation of vast areas into new plantations, slave prices mount steadily for the next fifteen years.

The defining shape of the slave South finally becomes apparent, as enslaved people are concentrated along the Black Belt, stretching from Georgia to Mississippi. The domestic slave trade extracts a brutal toll not only in the oldest enslaved areas of Virginia and South Carolina but also in the more recently enslaved areas of the Georgia Piedmont, Kentucky, and Tennessee. The sugar plantations of Louisiana demand ever more enslaved workers.

21

The free Black population of the South, which had grown rapidly in the wake of the Revolution and the awakening of conscience among some newly converted evangelical Christians, slowed with each decade that followed. Alarmed by rebellions and resistance, states made it increasingly difficult for slaveowners to manumit enslaved people and for free African Americans to remain in the places where they had lived. Some free Black people migrated westward, along the same paths as propertyless white people, moving from Virginia and North Carolina to Kentucky and Tennessee, avoiding plantation districts. Few free African Americans lived in the Lower South; those who did clustered in communities in Charleston and New Orleans.[33]

Most free Black people moved to cities in the South or along the border with the North. From the border regions, they might find relative safety as political winds shifted. Cities on the edge of the South, such as Saint Louis, Louisville, Baltimore, and Cincinnati, saw a steady growth of their free Black populations, as did large port cities such as Boston and New York. Free Black people also moved throughout the North and Midwest so that, by 1860, Pennsylvania had more than 57,000 African American residents; Ohio, 37,000; Indiana, more than 11,000; and Michigan, 6,800. Tens of thousands of others emigrated to Canada.[34]

Some of these Black residents of the North and Midwest had escaped southern slavery. Through every stage of the institution's spread, enslaved people did all they could to free themselves. For areas in the Upper South, where the slave trade ripped away family members and loved ones with growing speed and force, escape seemed tantalizingly possible. Most of the successful flights from bondage took place in Maryland, Delaware, Virginia, and Kentucky, places where one could escape by foot or boat. For the parts of the South to which people were being taken and shipped, escape was increasingly impossible. Any promise of freedom in the North or Canada lay hundreds of miles away, with only danger and death in between.[35]

Several thousand enslaved people managed to free themselves each year. Most of the successful refugees were young men, many of whom worked to bring family members to them after they became established. Slave catchers worked along the border and in northern cities, where Black people sought safety in anonymity. Escape grew increasingly dangerous as white southerners demanded the support of the federal government in returning those who crossed the line into freedom.

The desperate movements of free Black people and those escaping slavery fed a silent and invisible migration. Constantly shifting their routes as northern allies emerged and disappeared, adapting to the rise of steamships and railroads, and confronting suspicion and vigilance at every step of the journey, people fleeing slavery and the clampdown on the free Black population made their way to cities and towns across the North and into Canada. Over the three decades after 1830, as the proportion of free Blacks in the South declined amid a growing slave population, their numbers slowly increased outside the South. By 1860, about equal numbers of free Black people lived in the South and in states beyond its bounds: about 262,000 in the South and 226,000 in the North. Their determined migration established foundations for the churches, businesses, and organizations on which Black freedom would build.[36]

THE NATIVE DIASPORA

The 1830s culminated a displacement of the indigenous people that had already taken 100 million acres from them in the South. Most of these Natives lived in areas directly in the path of the expanding plantation empire. Having sought out rich soil along rivers for their own farms and towns, Cherokees, Creeks, Choctaws, and Chickasaws lived on the most valuable lands in the South. Having hunted seasonally across large expanses of territory, they depended on access to land they did not occupy. Having adapted to cash crops and livestock, Native farms testified to the possibilities of the land they settled.

The Indian Removal Act of 1830, demanded by southern states and President Jackson, threw the weight and power of the federal government to the displacement of Native peoples to the Indian Territory on the western side of the Mississippi River. Officials and speculators induced, often with bribery, putative indigenous leaders to cede the lands of their people without the consent of others. The government spent millions of dollars to then move these peoples, insisting that the investment would pay for itself in the white development of lands the Indians were forced to leave.[37]

Despite white claims that removal would save American Indians from extinction, leaders of the Native peoples argued that the removal schemes themselves posed the greatest danger. Unfortunately, the indigenous people proved correct. Of the 64,000 American Indians forcibly moved in the South, between 11,000 and 14,000 died. Most perished from disease spread by dirty water, horrible food, poor shelter, and crowding in encampments before the

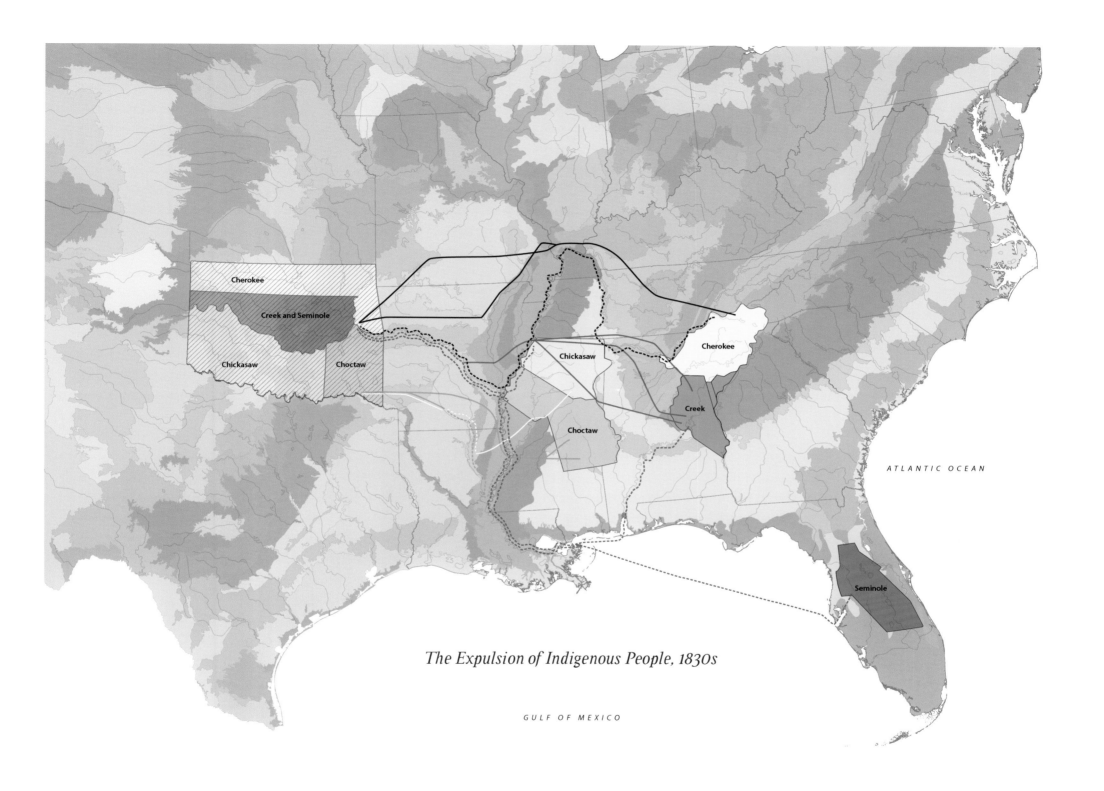

The Expulsion of Indigenous People, 1830s

After generations of wars, treaties, cessions, and dispossessions, the United States uses the power of the federal government to drive the Cherokee, Choctaw, Chickasaw, Creek, and Seminole peoples from their remaining lands. The long and deadly journeys of these indigenous peoples to the Indian Territory mark a capitulation to the demands of white speculators as well as settlers.

23

march to the west. In Alabama, contractors forced young and old Creeks, healthy and sick, to walk more than four hundred miles before boarding steamboats to travel up the Mississippi and Arkansas Rivers, chaos and resistance bedeviling the journey. The boats were so dangerous and crowded that some Creeks chose to walk the remaining hundreds of miles to Arkansas Territory rather than risk their lives on the water. Nearly a quarter of the six hundred relocated Creeks died along the way.[38]

Between 12,000 and 15,000 Cherokees, divided into groups of 700, were driven along a journey that came to be called the Trail of Tears. Under guard of U.S. soldiers, the Cherokees were marched, in brutally cold winter weather, a thousand miles through Tennessee and Kentucky and across Missouri. The last bands, often walking barefoot through areas stripped of food by previous migrants, suffered from exposure and hunger. White towns along the way refused to allow the forced migrants to pass through or gain shelter. As a result, a third of the Cherokee people died. About 1,100 found ways to stay behind in the eastern mountains.

In Florida, the Seminoles went on the offensive, attacking settlers and destroying over eight million dollars' worth of farms, homes, and livestock. The United States launched the Second Seminole War in retaliation, fighting from 1835 to 1842 and spending forty million dollars, a sum greater than the entire annual national budget. Failing to defeat the Natives on their own ground, the United States eventually resorted to deceit and bribery to persuade Seminole leaders to move across the Mississippi River. Half of the six thousand remaining Seminole people died during the years of war and deprivation in Florida. Three thousand went west, while a few hundred remained behind in the Everglades, far from American settlements.[39]

Though thousands of Native peoples were removed in the 1830s, thousands remained in the Southeast. Though most lost their land, others managed to retain theirs. Though white people proclaimed their differences with and superiority to indigenous peoples, many intermarried with those who had American Indian ancestry. Though Black people were held in bonds of law and surveillance, they too found companions among Native peoples. Lumbee Indians remained in eastern North Carolina, and Pamunkey and Monacan people remained in Virginia. The Cherokees of Georgia and North Carolina and the Seminoles of Florida demonstrated one generation after another the flexibility and fluidity of American Indian life, the durability of their people's self-understanding and identity with one another and with their pasts.[40]

The census taken by the federal government—and thus the maps made from them—did not acknowledge the presence of Native peoples on the lands they had occupied for so long. This helped create the false sense that the American Indians of the South had been completely "removed" when in fact hundreds of each people remained, although out of sight of federal officials. Moreover, the Native peoples who moved to the Indian Territory maintained their identities there despite suffering social dislocation, disease, and death in the new lands. The Cherokees, Choctaws, Creeks, Chickasaws, and Seminoles sustained their culture through ritual and remembrance even as they rebuilt their governance in new forms and even jostled with one another. They continued to maintain spiritual connection to lands on which they no longer lived.[41]

The Native peoples in the Indian Territory also maintained African American slaves. Hundreds of enslaved people had been driven west with their indigenous owners, laboring on the trails of removal and dying of the same sicknesses and neglect. The wealthiest Native families sustained slavery in the Indian Territory, identifying with the white slaveholders of the South and finding themselves on the front lines in debates about how far slavery would extend. The enslaved people taken there escaped as often as they could, while those who could not established connection with each other as best they might.[42]

THE BOOM IN THE SOUTHWEST

Slavery went everywhere in the South, unifying white people in support of the institution, and yet slaves and the wealth they created increasingly became concentrated in relatively few white families. Slavery paid everywhere, but it produced the largest and quickest returns where soil, weather, and transportation conspired to create a rapid return on planters' investment.

Mississippi embodied these trends. The public sales of the Choctaw lands there opened a broad diagonal band across the state, stretching from the prairies and pines on the Alabama border to the Delta along the Mississippi River. Speculators and well-connected politicians bought up much of the richest areas within that band. Poorer settlers descended on the Choctaw lands with or without legal sanction because those who established homesteads could win the right to buy 160 acres at the minimum price of $1.25 per acre before a public lottery began. Conflicts among competing speculators and lawyers dragged out the process of clarifying sales and titles through the 1830s. The Choctaw and Chickasaw people who remained, now dispossessed, became laborers on lands that had been their homes.[43]

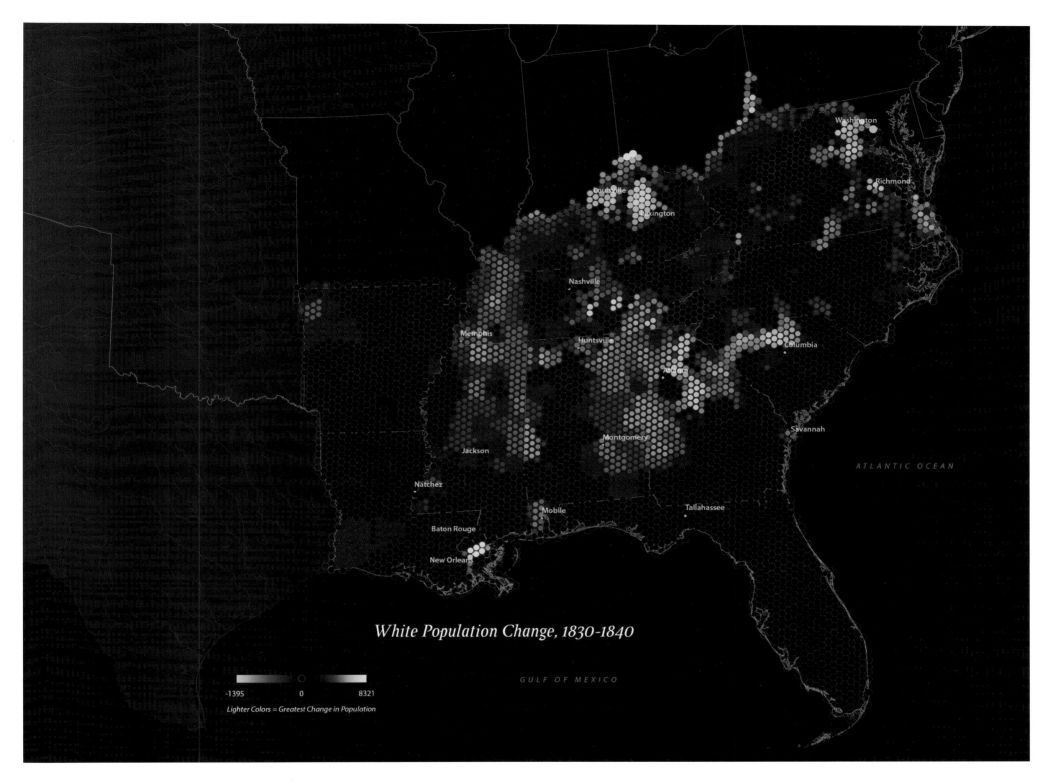

White Population Change, 1830-1840

-1395 0 8321

Lighter Colors = Greatest Change in Population

After the dispossession of the Native peoples, white settlers flood into their lands, leaving much of the older South, from Virginia through Georgia, virtually stagnant. The Piedmont, the first cotton frontier, sees massive departures.

The growth of steamboat traffic on the Mississippi River allowed settlers, traders, slaves, and cotton to move to and from the rich lands with a speed no other settlement period had seen. New Orleans, growing into the great shipping point for Mississippi's crop, surpassed New York to become the leading export city in the nation. Money flowed into the region from New York, Philadelphia, Boston, and London, finding its way to companies, banks, and individuals invested in the cotton and planting business, with credit growing tenfold in less than a decade. The planters and merchants of Natchez—the richest of all Americans—pumped cash and credit into their state. Slaveowners mortgaged their slaves, for which they had only partially paid, to borrow money to purchase more slaves on time. They built their schemes on the expectation of steadily rising cotton, slave, and land prices.[44]

The Mississippi boom collapsed even faster than it rose. When a bank in Natchez suspended payments, the Panic of 1837 swept across the United States. Public-land sales fell from three million acres in 1836 to less than half

a million the year after. Land that had sold for fifty dollars an acre a few years before now went on sale for five dollars. People rushed to sue one another while they might still have something worth suing for. Sheriff's sales announced the failure of one farm and plantation after another.

Many families stole out at night in their wagons, leaving their cabins—and their debts—behind as they headed to Texas, where American law did not extend. They often took the only property they could take: the enslaved people who had so recently arrived in the promising new lands of Mississippi.

The sugar plantations did better. With friendly tariffs protecting American sugar producers, by the 1850s, Louisiana planters produced a quarter of the world's sugar. A labor force of 125,000 enslaved people worked in crews of up to 100 in the sweltering fields. In the sugar parishes, Black people outnumbered white people, often more than two to one. Planters, notorious for their hard use of slaves, adapted the latest steam-driven machinery to extract as much as possible from their investments in land and people.[45]

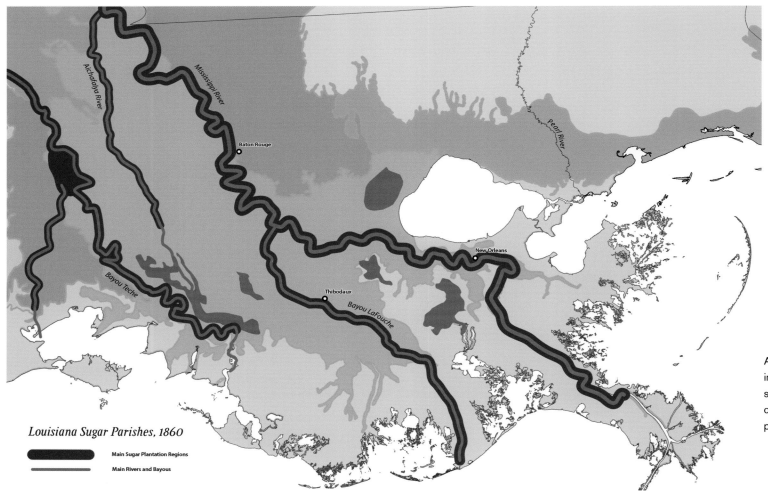

Louisiana Sugar Parishes, 1860

■ Main Sugar Plantation Regions

— Main Rivers and Bayous

After decades of development and the massive importation of enslaved people, the rivers of southern Louisiana are lined with long strands of sugar plantations, the wealthiest agricultural properties in the nation.

Men accounted for up to 85 percent of the enslaved people that sugar planters bought. These owners paid top dollar for taller and younger enslaved men, acknowledging the brutal work on which they were about to embark. More than 90 percent of the males bought in New Orleans were between the ages of eleven and thirty—"prime" hands. The young women the planters sought, generally between thirteen and twenty years of age, were eyed for their reproductive capacity as well as for their labor in the fields. Enslaved women in the sugar districts were forced to have children as long as they could bear them; purchasers preferred teenagers to extend that productivity. As slave prices mounted during the 1850s, planters could not afford to be as selective by gender and so purchased more women.

The Louisiana sugar districts saw terrifying death rates of enslaved people. Elsewhere in the slave South, the natural rate of population growth for enslaved people was about 28 percent; in Louisiana, it was only 6 or 7 percent. Women, especially, suffered in the sugar districts, pushed into having as many babies as possible despite the demands of working in the cane fields. Infants, bearing the burden of the poor nutrition and overwork of their mothers, died in heartbreaking numbers. On some plantations, as many as half of babies died while only a few months or years old. Forced to wean their children as quickly as possible, mothers watched them perish from malnutrition and diseases brought on by inadequate diets.[46]

THE 1840S

White migration slowed during the 1840s. Large parts of the South became relatively stagnant for the white population as low cotton prices combined with high slave prices to slow migration of all kinds. Yet Virginia continued to lose many of its people. Most white people left that state for the North: 163,000 moved to free states during the 1830s and 1840s, compared to the 105,500 people who migrated to other slave states. Nearly 86,000 moved to Ohio alone, while Indiana, Illinois, and Pennsylvania each absorbed tens of thousands of white Virginians.[47]

White population stagnated in other places as well, including the Piedmont cotton belt of South Carolina and Georgia, so promising only a generation earlier. Emigration outran natural population growth among white people in those places during the 1850s, and the reason did not seem hard to find: cotton farming had depleted much of the land. The Piedmont, once so rich, had become vulnerable because the hard rains captured by the Appalachian Mountains to the northwest removed the red clay from the rolling hills as the water ran to the Atlantic.

"The successful cotton planter," a South Carolinian explained, "sits down in the choicest of his lands, slaughters the forest, and murders the soil." After consuming his own land, he "buys up all that he can from his neighbors . . . and continues the work of destruction until he has created a desert of old fields around him, and when he thinks he can be no better, sells his land for what he can get . . . and marches off to a new country to recommense the same process."[48]

In the "new country" of Mississippi, the rich but loose soil that beckoned so many also became vulnerable as soon as the trees had been cut, rows plowed, and cotton planted. After just a few years, valuable topsoil had washed away in the heavy Mississippi rains, exposing the clay underneath. Facing such conditions, people decided to move once again. Some places that had recently seen white people arrive now saw people leave westward. Only about four of ten families who lived in Mississippi in 1840 still lived there in 1850. The two-thirds of Mississippi settlers who squatted felt little reason to stay if new land free for the taking could be theirs by moving again. The new arrivals to Mississippi were even younger and poorer than those who left.[49]

Most of those who left Mississippi, and Alabama as well, headed to Arkansas and Texas. Their movement began in the 1840s and accelerated during the 1850s. Arkansas, lightly settled by indigenous peoples, saw its population double in the 1820s, triple in the 1830s, and then double again in the 1840s. Becoming a state in 1836, Arkansas claimed more than 200,000 people, about a quarter of them enslaved, by 1850. While white people spread across the state, Black people were taken to its new plantation districts. Farming families who did not claim a slave—the great majority of settlers—moved to the higher lands in Arkansas, away from the rivers.

The arrival of the larger plantations swelled the enslaved population of the eastern part of Arkansas at rates equal to those of the Mississippi-Yazoo Delta. On both sides of the Mississippi River, from Memphis down to Vicksburg, Natchez, Baton Rouge, and New Orleans, slavery boomed during the 1850s. High cotton and slave prices made possible the heavy investment necessary to clear bottomlands for plantations. With a flourishing steamboat business that pushed vessels up even the small rivers branching off the Mississippi, planters enjoyed rapid and dependable transportation for the enormous pyramids of cotton bales they delivered to New Orleans, from where they traveled on to New York and Liverpool.

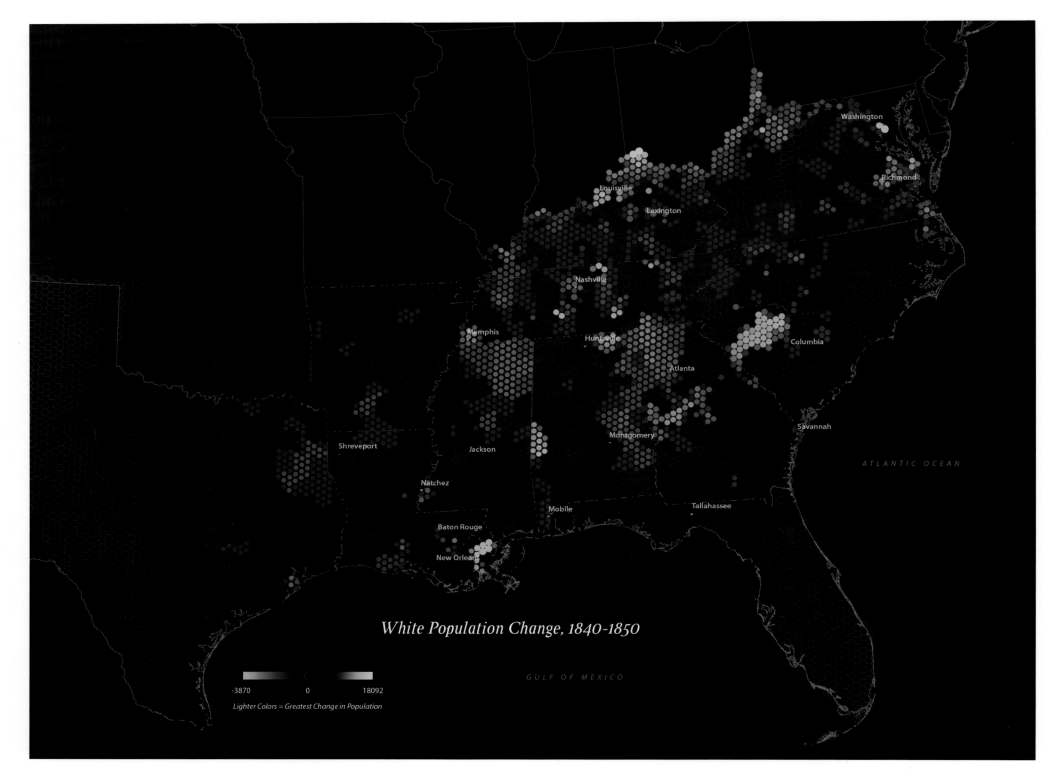

White Population Change, 1840-1850

-3870   0   18092

Lighter Colors = Greatest Change in Population

Relatively few white people move into the burgeoning plantation districts being filled with enslaved people. Instead, white settlers, abandoning the Piedmont of South Carolina and Georgia, move into the Upper South, Arkansas, northern Louisiana, and East Texas.

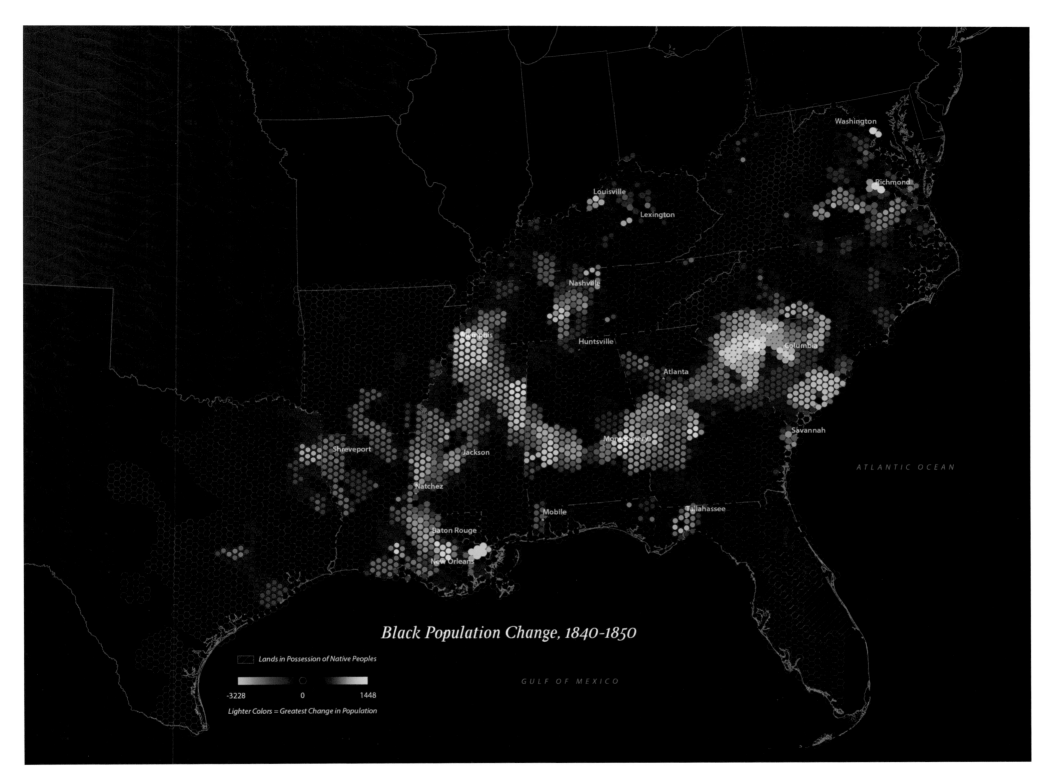

Black Population Change, 1840-1850

Lands in Possession of Native Peoples

-3228　　　0　　　1448

Lighter Colors = Greatest Change in Population

The concentration of enslaved people in the new plantation districts expands into Arkansas
and Texas, while the drain of the slave trade in the East slows during hard times.

Hundreds of thousands of white Americans moved to Texas, the new promised land for all classes of white people, during the 1840s and 1850s. Land remained inexpensive there, only five or six dollars an acre for remarkably rich soil that had never been farmed, and settlers poured in after Texas entered the United States as a state in 1845. Almost all those settlers came from other southern states and arrived with the expectation that Texas would be a richer and newer version of Mississippi, with cheaper lands, fewer legal complications, and fewer struggles with indigenous peoples. About half the families who moved there had started in Alabama or Tennessee but paused long enough in Mississippi, Louisiana, or Arkansas for a child to have been born in one of these places. Arriving in Texas, they dispersed themselves across the state evenly.[50]

The enslaved population of Texas grew even faster than the white, the 58,000 enslaved people in the state in 1850 expanding to more than 182,000 by 1860. Enslaved people were shipped to plantations to the south of Dallas and Fort Worth and between Austin and Houston, creating a vast new slaveholding region in the rich Blackland Prairie. By 1860, Black people constituted a third of the population, and enslaved labor produced 90 percent of the state's cotton. In 1850, the new plantations yielded about 59,000 bales of cotton; ten years later, they produced 432,000 bales.

Texas was in many ways a distillation of southern history, the virtual embodiment of its settler-slave hybrid. Its growth began with the appropriation of land—in this case from the Mexican government and the Comanche—quickly followed by the division and selling of that property. There was none of the chaos that had marked land sales in Kentucky during the 1790s or Mississippi in the 1830s. Planters and slaveholders by this time had learned how to use forced labor to stake out plantations with remarkable speed, bringing in squads of slaves to clear land and put it into production in a matter of months. The settlement of Texas coincided with a long boom in cotton prices during the 1850s, creating the impression that its prosperity was a permanent creation of the settler-slave complex.

But Texans of the 1850s might have looked back at the experiment of the Republic of Texas between 1836 and 1846 as a warning. That government had bet everything on the international standing and power that would come from producing cotton, the world's most valuable commodity. They built what they hoped would be a new nation as a safe haven for slavery, based on widespread landholding, a booming crop, and a place secure from the threats of abolitionists in the American North, England, and Mexico. But that republic, staking its existence on the power that would come from that sturdy settler-slave formulation, failed when the international market for cotton betrayed them in the late 1830s and the years afterward. The powerful formula of slavery and cotton proved surprisingly brittle in the face of prolonged economic challenge.[51]

THE 1850S

By the early 1850s, moving had become a way of life in the South. White families expected and hoped to uproot themselves for something better. Black people expected and dreaded sale and forced migration. The slave trade had developed into a big business, with prices instantly conveyed hundreds of miles on new telegraph lines and thousands of slaves shipped by sea from the docks of Richmond and Charleston to the docks of New Orleans and Galveston. Hundreds of steamboats plowed through the currents of the Mississippi and lesser rivers, carrying enslaved people to the plantations where they would labor for and among strangers.

Slave traders established their operations near the railroads and telegraph lines, ready to ship workers in gangs or as individuals. States financed railroad construction with hundreds of millions of dollars of debt as they raced to build lines to new cotton lands. Southern states built more than 8,300 miles of track during the 1850s, creating one of the largest rail networks in the world and connecting with a vast system of rivers and steamboats. This infrastructure construction contributed to the rising prices for enslaved people in years when cotton prices remained flat, for more than ten thousand bondsmen worked on railroad crews every year of the 1850s.[52]

Fed by the railroads, towns and cities grew rapidly during the 1850s. Though the absolute numbers were smaller than those of the North, the rates of urban growth were just as high. Raleigh, Columbia, Augusta, and Atlanta attracted new residents, while Richmond, New Orleans, Nashville, Mobile, and Memphis grew steadily as well. The new cities of Texas—Dallas, Houston, Austin, and San Antonio—boomed.[53]

While the Black population of towns and cities did not grow as fast as the white population, the cities of the South accommodated slavery. Nearly half of white families in cities owned at least one enslaved person. While most enslaved people, disproportionately women, worked as domestics in white people's homes, slaves in Richmond and Lynchburg, hired out by their owners,

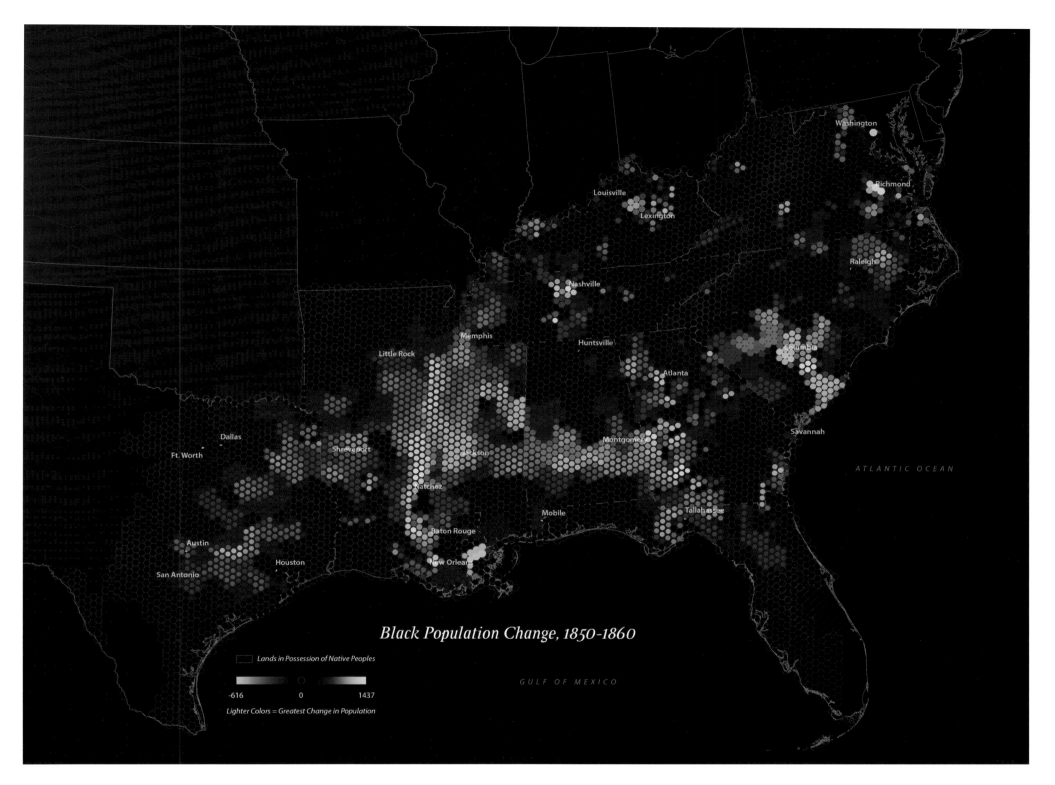

Black Population Change, 1850-1860

☐ *Lands in Possession of Native Peoples*

-616   0   1437

Lighter Colors = Greatest Change in Population

Slavery grows ever-more-intensely focused on the most fertile lands during this decade
of high prices for enslaved people. These laborers convert the Mississippi-Yazoo Delta
into raw plantations. The enslaved population of the Upper South barely grows, as young
people are shipped farther south and away from their families.

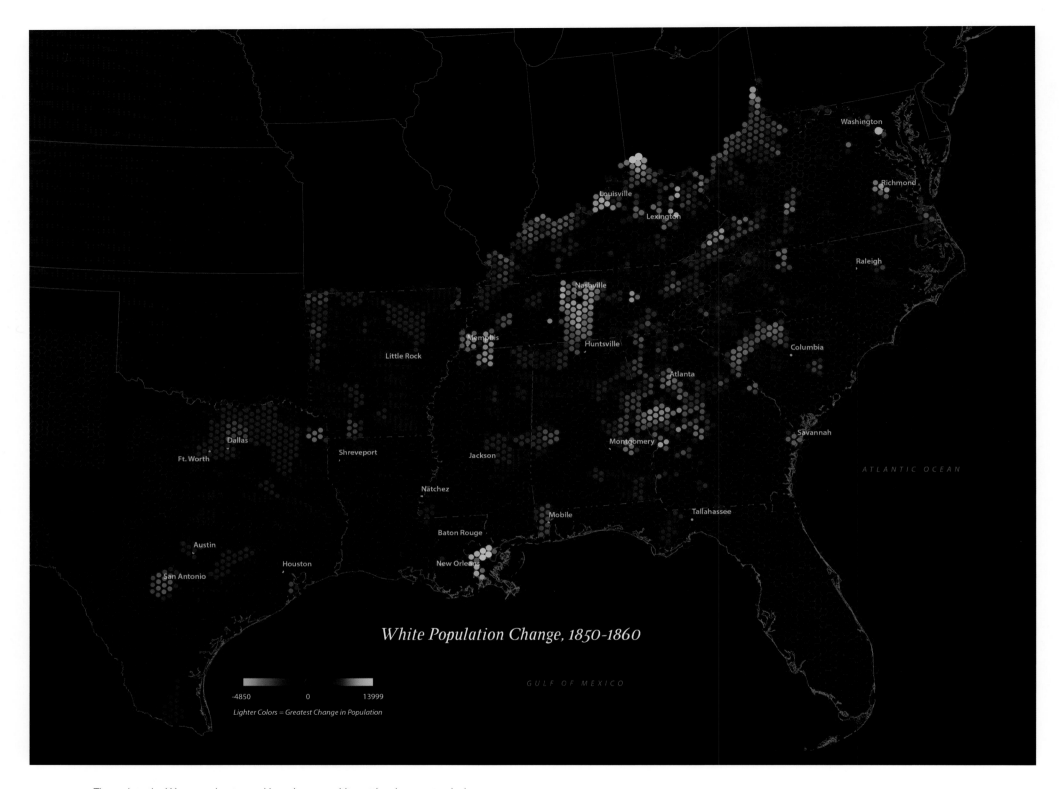

White Population Change, 1850-1860

-4850   0   13999

Lighter Colors = Greatest Change in Population

The rush to the West accelerates and broadens, as white settlers leave not only the
Piedmont but also the Cumberland Plateau of Middle Tennessee for Texas and Arkansas.

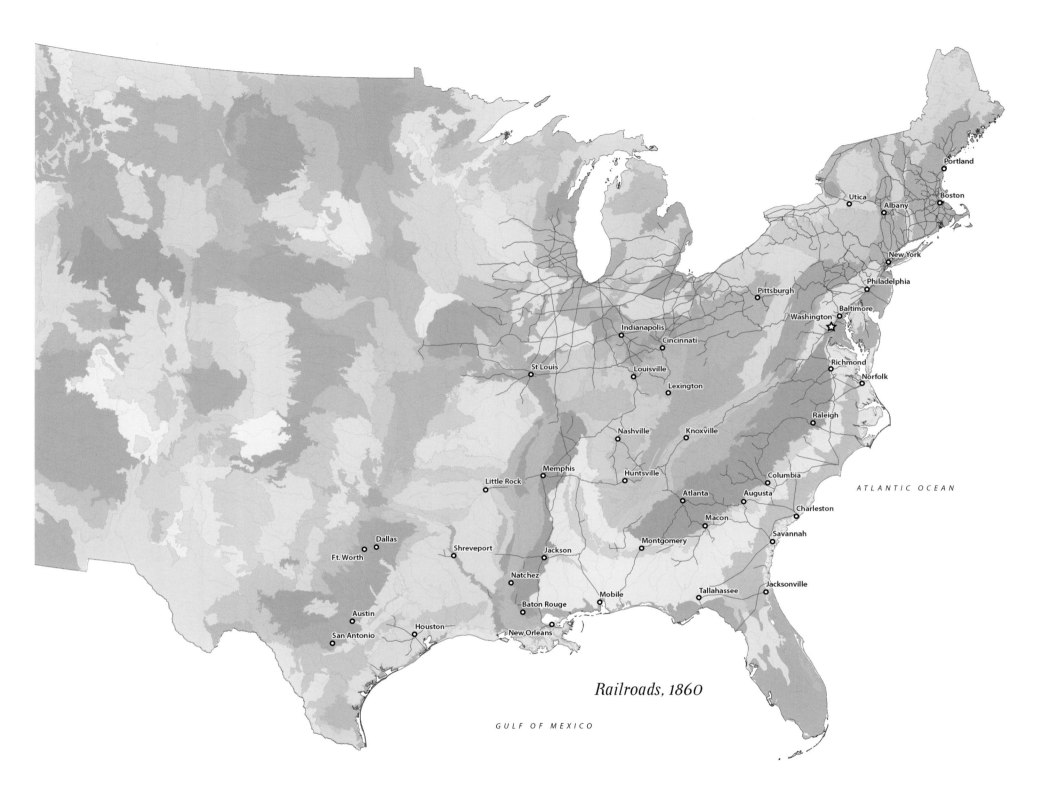

Portland
Utica
Albany
Boston
New York
Philadelphia
Pittsburgh
Baltimore
Washington
Indianapolis
Cincinnati
St Louis
Louisville
Richmond
Norfolk
Lexington
Raleigh
Nashville
Knoxville
Memphis
Huntsville
Columbia
Little Rock
Atlanta
Augusta
Charleston
Macon
Montgomery
Savannah
Dallas
Shreveport
Jackson
Ft. Worth
Natchez
Jacksonville
Tallahassee
Austin
Baton Rouge
Mobile
Houston
New Orleans
San Antonio

ATLANTIC OCEAN

Railroads, 1860

GULF OF MEXICO

Complementing the South's extensive system of rivers, railroads grow rapidly during the 1850s. While not as extensive as those of the North and Midwest, the South develops a large, new network of transportation and communication.

worked in factories and sometimes lived on their own. In Charleston, Savannah, and Mobile, African Americans labored on docks and in shops. Slavery proved alarmingly adaptable to different economic purposes.

The older states of the South, especially Virginia, began to see a new kind of growth and development during the 1850s. Despite decades of white emigration and forced Black migration, Virginia remained the largest state in the South for both white and Black people, its population growing by nearly a third between 1840 and 1860 through natural reproduction. Hiring and renting of enslaved people provided a flexible way for slaveowners to derive revenue from their "excess" human property. Planters and farmers, meanwhile, shifted their crops toward vegetables and wheat. Giant flour-mills in Richmond ground wheat for distant markets, both domestic and international, and enslaved workers processed tobacco and forged iron in new factories.

Even the upcountry of South Carolina, which had seen so many of its white residents leave, rebounded. People invested the returns from the high cotton prices of the decade into railroads, banks, and towns. As one farmer wrote his brothers in Alabama in 1852, "There is nothing like a railroad running through a country." His brothers spoke of moving to Arkansas "or some other new country and advise[d] me to leave this old place—in reply I would advise you to return to this country. It has become an entirely new place." South Carolinians saw signs of a new commercial spirit throughout the region and welcomed that spirit. Newspapers grew throughout the region, as did telegraphs and railroads.[54]

Slavery in the 1850s extended into places it had not been strong before: into the mountains of Appalachia and the piney woods of the coasts, into railroad camps and iron foundries, and into hiring and leasing of laborers among emerging businesses in the Chesapeake. Slavery had never been more profitable, more adaptable, and—critical to every other attribute—more portable than in the 1850s. White southerners saw no reason their slave society could not expand into Cuba and Central America if the United States would help enable that expansion of empire as it had enabled the removal of the American Indians and the defeat of the Mexicans.[55]

Relationships and categories had to be constantly renegotiated on the perpetual frontier of the South as people left, traveled, arrived, and often departed again. For individual families, the flux created both the impression and reality of possibility. Chances were that the land to which people moved was more productive than the land they had left, the places for cattle and hogs to graze more plentiful. Chances were that a new cotton plantation would produce greater profits than an old wheat or tobacco plantation. Chances were that propertyless families would find at least the opportunity of claiming a homestead in a remote, unsettled area.[56]

These individual possibilities, however, did not add up to a more democratic social order. The possibilities for greater slaveholding fell to those who already held or inherited enslaved people, for they could convert the rising prices for the people they already held into collateral for the additional people they wanted to buy. The opportunities for rich land came to those who had the cash to pay speculators or to collude with other wealthy men to purchase expansive tracts of the best lands as they came on the market from the Choctaws, Creeks, Chickasaws, or Cherokees. Families who possessed a few slaves, along with some cash or access to credit, could prosper on the moving frontiers of the South.

The percentages of white families owning enslaved people neither decreased nor increased in the western states. Slavery became neither more concentrated nor more distributed as white people moved. The percentage of land in a state that could support plantation agriculture, not the duration of settlement, determined its percentage of slaveholders. South Carolina and Mississippi, claiming the highest ratios of land suitable for producing staples, shared the highest percentage of slaveowners in 1860: 46 and 49 percent, respectively. Georgia and Alabama, despite white people leaving the former for the latter, each saw about 35 percent of white people owning slaves. The older southern states of Virginia and North Carolina claimed about the same percentage of slaveholders—a little over a quarter—as the new state of Texas and the sugar-producing state of Louisiana.

THE PARADOXES OF THE SLAVE SOUTH

Settlement made the South resemble the North in critical ways. The slave South spread as rapidly as the slaveless North, often through the same stages. The rates of population turnover were about the same in both regions, with most people in a given place leaving each decade. Mobility worked as a kind of gyroscope in both the North and the South, the rapid spinning of the population stabilizing relationships in a society filled with strangers.[57]

As in other settler societies, much of the enormous labor of economic, cultural, and political construction in the slave South was privatized. After the federal government had driven out the indigenous people—their removal often paid for by returns from selling their land—it expended little more. Local taxpayers put up courthouses as one of their first acts and then paid to have their land surveyed and registered. Merchants took it upon themselves to create stores and towns and to lobby for railroads to come to the county. Politicians produced newspapers that would tie their new communities to national and state political parties. Evangelical settlers quickly formed churches in their communities, anchoring raw settlements with the Protestant morality whose authority everyone acknowledged, even if they did not obey it. Slaveowners relied on a combination of state law, policing by every white man, and vibrant commercial markets in human flesh to institute an instant labor force on new plantations.

The massive and mobile enslaved population of the American South differentiated it from other settler societies. Slavery prevented the South's settler society from developing as it did elsewhere, with densely populated towns and farms. No matter how long they had been established, from the oldest parts of Virginia to the newest districts in Texas, counties in the South generated a population density about half that of the North. Plantations pulled development into themselves. Wealthy settlers used up the land because it was cheaper than labor; new slaves were expensive and risky, but more rich soil always lay nearby. Slaveholders needed to make the most from each slave, not from each acre. Larger plantations with larger labor forces were more efficient than small farms.[58]

While the North grew denser in the 1850s, the South did not. The southern economy and social order moved enormous numbers of people according to the dictates of the slave economy, creating a society that was both efficiently mobile and relatively undeveloped at the same time. While cotton did not grow everywhere in the South, the crop acted as a gravitational field that concentrated Black populations. The overall population density was greatest where the largest numbers of Black people lived, but enslaved people did not foster the commercial development or community building that free people did.

Southern white settlers possessed in slave labor a tool that accelerated primary settlement but reduced advanced settlement. That dispersed pattern meant there were fewer businesses, fewer schools, fewer villages, and fewer artisans in wealthy plantation districts. While the North attracted many immigrants from abroad, especially from Germany and Ireland, the rapid population movement of the South remained almost entirely internal. Immigrants

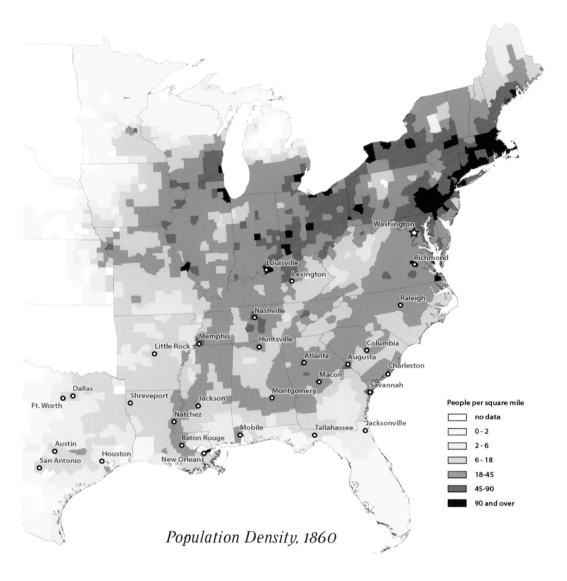

Population Density, 1860

People per square mile
- no data
- 0 - 2
- 2 - 6
- 6 - 18
- 18 - 45
- 45 - 90
- 90 and over

The areas of greatest population density are those where enslaved people labor on plantations, not where white people create the dense rural, town, and urban communities emerging in the North and Midwest.

Percentage of Foreign-Born Population, 1860

people per sq/mi

percentage of foreign-born people

40%

0%

50+   0

While some immigrants come to southern cities and parts of Texas, the divergence between
the North and the South has grown extreme by 1860. The enormous population movement
within the South, both white and African American, is almost entirely native-born.

seldom moved to the rural South because enslaved labor choked off nearly all opportunity for propertyless-white arrivals.[59]

Some white southerners worried about the lack of social development, but many preferred, they said, their uncrowded, egalitarian, independent, low-tax, low-land-price, and unregulated rural society to that of the North. They did not want the immigrants and landless people who arrived in the free states, they said; they wanted to maintain things as they were and to extend that social order across space. Their ideal society required space, mobility, and movement, which is what they briefly enjoyed.

White southern men came to consider the prerogatives of a settler-slave society their birthright. Having the right to move when and where a man pleased demonstrated his property rights, gender rights, and racial rights—and this required commensurate political rights. This ideology would remain the bedrock of white southern political identity for generations to come, long after the plantations and farms had been plowed under or paved over.

Migration prevented the great disparities of wealth and poverty from dividing the South more profoundly. New land was not so much a safety valve as it was a sifter, depositing the largest slaveholders in places nonslaveholders did not particularly covet because those regions did not suit their purposes or realistic expectations. Similarly, slaveowners in the older states benefited from the growth westward, from the demand for cotton, and from the increase in the value of their slaves. Slavery's expansion did not leave the older South short of Black labor and, in fact, converted this resource into cash. Mobility unified the South across space.[60]

As American slavery spread across the southern landscape, enslaved people found no place of refuge. The areas with wide and deep connections among enslaved people in the eastern and Upper South were also the places where the slave trade worked insidiously to select young men and women, boys and girls, to take from their parents and those they loved for sale westward. The places where the greatest numbers of enslaved people moved demanded the hardest labor of clearing new plantations and gang work in cotton fields. Directed at the single goal of extracting as much cotton from the land in the shortest time possible, slavery as well as agriculture turned ever more toward monoculture, toward repetition and routinization.

That profound shift for the South's Black population pulled families apart with a silent but relentless logic, reflected in the ratios between enslaved men and enslaved women. The greatest imbalances grew in the places where families were separated—Virginia and North Carolina, in particular—and in the places where men were shipped to start new plantations along the Mississippi River and especially in the sugar regions of Louisiana.

While it is obvious why men would far outnumber women in the new plantation districts, where massive trees were felled and drainage ditches dug, the predominance of men in the older areas is less understandable. The skewed ratio may have resulted from the decisions of smaller slaveholders, six of ten of whom purchased a woman as their first slave property. As a result, in the many parts of the South where smaller slaveholding predominated, so did the proportion of enslaved females. A woman could work in the fields as well as in the home, after all, and one of childbearing years could also increase the number of slaves the white family owned. Thus, demand for women seems to have selected them out of Virginia and scattered them across the region, leaving the men behind.

Enslaved people confronted this process as a set of harrowing changes. Not only were individuals torn from their families and communities, but they were also taken to places where the work was even more dangerous, deadly, and brutal. Digging and grubbing plantations out of the river land of the South took a horrific toll on the young men and women dragged there to do that work. Disease and accident killed many. The opportunity to start a family or learn a trade were stripped away when males worked in gangs and housed in log lean-tos far from any settlement or church. With no apologies and no apparent guilt, white Americans systematically mined the enslaved people of the Atlantic Seaboard just as they mined the soil of the Southwest.

The indigenous peoples relocated to the Indian Territory had gained some demographic stability by the 1850s, after devastating contagious disease had killed up to a third of the Native peoples who had survived the forced marches of the 1830s. Each of the nations settled in the eastern part of the territory, where the landscape resembled those from which they had been driven east of the Mississippi River. The three largest nations—the Cherokees, the Choctaws, and the Creeks—claimed about 13,000 people each in 1860, while the Chickasaws had 4,260 people and the Seminoles 2,630.

Each of these Native American peoples owned large numbers of enslaved African Americans. The Cherokees and Choctaws registered 2,511 and 2,349 slaves, respectively, or about 15 percent of their total population. Enslaved people accounted for an even larger share of the populations of the Chickasaws and Seminoles, with nearly a third of the total Seminole population held

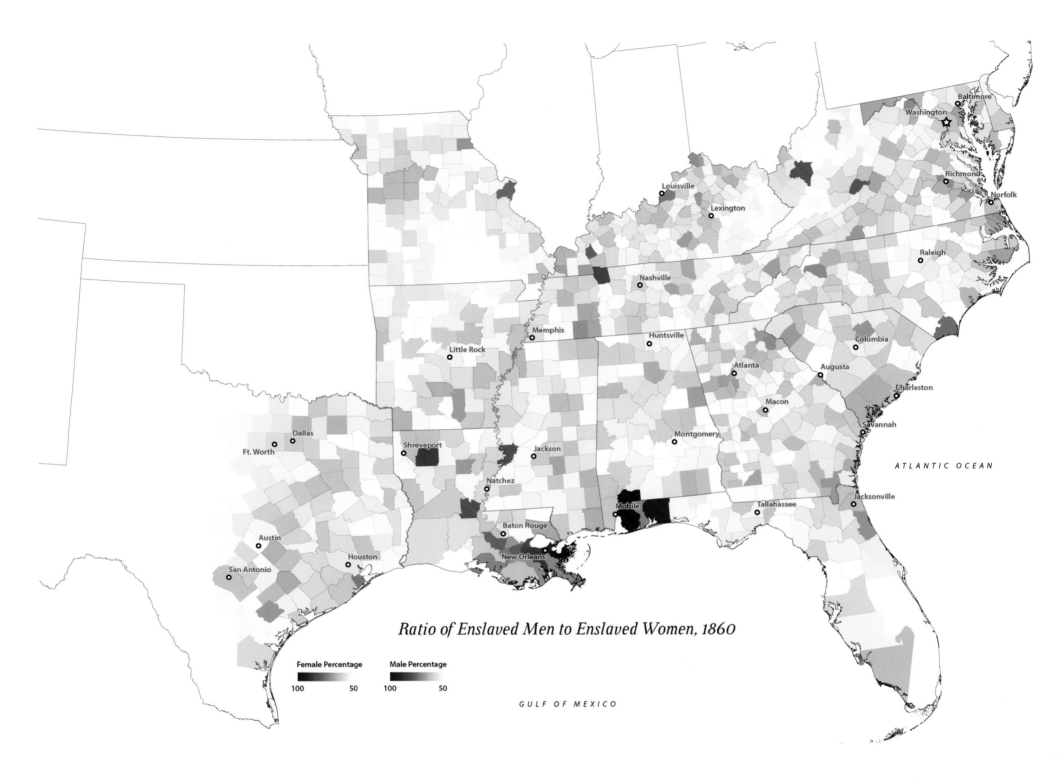

Ratio of Enslaved Men to Enslaved Women, 1860

Female Percentage   Male Percentage

100   50   100   50

GULF OF MEXICO

ATLANTIC OCEAN

The domestic slave trade separates men from women, as traders and planters ship male
workers to the sugar fields of Louisiana and Texas as well as to the new plantation areas
along the Mississippi River. Most parts of the South, by contrast, display a disproportionate
share of enslaved females, as small slaveholders purchase women who perform a wide
range of work as well as bear children claimed by the owner of the mother. The older
areas of slavery, especially in Virginia, are left with a larger share of men.

in slavery. Some of the enslaved people, especially near the Red River, raised cotton; others gathered salt. Most labored on smaller farms that produced few cash crops.[61]

SOUTHERN MIGRATION AND THE CRISIS OF THE NATION

The 1850s saw the movement of the preceding twenty years pay dividends to white southerners. More farmers produced more cotton in more places, with the South doubling its production from two million pounds in 1850 to four million pounds a decade later—two-thirds of the world's supply. Louisiana's sugar harvest of 1860 was the largest ever recorded. More than a million new acres were farmed in Arkansas and Louisiana, more than a million and a half in Mississippi and Tennessee, and more than two million in Alabama. Isolated crossroads grew into towns of hundreds of people. Sawmills and cotton gins developed alongside churches and schools. The newest state, Texas, already published seventy-one newspapers and boasted nine railroad companies by 1860.

In all these ways, the expansion of the settler-slave society of the preceding half century emboldened the South to demand ever more space to expand within the nation and beyond. The South's insistence on its rights grew less from desperation than it did from confidence that it had found the formula for its very nature, its very "way of life," as apologists would call it. That way of life was based on a dynamic slavery: mobile, hired and rented, urban and industrial, expanding, and self-perpetuating.

As the future of slavery became the defining issue of American politics in the late 1850s, the logic of migration became the logic of voting. Hundreds of thousands of southern white men had already voted with their feet, casting their lot with movement, with the expansion of the South. Their experience primed them for resistance to newly emerging Republican opponents who challenged that assertion. Those southerners had seen their society move fast, slavery expand fast, places fill up fast. They had also seen soil exhausted in a few years and the best lands taken by the richest men. Those who voted for southern rights voted for their right to keep moving, either to protect slavery or to escape the consequences of slavery.[62]

The patterns of voting in the South in 1860 embodied this history of migration. Places that witnessed stagnant or even declining white population movement tended to vote for John Bell, the Constitutional Unionist, while those where the largest numbers of new settlers had recently arrived supported John C. Breckinridge, the secession candidate. South Carolina did not have a direct election for president in 1860 (and thus did not record votes), but it was the first state to secede. The massive outmigration and sale of enslaved people over the preceding two generations tied South Carolina to expansion and gave white Carolinians reason to worry about what would happen if that expansion stopped.

The strongest indicator of who voted for Breckinridge was not slaveholding itself—since every candidate declared himself the defender of slavery—but the rate of white and Black population growth in the preceding decade. The Breckenridge vote in Alabama and Mississippi proved strongest in counties where plantations were growing most rapidly, weakest where that economy had already peaked. The energy for political rebellion radiated from men who had recently moved and who demanded the right to move again should they choose.[63]

●●●

Migration defined the enduring character of the United States. The new nation, amorphous in 1790, quickly defined itself as a settler society, a nation built by pioneers who took land from indigenous people and filled it with migrants. The course of American political, legal, and military history reenacted the sequence over and over across a vast expanse: military and governmental power made property out of territory, law expanded to protect that property, and the nation celebrated the opportunity to gain property as the essence of the American dream.

The South shared that course of nation building along with the North, claiming the principles of a settler society as its own and building a shared political language of white male independence. But, in a crucial and defining difference, the white South forged a modern network of racial slavery entangled within and resting upon that settler society. Slavery took advantage of the power, wealth, and mobility of a settler society, but it undermined the drive toward full "settlement"—a dense community of farms and towns. By 1860, the settler societies of the North and South had run out of room for their parallel settlement, for their future of unlimited expansion, and for their demands of perpetual replication. Migration had created a vast new nation with breathtaking speed; now it threatened that nation's existence.

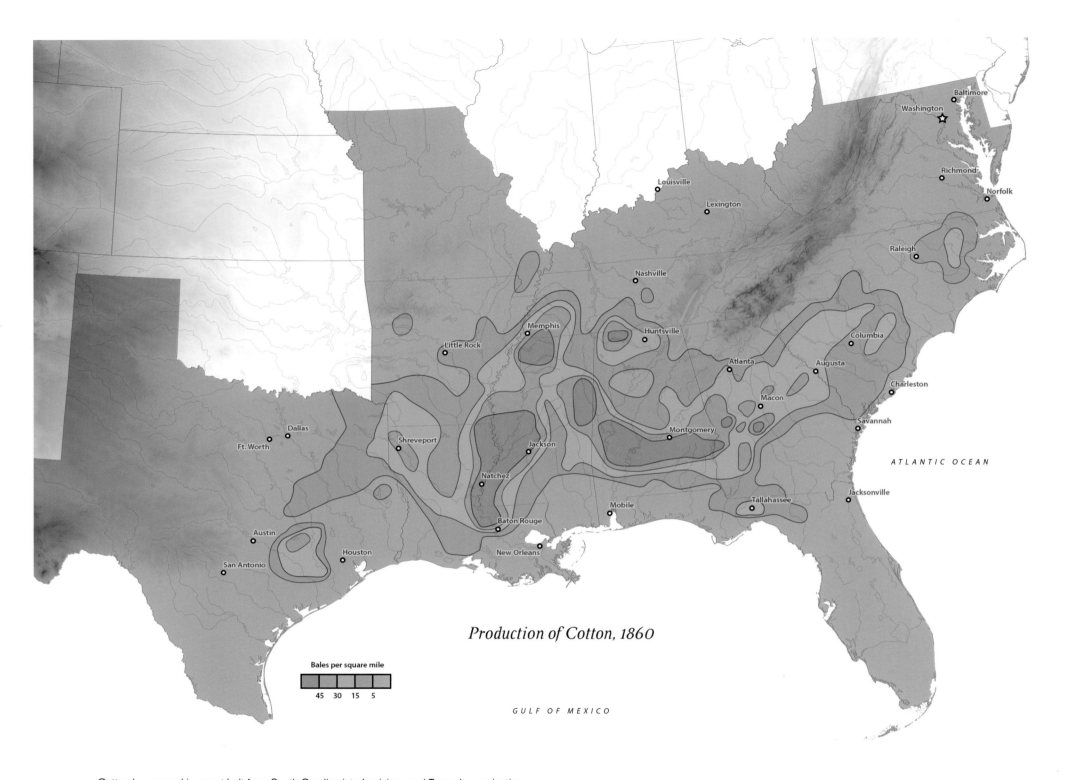

Production of Cotton, 1860

Bales per square mile

45	30	15	5	

GULF OF MEXICO

ATLANTIC OCEAN

Cotton has spread in a vast belt from South Carolina into Louisiana and Texas. Its production is anchored in the Black Belt and along the Mississippi River from Baton Rouge to Memphis, establishing itself in Arkansas, Louisiana, and Texas as well as in the Mississippi-Yazoo Delta.

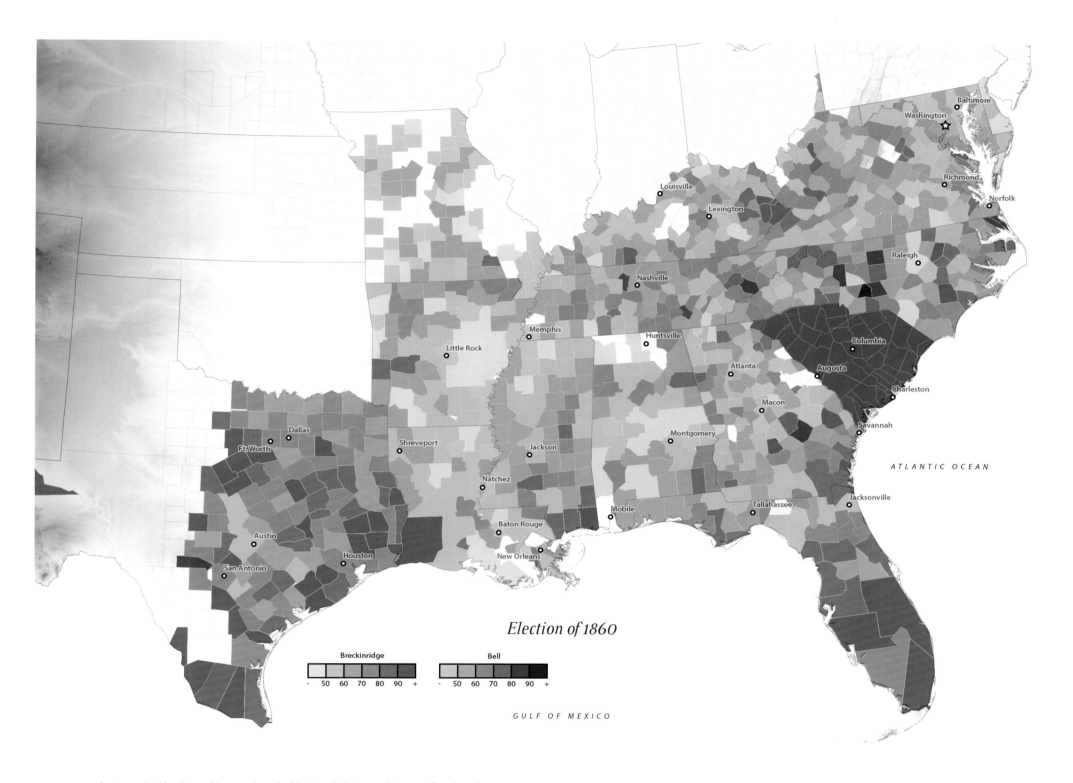

Election of 1860

Breckinridge
- 50 60 70 80 90 +

Bell
- 50 60 70 80 90 +

GULF OF MEXICO

ATLANTIC OCEAN

Baltimore
Washington
Richmond
Norfolk
Louisville
Lexington
Raleigh
Nashville
Memphis
Huntsville
Little Rock
Columbia
Atlanta
Augusta
Macon
Charleston
Dallas
Ft. Worth
Shreveport
Jackson
Montgomery
Savannah
Natchez
Austin
Baton Rouge
Mobile
Tallahassee
Jacksonville
Houston
San Antonio
New Orleans

Areas marked by the rapid expansion of white population over the preceding decade—
especially Alabama, Mississippi, Florida, Arkansas, and Texas—vote heavily for the states'
rights Democrat, John C. Breckinridge. Areas with great concentrations of enslaved people,
on the other hand, across the entire Upper South as well as in the Georgia Piedmont and
the Mississippi Delta, vote for the Constitutional Union Party and its platform of protecting
slavery where it is already entrenched.

TWO

THE RESTLESS SOUTH, 1860–1940

The settler-slave society of the South was destroyed at a peak of expansion, prosperity, and confidence. The leaders of the would-be nation of the Confederacy demanded the right to take their human property into yet more territory to be taken from yet more Native peoples. They gambled everything on that vision of the future, a vision based on generations of migration. The defeat of the Confederacy and the end of slavery transformed the South from a unique settler-slave society to a new society, one without a blueprint or an example to follow.

MIGRANTS OF WAR

White Confederate civilians who fled before the arrival of U.S. troops called themselves "refugees," innocent people seeking refuge in some place not their home. Members of wealthy families believed the Union army would humiliate them and destroy their homes. Slaveholders sent enslaved people away from potentially liberating armies, pushing tens of thousands of African Americans from their families. Some were transported to distant plantations in the interior South, while others were hired out to safer locales.[1]

Thousands of white refugees swept into the cities of the Confederacy. Families abandoned farms and plantations to move to New Orleans and Baton Rouge, to Nashville and Memphis, to Savannah and Charleston, or to Richmond, Atlanta, and Columbia, seeking safety in numbers. As one southern city after another fell to Union armies and navies, refugees fled to another city that seemed safer. Planters drifted into the mountains and into the Carolinas, into Confederate-protected territory in Mississippi, and into Texas. Such refugees, welcomed at first by local people, confronted increasing resistance as food and housing shortages worsened. Wealthy arrivals made few efforts to hide their sense of superiority over their reluctant hosts.[2]

Southern Unionists became different kinds of refugees, intimidated into leaving their homes by their neighbors and by the Confederate government. They sold what they owned, often at great loss, and fled the South if they could. Unionists took their families into East Tennessee, western North Carolina, or western Virginia, but they found only uncertain safety there as neighbor fought neighbor in the mountains. Poor families on the move, political outcasts without the resources of the wealthy, found few allies other than enslaved people who might try to help as they could.

Most Confederate refugees would probably have been safer had they remained at their homes, for their flight came at great expense and risk. Abandoned plantations fell easy prey to enemy soldiers, who took great pleasure in destroying fine furniture and furnishings, and enslaved people took advantage of the dislocations to escape bondage. The desperate and scattered flight of white refugees from the countryside began a migration from plantation districts that would proceed for generations.

While white refugees fled from the Union army, Black refugees fled from slavery. Hundreds of thousands of enslaved people came into contact with the U.S. Army and Navy during the war. African American people and the army confronted one another along the Atlantic coast, from Virginia to Florida; along the Mississippi River from New Orleans to the Ohio River; along the Tennessee River, sweeping across the two ends of the state that bore its name as well as far northern Alabama; and ever deeper into the Confederate interior as the war progressed. Every exchange was unpredictable, shaped by the military situation, the character of the soldiers, the identity of the enslaved, and the circumstances, which were often beyond anyone's control.

Enslaved people rushed to Union troops in gratitude and hope, aiding the troops with information and labor, often leaving with them when the soldiers marched on. Sometimes the army welcomed the enslaved people and gave them refuge; at other times and places, those in flight received only violence, disdain, and rejection. Some fugitives followed the soldiers regardless of invitation, carrying what they could, trying to keep up with the ranks. Sometimes failing, they would find themselves abandoned along the road, uncertain of whether to return to their former owners, where they were sure to be punished, or to look for new refuge elsewhere.[3]

With or without the aid of the Union army, enslaved people took advantage of war's chaos to seek freedom. Many followed roads and trails to uncertain destinations. Fighting hunger as well as white patrols, fugitives from slavery risked and sometimes lost their lives on the way. The long border between the United States and Mexico offered freedom during the Civil War to enslaved people sent to Texas by their owners, sympathetic Mexican people helping the fugitives cross the Rio Grande.[4]

Half a million enslaved people, as individuals, families, and communities, escaped slavery during the war and fled to Union posts, where they constructed makeshift camps. The refugees moved into abandoned buildings or propped up ragged canvas tents and lean-tos outside the camps' boundaries.

Some army commanders provided for the nearby refugees; others neglected, resented, or resisted them. Called "contrabands" by the U.S. Army, those who fled slavery were more than that word conveyed, more than property seized from military enemies. They were refugees from the world of slavery.

Beginning in the first days of the war, at Fort Monroe in Virginia, more than three hundred refugee camps developed, from the Atlantic coast to the Mississippi River. Some of them, especially those established in the East early in the conflict, lasted years and grew into large and lasting communities. Others, especially those thrown together along the rivers and railroads in the western theater, lasted only as long as Union forces paused.

Women, children, the elderly, and the ill filled these camps as military-aged men enlisted in the U.S. Army or were sent to labor on fortifications and railroads. Women cooked or did laundry for the soldiers, trying to keep their children nourished and safe from the disease that ravaged these sites, where mosquitoes bred and sewage festered. A hundred thousand people died in the camps.

When the war came to an end, so did the refugee camps. More than eight of ten white U.S. soldiers went home within six months after Appomattox, removing security as the refugee camps dissolved and former Confederates returned home. Black people streamed into Union-occupied cities such as Norfolk, New Orleans, and Memphis, where racial massacres of African Americans descended in 1866 as white police led riots against Black migrants.

More than eighty thousand enslaved people escaped the Upper South into the Midwest during the war and in the chaos that followed. Refugees often settled in cities near the Ohio River, but thousands more pushed into the upper Midwest. Steamboats provided free passage for those who would help stoke the fires that drove their engines. Most of the early migrants moved as families and established households in small cities and small towns. In the East recently enslaved people followed different routes out of the South. African Americans fled Virginia for cities from Washington, D.C., to Boston. Nearly twenty thousand Black people escaped Virginia during the war itself, and thousands more followed in the first years of freedom. New England's white population had long displayed liberal attitudes toward the enslaved people of the South, and during and immediately following the Civil War, they lived up to their word. In some places in Massachusetts, such as Worcester, white soldiers and their families sponsored the migration of individual African American families, helping them become established in new homes.[5]

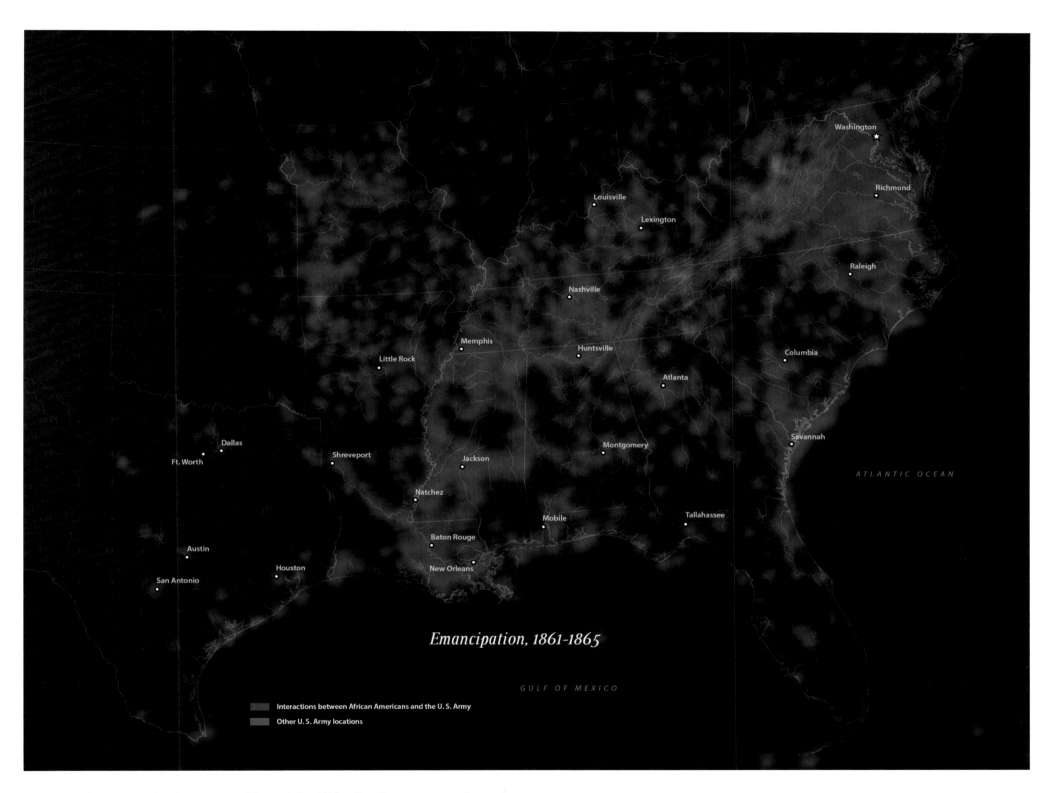

Emancipation, 1861-1865

Washington

Richmond

Louisville

Lexington

Raleigh

Nashville

Memphis

Huntsville

Columbia

Little Rock

Atlanta

Savannah

Dallas

Montgomery

ATLANTIC OCEAN

Ft. Worth

Shreveport

Jackson

Natchez

Mobile

Tallahassee

Austin

Baton Rouge

Houston

New Orleans

San Antonio

GULF OF MEXICO

Interactions between African Americans and the U. S. Army

Other U. S. Army locations

Enslaved people take advantage of the proximity of U.S. military forces to escape slavery
and seek refuge. That proximity is widespread but not universal. Most slaves never come
within reach of the Union army.

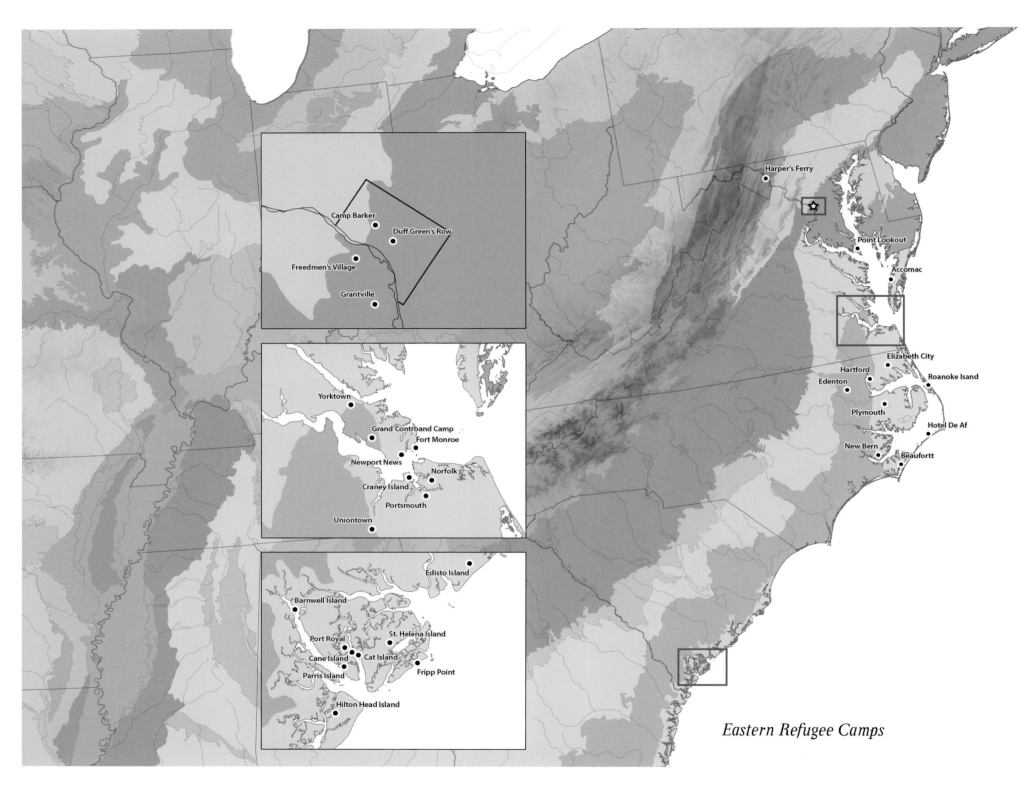

Camp Barker
Duff Green's Row
Freedmen's Village
Grantville

Yorktown
Grand Contraband Camp
Fort Monroe
Newport News
Norfolk
Craney Island
Portsmouth
Uniontown

Edisto Island
Barnwell Island
Port Royal
St. Helena Island
Cane Island
Cat Island
Parris Island
Fripp Point
Hilton Head Island

Harper's Ferry
Point Lookout
Accomac
Elizabeth City
Hartford
Roanoke Isand
Edenton
Plymouth
Hotel De Af
New Bern
Beaufortt

Eastern Refugee Camps

Most camps for refugees from slavery are established along the Atlantic coast and along the
Mississippi River, where large numbers of people live in slavery and the U.S. military wins early
victories and establishes secure bases.

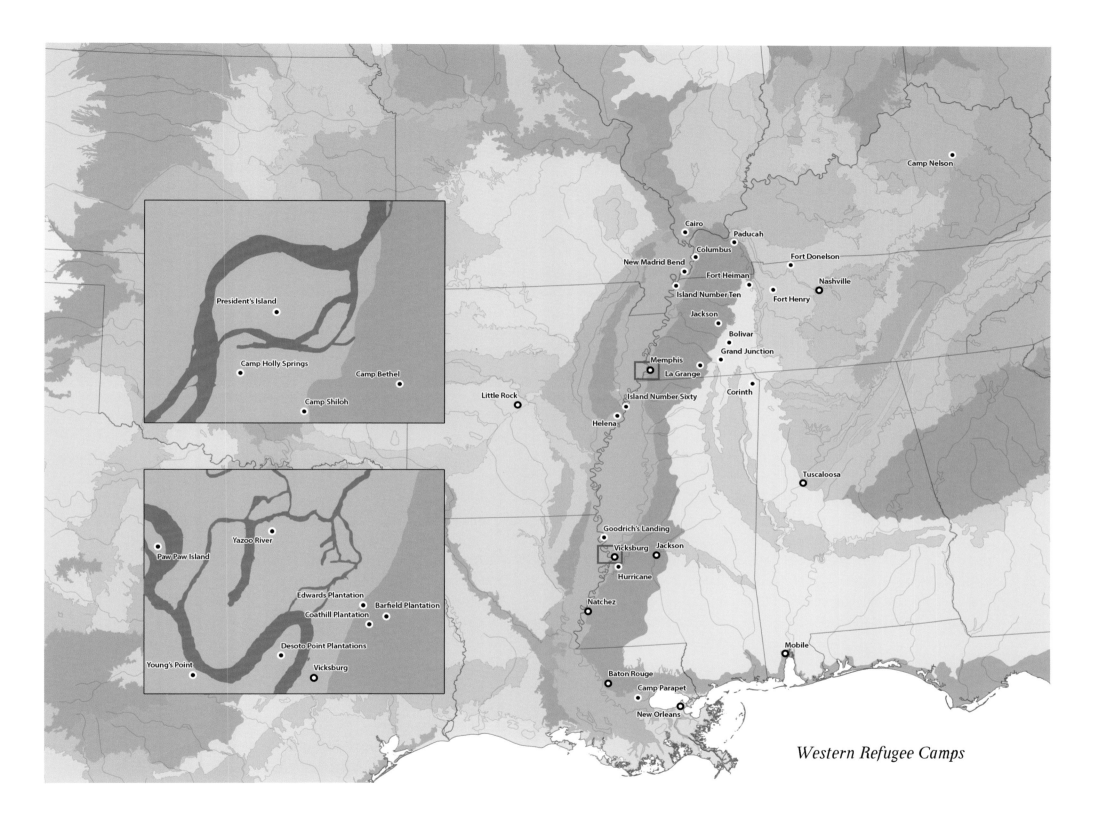

Cairo

Paducah

Columbus

New Madrid Bend

Fort Donelson

Fort Heiman

Nashville

Island Number Ten

Fort Henry

Jackson

Bolivar

Grand Junction

Memphis

La Grange

Little Rock

Island Number Sixty

Corinth

Helena

Tuscaloosa

Goodrich's Landing

Vicksburg   Jackson

Hurricane

Natchez

Mobile

Baton Rouge

Camp Parapet

New Orleans

President's Island

Camp Holly Springs

Camp Bethel

Camp Shiloh

Yazoo River

Paw Paw Island

Edwards Plantation

Barfield Plantation

Coathill Plantation

Desoto Point Plantations

Young's Point

Vicksburg

Western Refugee Camps

MIGRANTS OF FREEDOM

For the first time since the nation's founding, white southerners seemed frozen in place after their defeat in the Civil War. The Confederacy had sacrificed a quarter of its military-age male population; men who would have started families lay buried in graves across the South. The widows and orphans they left behind, like the elderly and the maimed, could not move on their own, no matter how desperate they might be. Families mourned the loss of a generation and white communities suffered stagnation and despair.[6]

Many white people fled plantation districts in the wake of the war, moving to the edge of white settlement in Texas and toward the white communities of the Upper South, where they would not compete with Black people for work. Even more than under slavery, most white people did not wish to live among Black people unless they benefited directly from their labor. White-majority cities such as Atlanta, Little Rock, and Jacksonville grew rapidly from white migrants.

State legislatures passed harsh Black codes to curtail the freedom of the people emerging from slavery, preventing them from moving from one land-owner to another. Sheriffs, constables, and courts rounded up migrants, charging them as vagrants and turning petty thieves into felons. Vigilantes, hidden behind masks and hoods, inflicted terror on Black people who dared enact freedom.

No one knew what might replace slavery in the countryside, for the formerly enslaved people owned virtually nothing, and the landowners had no cash to pay labor. Freedpeople refused to work in gangs, as they had under slavery, determined to create independence for their own families, to make the family the focus of work. Freedpeople preferred to exchange their labor for a share of the crop they grew, with land and housing provided by planters, who also sold workers clothing and food on credit. The hard and unequal bargain of sharecropping spread across the South, generating deceit, anger, and disappointment.[7]

Sharecropping fed Black migration as people sought out plantations, counties, or towns that held even a faint promise of greater opportunity, fairness, and security. Some landowners resorted to violence and coercion to force men and women to work on their plantations, but such strategies soon backfired as word spread among the laborers they needed. Particularly callous landowners turned to convict labor, work gangs fed by cynical laws and greedy sheriffs.[8]

Despite the efforts to hold them in place, Black people left the Piedmont from Virginia to Atlanta, the rich cotton lands of northern Alabama and Mississippi, and the bluegrass of Kentucky. Eastern Virginia saw vast numbers of African Americans leave the region between 1860 and 1870, enabled by the presence of the U.S. Army and enticed by the proximity of Washington, Richmond, and Norfolk. The once-rich rice plantations of the South Carolina low country, devastated by war, enemy occupation, and natural disasters, saw Black people flee to Charleston or Savannah.

Wartime movements of Black refugees became clearly legible in the federal census published five years after the war. Though that count overlooked more people than any other census in American history—nearly 7 percent, historians estimate, with a disproportionate number of African Americans left out—the patterns were striking nevertheless: wherever the U.S. Army had stayed for months or years, the Black population abandoned the countryside.

The river counties in Mississippi, Louisiana, and Arkansas saw an exodus as the U.S. Army recruited heavily among young African American men. In 1865 and 1866, flooding drove rivers over damaged levees, and armyworms consumed vast areas of cotton. Planters of enormous wealth five years earlier now fell deep into debt. As one wrote: "How still and lifeless everything seems. . . . The bare echoing rooms, the neglect and defacement of all. . . . Everything seems sadly out of time."[9]

The freedpeople of the river districts judged the situation and decided to leave. "They say that they have tried their old masters, know what they require, and how they will be treated," a Freedmen's Bureau official explained in the summer of 1865. "As they are now free, they will try some other place and some other way of working." The particularly harsh Black codes of Mississippi and Louisiana, rather than stopping migration, fed it. Landowners promptly ignored the laws they had demanded from legislators, bargaining with Black families to stay.[10]

Planters in the cotton South recruited Black workers from Virginia and the Carolinas. The Freedmen's Bureau helped transport people to the plantation districts of Alabama, western Georgia, northern Florida, and East Texas, thinking that the freedpeople would do better in these newer areas than among the used-up and washed-out fields of the East. With these tentative migrations of the immediate postwar years, a massive internal shifting of the African American population began.[11]

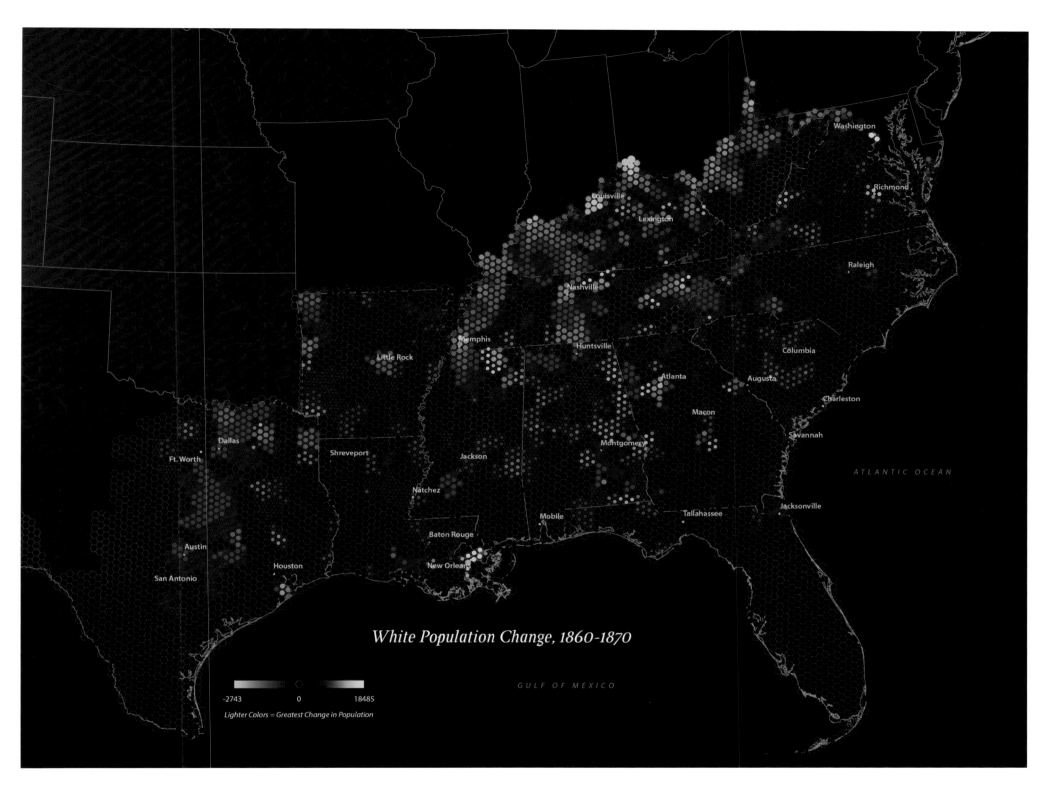

White Population Change, 1860-1870

-2743   0   18485

Lighter Colors = Greatest Change in Population

White people retreat from plantation areas in the decade of war and emancipation. Towns grow,
but migration remains relatively quiet because people do not possess the resources to move.

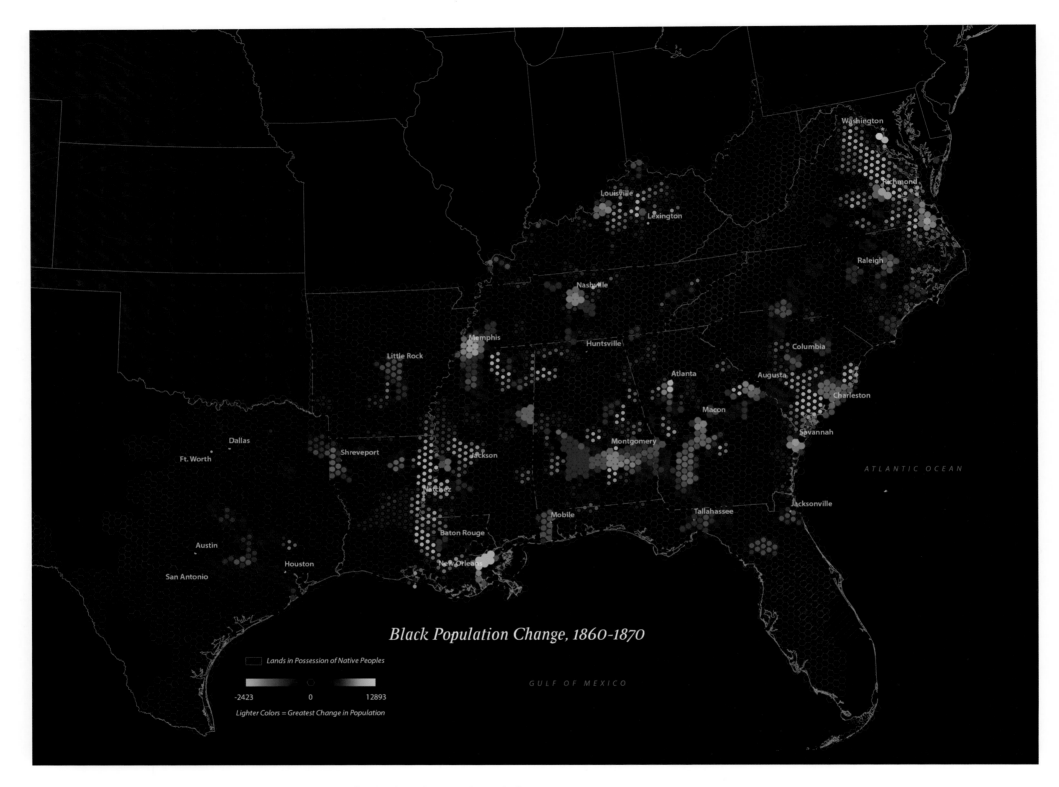

Black Population Change, 1860-1870

Lands in Possession of Native Peoples

-2423   0   12893

Lighter Colors = Greatest Change in Population

Many Black people move to the Black Belt of the Lower South, where sharecropping on fertile land promises some return for labor. The dislocations of wartime and its aftermath lead Black southerners to leave the districts along the Mississippi River and along the Virginia and South Carolina coasts.

A NEW SOUTH

Pushed and pulled by deep and rapid changes, the rural people of the South moved repeatedly after 1880. More than half of all tenants moved every year, and farm laborers moved from one season to the next. White tenants and laborers moved even more often than their Black counterparts. High birthrates filled tenant shacks and farmhouses.

The migrations of the New South were purposeful but not as coordinated as they had been in the slave South. State-sponsored lotteries of indigenous lands no longer existed, nor did slave traders working to distribute African American people exactly where the market demanded, though labor agents recruited men and women to work in some of the more isolated places. Railroads reached into some remote areas, creating towns and markets where they had not existed before. Logging companies bought land, stripped it of its trees, and abandoned the used-up acreage. Black and white families followed, trying to benefit from the dislocations and newly cleared land. Manufacturing pulled in ever more people to textile factories and mill villages.[12]

Towns and cities replaced rural settlement as the engines of growth. Those places drew people out of the country, either as refugees from dismal rural areas or as ambitious seekers of new opportunities. Once people of either race moved to a town, they were unlikely to return; young people left the countryside more frequently than their elders.

Across the South, towns of fewer than 2,500 people doubled in the 1870s and then doubled again by 1900, when more than 1.2 million people lived in two thousand such communities. More than 90 percent of southerners by 1890 lived in a county crossed by a railroad, altering the rhythms of daily life and transforming agriculture, industry, and politics. The cities of the South grew as fast as those of the North and West, two of the most rapidly urbanizing places in the world.

Railroads extended the reach of a new cotton empire far beyond the cotton kingdom of slavery. By 1891, the South grew twice as much cotton as it had in 1861. The rail lines brought in guano, fertilizer that allowed the plants to flourish where before they would not grow profitably. Landlords demanded that sharecroppers, Black and white, grow only cotton; their food would be purchased, on credit, at a plantation store. Landowners and merchants wrung all they could from white and Black farmers alike, deploying expensive credit, liens, mortgages, and high prices at stores.[13]

The harder southern farmers, Black and white, worked—the more cotton they planted, picked, ginned, baled, and shipped—the further they fell behind. The price of cotton relentlessly declined, from twenty-four cents in 1870 to seven cents in 1894. The South's near monopoly of cotton had been sacrificed during the Civil War; now, India and Egypt offered laborers paid even less than those in the American South. Consumers around the world drove prices lower as millions of them purchased inexpensive cotton clothing from burgeoning suppliers. Global demand doubled between 1860 and 1890 and then doubled again by 1920.[14]

Driven by the same machinery of transportation, communication, and commerce that powered other settler societies, including the North, the South became a failed settler society whose essential ingredient—a commodity to sell on the world market—suffered falling prices and overproduction. Black southerners barely had a chance. Without the advantages enjoyed by white southerners before emancipation—inexpensive land, easy credit, and high prices for cotton—former slaves and their descendants struggled. They could not establish farms even though they shared the ideal of household autonomy that had driven the South's original settler society. The federal government did not support Black farmers as it had white farmers in the South nor as it was then doing with white farmers in the West.

Farms shrank as rural districts became crowded through natural increase and as parents divided acreage among children. The open range on which farmers had relied disappeared; laws declared that hogs and cattle now had to be fenced in and kept out of other people's fields. Fertilizer, seed, work animals, and implements became expensive necessities. Pushed ever more intensively, farms suffered from eroded soil, cut-over woods, and abandoned fields. White tenancy spread like a cancer.[15]

Black migration responded quickly to both constraint and possibility. In the 1870s, when a massive depression wracked the region and the nation, Black people moved in great numbers to the upper Piedmont of South Carolina and Georgia, where cotton grew in new fields. Others migrated to a strip of Alabama's Black Belt connected to markets by new railroads. The largest numbers of African American migrants traveled to the Mississippi Delta and the plantation districts of Arkansas and Louisiana as the dislocations of war faded and the richest soil in the nation beckoned.[16]

Some Black southerners banded together to establish their own communities through migration. Most famously, the "Exodusters," fired by religious belief as well as a determination to escape the violence and intimidation of

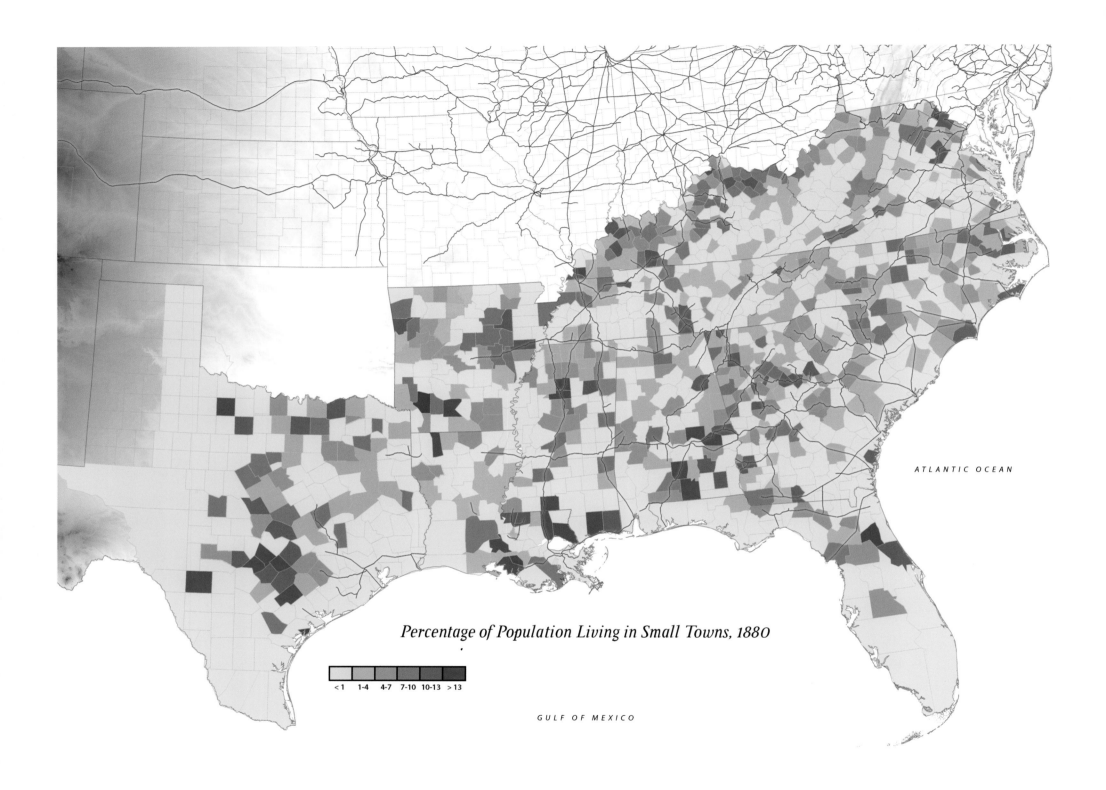

Percentage of Population Living in Small Towns, 1880

< 1   1-4   4-7   7-10   10-13   > 13

ATLANTIC OCEAN

GULF OF MEXICO

Much of the migration of the New South appears in named places of fewer than 2,500
people, the threshold of "urban" communities. Across the entire South, in areas long settled
and recently settled, people move to hamlets and towns along the new railroads.

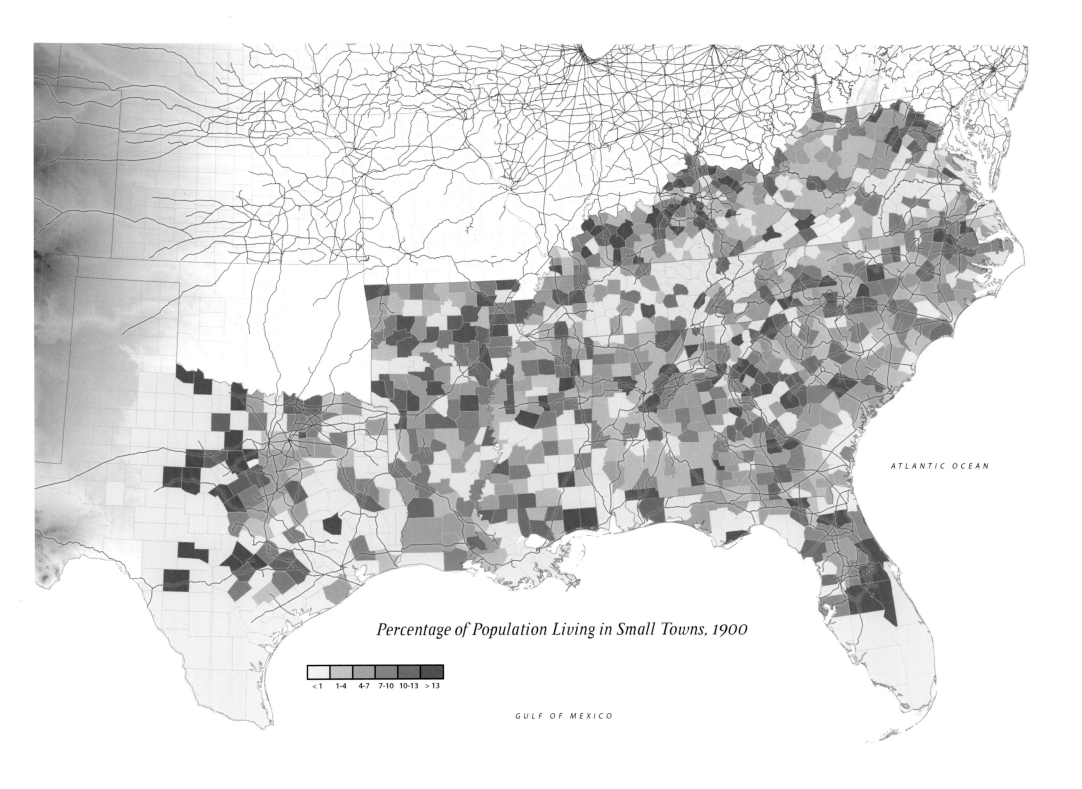

Percentage of Population Living in Small Towns, 1900

< 1   1-4   4-7   7-10   10-13   > 13

ATLANTIC OCEAN

GULF OF MEXICO

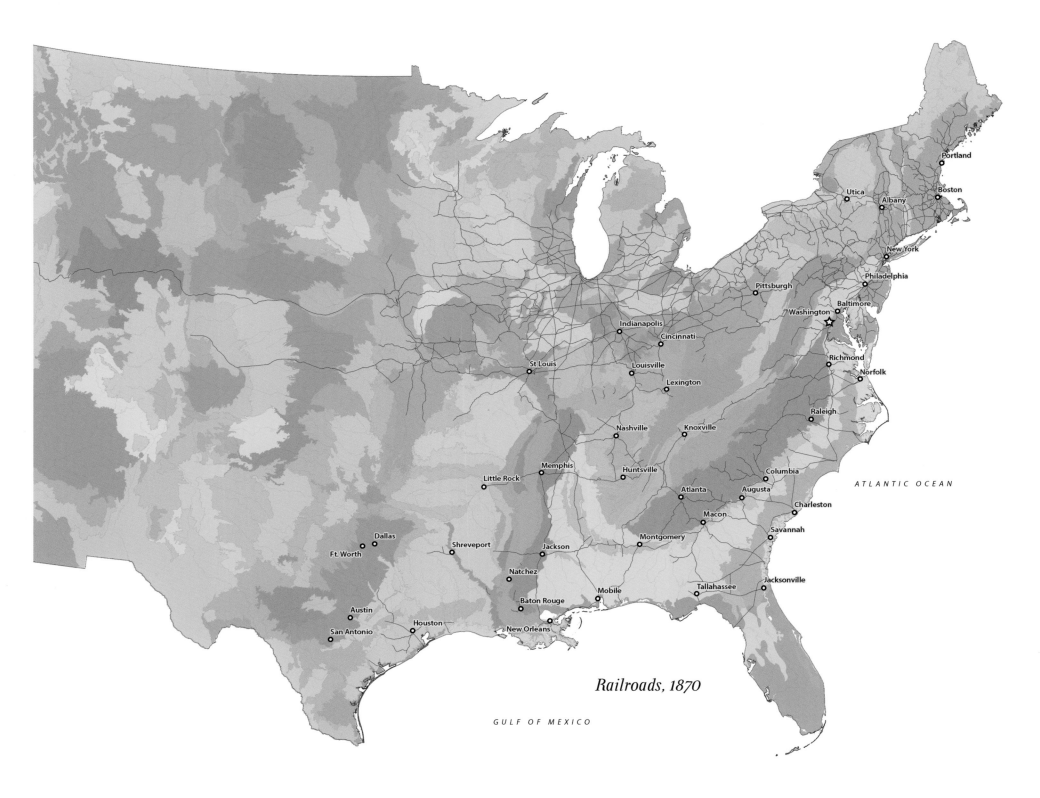

Railroads, 1870

The twenty years after 1870 witness the rapid rebuilding and then expansion of the southern
rail network. By 1890, railroads weave across vast new expanses from east to west.

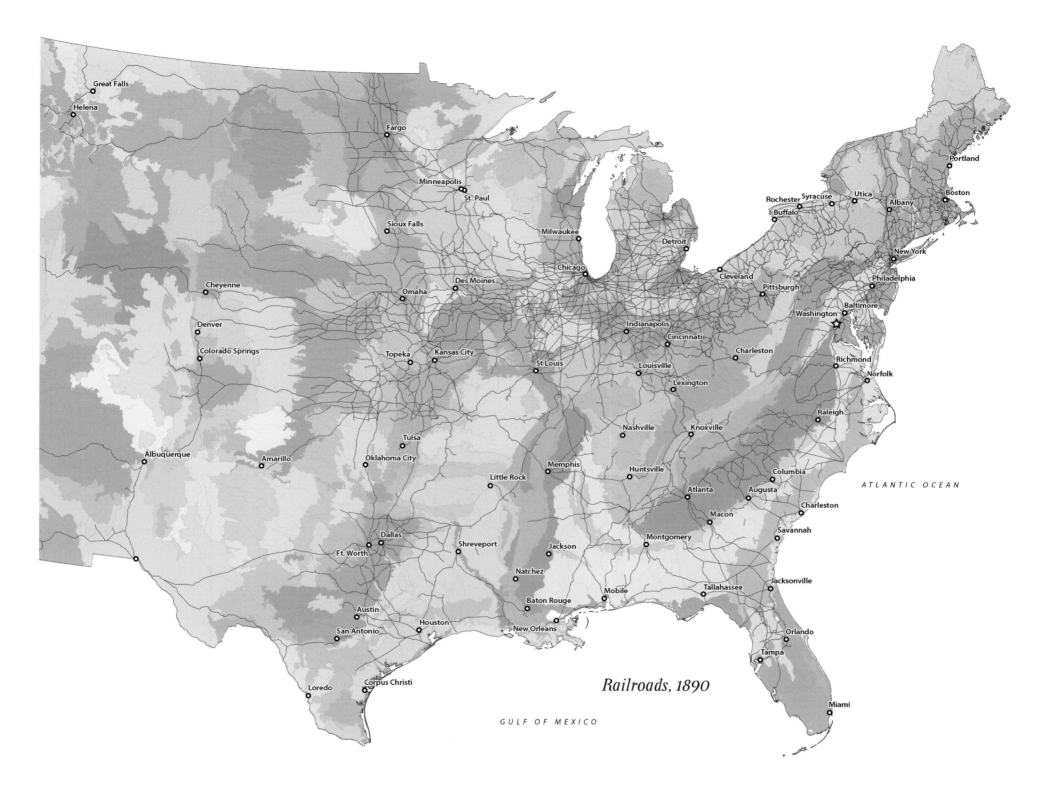

Railroads, 1890

Great Falls
Helena
Fargo
Minneapolis
St. Paul
Sioux Falls
Milwaukee
Detroit
Chicago
Cheyenne
Omaha
Des Moines
Cleveland
Pittsburgh
Denver
Indianapolis
Cincinnati
Colorado Springs
Topeka
Kansas City
St Louis
Charleston
Louisville
Richmond
Norfolk
Lexington
Nashville
Knoxville
Raleigh
Tulsa
Albuquerque
Amarillo
Oklahoma City
Memphis
Huntsville
Columbia
Little Rock
Atlanta
Augusta
Charleston
Macon
Savannah
Dallas
Shreveport
Jackson
Montgomery
Ft. Worth
Natchez
Mobile
Tallahassee
Jacksonville
Austin
Baton Rouge
San Antonio
Houston
New Orleans
Orlando
Tampa
Loredo
Corpus Christi
Miami

Rochester Syracuse Utica Albany
Buffalo
New York
Philadelphia
Baltimore
Washington
Portland
Boston

ATLANTIC OCEAN

GULF OF MEXICO

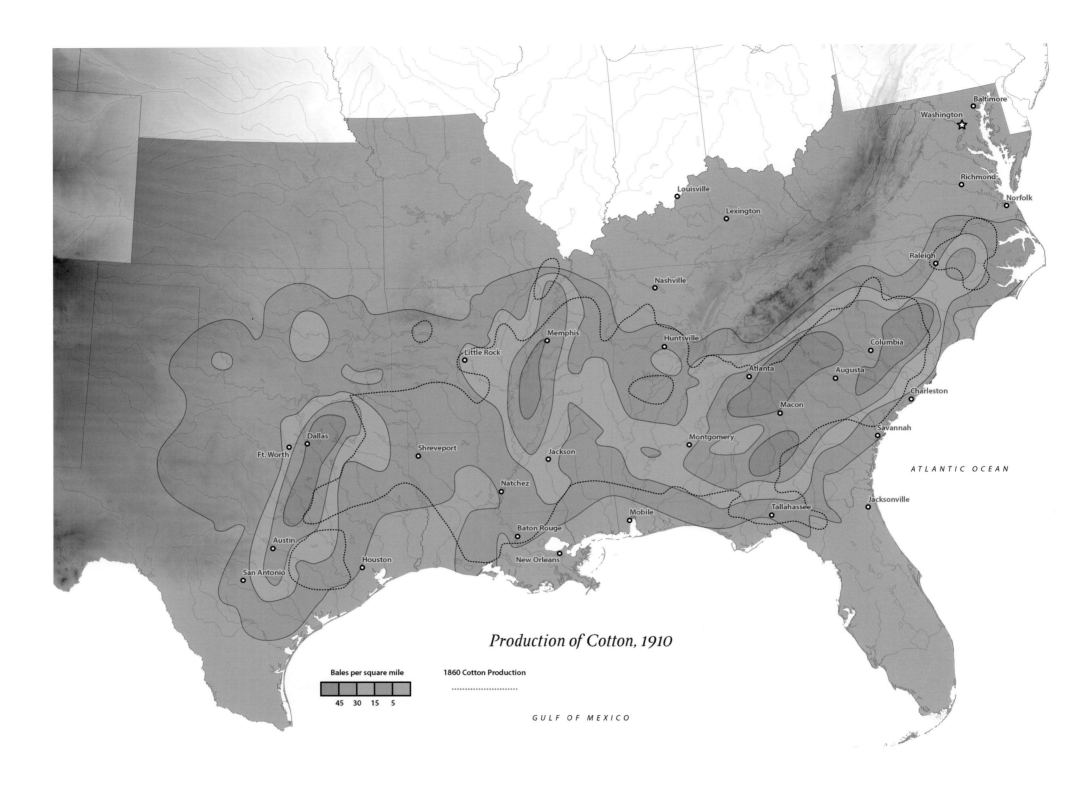

Production of Cotton, 1910

Bales per square mile

45 30 15 5

1860 Cotton Production

. . . .

GULF OF MEXICO

ATLANTIC OCEAN

The South grows far more cotton in the early twentieth century than it had at the peak of
slavery. Enabled by fertilizer and railroads, farmers there plant cotton over a much more
expansive range and with much greater intensity than before the Civil War.

the post-Reconstruction South, organized a mass migration to Kansas from Mississippi River districts. Tens of thousands of men, women, and children made the move in the decade after 1879, many of them going to the cities and others to the uplands of Kansas, the only land they could afford. At the same time, Black people formed independent communities in Texas, Florida, and the Indian Territory. Thousands of Black southerners dreamed of moving to Africa to build new lives for themselves, contributing money and organizing support for a large effort soon smothered by opposition and lack of resources.[17]

The future state of Oklahoma witnessed the history of the New South in especially concentrated form. After the Civil War, the federal government punished the Native peoples who had aligned with the Confederacy. The members of the Five Tribes—Cherokees, Choctaws, Chickasaws, Creeks, and Seminoles—were forced to relinquish their land rights to various railroad companies. Their territory also took on a new name, Oklahoma, "red people" in the language of the Choctaws. The federal government forced them to give up the practice of shared land and settle on individual allotments. Year after year, land originally reserved for Native peoples was taken until only a small portion of the territory remained in their hands.

White officials and reformers worked to dissolve tribal bonds and make American Indians into independent citizens. Over several decades and after a series of legal decisions, tribal identity and sovereignty shifted from a focus on the land the people occupied to their membership in a particular Native nation. This transition alienated American Indians from their land even as it made their bodies the vehicles of their identity—a particularly dangerous development in the time when legal racial segregation gripped the South and overt racial prejudice filled the nation. White southerners viewed anyone claiming Native identity with misgivings, suspecting that they were actually "colored" by association with African Americans. Claiming membership in a tribe, nevertheless, granted some security as a citizen as well as claims to any tribal property. American Indians found strong incentives to maintain this identity. Tribes began keeping rolls of those recognized as tribal citizens, though practices varied and generated conflict among American Indians and with white officials and claimants.

As decades passed, confusion and uncertainty persisted. Though many Native peoples had roots in the South and lived and moved within the region, they could not be counted or mapped in consistent ways. The displacement and erasure of Native communities in the settler-slave society of the early nineteenth century continued under a different guise at the beginning of the twentieth. As in the earlier displacement, though, legal removal did not remove actual people. Native southerners did not disappear, even if they remained invisible to white people. American Indians used their extended families, flexible gender roles, separate Christian churches, and movement itself to sustain their tribal identities.[18]

In 1889, land in the Oklahoma Territory was thrown open to white settlement, and by 1890, white people numbered more than 128,000 residents, far greater than the 50,000 Natives living there. Eastern Oklahoma attracted white migrants from Arkansas, Missouri, and Texas. The rest of Oklahoma filled with a mix of migrants from the Midwest and Upper South.[19]

Black settlers accounted for about 10 percent of the non-Native population in Oklahoma, many of them settling in "all-Black" communities established earlier by railroad companies in the Indian Territory. Some formerly enslaved people of the region took advantage of the racial complexity of Oklahoma to move among Black, Native, and white communities. More than 100,000 Black people moved to Oklahoma between 1890 and 1910 but found their ambitions frustrated when the legislators of the new state instituted racial segregation as one of their first acts. Thousands of African American settlers in Oklahoma explored moving to Africa.[20]

Elsewhere in the South, the movement to cotton districts slowed and narrowed in the 1880s, as African Americans sought new opportunities for logging and turpentining in other regions and work in towns and cities, but accelerated again in the 1890s. Black people pushed into lands that had been cut over for lumber and now were offered at cheap prices that poorer people of both races might afford: the wiregrass regions of Georgia and Florida, the lowlands of Mississippi and Louisiana, and the piney woods across the lower parts of the Gulf states. Black farmers were also able to take advantage of low land prices in the Upper South as white people left. About half the Black farmers in those states managed to acquire at least some land, their numbers growing until 1910.[21]

The Mississippi Delta witnessed the transformations of the New South in especially concentrated and accelerated forms. New railroads pushed into areas that steamboats could not reach. Lumber crews followed, harvesting massive cypress and oak trees, in the process opening land for farms, stores, and towns. Propertyless Black farmers contracted with railroads and other

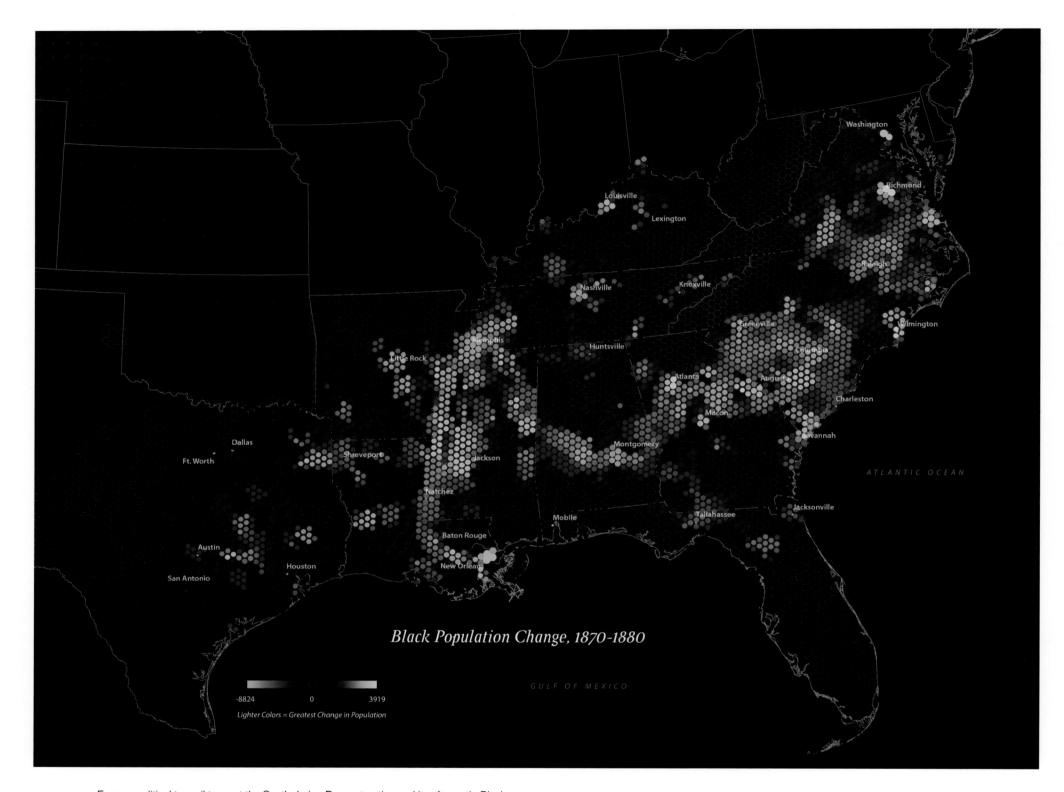

Black Population Change, 1870-1880

-8824   0   3919

Lighter Colors = Greatest Change in Population

Even as political turmoil tears at the South during Reconstruction and its aftermath, Black southerners seek out places where they might find safety in numbers in the most productive farming areas of the cotton South and in cities and towns.

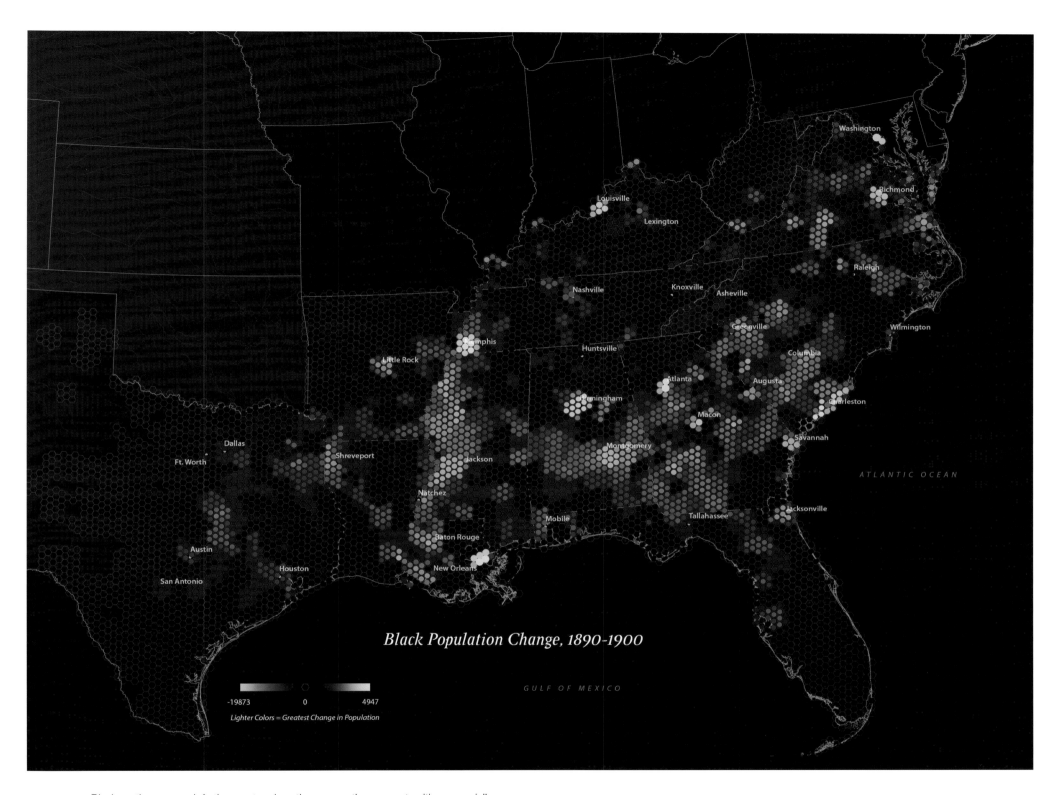

Black Population Change, 1890-1900

-19873   0   4947

Lighter Colors = Greatest Change in Population

Black southerners push farther west and south even as others move to cities, especially
Birmingham, New Orleans, and Memphis. Many Black people leave the Upper South,
sometimes for cities in the Midwest and Northeast.

landowners to finish clearing these lands. They hoped to crop a parcel of land, then rent it, and if fortunate buy it, glimpsing a chance at prosperity few farmers elsewhere in the South could enjoy. The fresh alluvial land produced cotton at prodigious rates. Once farms had been established, however, wealthy planters and conglomerates bought and consolidated them into enormous plantations with which smaller operators could not compete. Black migration to the Delta slowed as opportunities for autonomy disappeared. Many Black families decided they could do better on cheaper and less productive land where they would be left alone.

White and Black southerners moved to Texas in growing numbers in every decade, pressing ever farther west. Texas had, by its standards, grown modestly during the Civil War decade, its Black population barely increasing, its eastern areas stagnating as white people pushed into undeveloped lands. But the rush to Texas from elsewhere in the South renewed after the 1870s. The state's population surged from 800,000 to over 2 million people in 1890, especially into the rich Blackland Prairie, where the land required no fertilizer to produce astonishing yields of cotton. Dallas, Waco, Austin, and San Antonio flourished in that district. About a quarter of the migrants to Texas were African Americans, who tended to settle in towns and cities, but the proportion of Black Texans slowly declined as white people poured into the state.

Even as the brief post–Civil War period that became known as the "Old West" came and went, Texas became ever more southern, its cotton crop increasing by 300 percent. Landowners offered acreage at extremely low prices, hoping to bring in enough people to attract railroads. And railroads indeed came, the 500 miles of track in 1870 growing to 8,000 miles by 1890. By 1904, Texas had more railroad mileage than any other state in the Union.[22]

Mexican workers also came in to help fill the labor needs of the burgeoning state. First arriving in the 1880s, by the turn of the century, Mexicans had become an essential part of the cotton economy. Landowners preferred these laborers to either Black or white people because they worked for less and demanded fewer concessions. The Mexicans did not suffer the full extent of the indignities inflicted on Black southerners, nor did they enjoy the acceptance of white southerners. At first, single men came, then followed by the families that cotton growers preferred. Spanish-speaking people grew to about 7 percent of the Texas population in 1910, their numbers swelling after the Mexican revolution that began in that year.

Black southerners moved as technology transformed sugar and rice production. Sugar planters, buoyed by tariffs after 1890, poured money into advanced machinery and electrification. Rice flourished on the flooded prairies of southwestern Louisiana and southeastern Texas, enabled by the arrival of the railroad and farmers from the Midwest who used irrigation techniques adapted from wheat farming to grow the water-dependent grain. By the turn of the century, the new rice fields produced tens of millions of bushels. Black people found technical and management roles there routinely denied them elsewhere in the South.

Big money also reconfigured the plantations in the Mississippi Delta. With levees rebuilt during the late 1880s and railroads pushing into the canebrakes and cypress stands, conglomerates consolidated smaller farms into enormous plantations overseen by resident managers and riders, who traveled across the land to keep an eye on the workforce of Black migrants. Workers could only shop at plantation stores owned by the same people who owned the land and everything else. But the work paid well, and the Delta experienced one of the fastest-growing Black populations in the South.[23]

More than seven million southerners lived in towns and cities by 1910. The fastest-growing cities were new ones where the railroads met the fall line of the Piedmont—Charlotte, Winston-Salem, Columbia, Augusta, and Atlanta. Others, especially Dallas and Fort Worth, boomed on the western cotton frontier. Birmingham grew into the industrial center of the New South, while a town called Big Lick transformed into Roanoke, the nerve center of an extensive and expanding rail network.

In the cities, as in the South as a whole, white people withdrew from Black people, moving away from the city center, where Black arrivals congregated, and creating new suburbs along streetcars lines. Newer cities segregated more quickly than older ones, and the faster one grew, the faster the races divided. By the mid-1890s, most parts of Atlanta, Richmond, and Montgomery had become solely occupied by white people or Black people. Only whites who could not afford to leave remained in increasingly Black neighborhoods.

The dislocations of the southern population fed a range of political responses. White and Black farmers who held to the principles of settlers—hard work, independence, and self-reliance, all based on the land—launched a revolt of landowning farmers in the 1880s and 1890s. The Farmers' Alliance sought to mobilize the settler ideal in opposition to the business-oriented

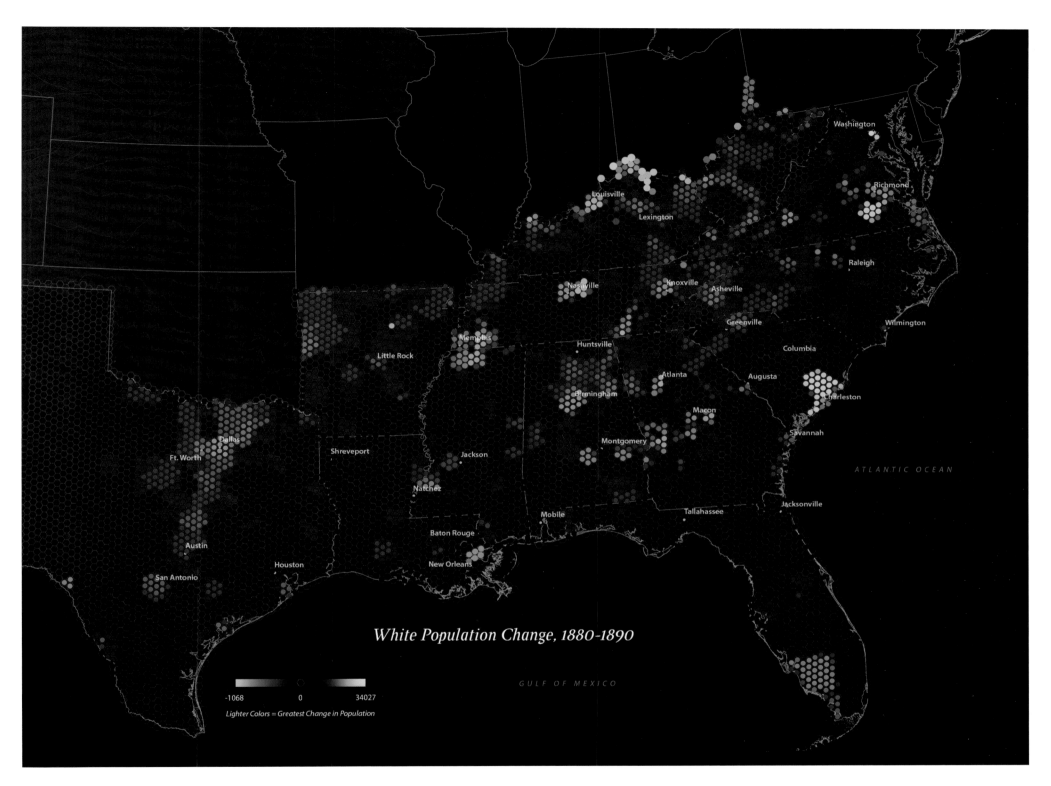

White Population Change, 1880-1890

-1068   0   34027

Lighter Colors = Greatest Change in Population

In a virtual reverse image of Black movement, white southerners flee old plantation districts
for the new lands of Texas and Arkansas and the old lands of the upland South.

Democrats who ruled the South after the end of Reconstruction. The movement began in Texas among farmers who had staked everything on a move west, only to confront poverty born of low cotton prices and a currency system built to benefit others. They called for reforms that would make it possible for farmers to recover the prosperity and social standing they had held when the ideals of settlers had dominated the South. The Populists launched a powerful political movement but fell short, absorbed and deflected by the Democrats.

Statewide segregation and disfranchisement presented a distinctly modern political response to the migrations and movements of the South. Railroads and other forms of transportation were the first places in the South subject to systematic legal segregation. It was on those railroads that Black and white strangers confronted one another without a script. Conflict and confusion troubled the trains as conductors had to decide who belonged to which race. After many lawsuits and editorials, state legislatures divided railroad cars into segregated areas as a way to regulate a mobile society of strangers. Once begun, segregation snaked into the new cities of the South, the "white" and "colored" signs markers of managed race relations among people who did not know one another.

Out of similar motives, legislatures and constitutional conventions enacted laws to deprive Black men of the vote. Requirements that a voter live in a place for a year before voting, or pay registration and poll taxes in advance at the local courthouse, sharply reduced voting among people who moved from one county to the next, who migrated into an area just emerging from logging, or who located in a strange city. While white legislators claimed that they only wanted to curtail voting among Black men, they ended up eviscerating white participation for generations as well, for white southerners moved just as often as Black southerners.

A plague of lynching in the South reached its most virulent levels in the last decades of the nineteenth century. The places with the highest rates of lynchings were, by and large, the places with the highest levels of Black transiency. And the most likely victims of lynching were unmarried young Black men migrating from one state to another, men whom no one in the local Black community knew or could vouch for.[24]

Half a million African Americans quietly left the South in the three decades after 1880, most of them to cities in the Midwest and Northeast. The Black population of those on the borders of the South—Washington, Baltimore, Saint Louis, and Louisville—grew especially rapidly. Closely attuned to economic cycles and opportunities in northern cities, young Black families, often with education, helped family and friends make the move out of the South. New arrivals found themselves crowded into the bottom of the job market, from which it was difficult to move, but they nevertheless felt safer and less systematically demeaned than in the South.[25]

Carter G. Woodson, born in 1875 in Virginia, worked in coalmines in West Virginia before attending Berea College in Kentucky and becoming the second African American to receive a doctorate at Harvard University. He published *A Century of Negro Migration* in 1918 to remind Americans that Black people had searched for opportunity and justice since the days of slavery. He showed with graphs that both the laboring class and the educated class, "tired of oppression in the South," had "migrated to the large cities in the East and Northwest, such as Philadelphia, New York, Indianapolis, Pittsburgh, Cleveland, Columbus, Detroit and Chicago."

But while celebrating the energy of Black migrants, Woodson recognized the limits and costs of this migration. African American migrants from the South, while attracted by economic opportunity, were sometimes led to believe, as he bitterly put it, "to think that they are citizens of the country." The departure of accomplished and confident Black people left southern communities bereft "of their due part of the talented tenth," but in the North "the enlightened Negro must live with his light under a bushel." African Americans found few places of true sanctuary beyond the South.[26]

Most Black people moved within the South, as more than 886,000 of them migrated to cities within the South during the first decade of the twentieth century. White southerners, too, flooded into new cities in the interior South and along the coastal plains of both the Atlantic and the Gulf, including Florida, where Tampa and Jacksonville rapidly expanded. They rushed into Oklahoma, to which the southeastern American Indian nations had been displaced seventy years before and now would be displaced again.[27]

A smaller percentage of white southerners abandoned the region at the beginning of the twentieth century than in previous decades. Growing rapidly from natural increase, they moved into every part of the region, including areas that had been bypassed by earlier migrations. Even though more than 1.2 million white people left the South between 1880 and 1910, twice as many of them moved within the region. In 1900, over 90 percent of white southerners born in those states still lived there. Those who did migrate from the Upper South—Kentucky, Tennessee, Virginia, and North Carolina—radiated

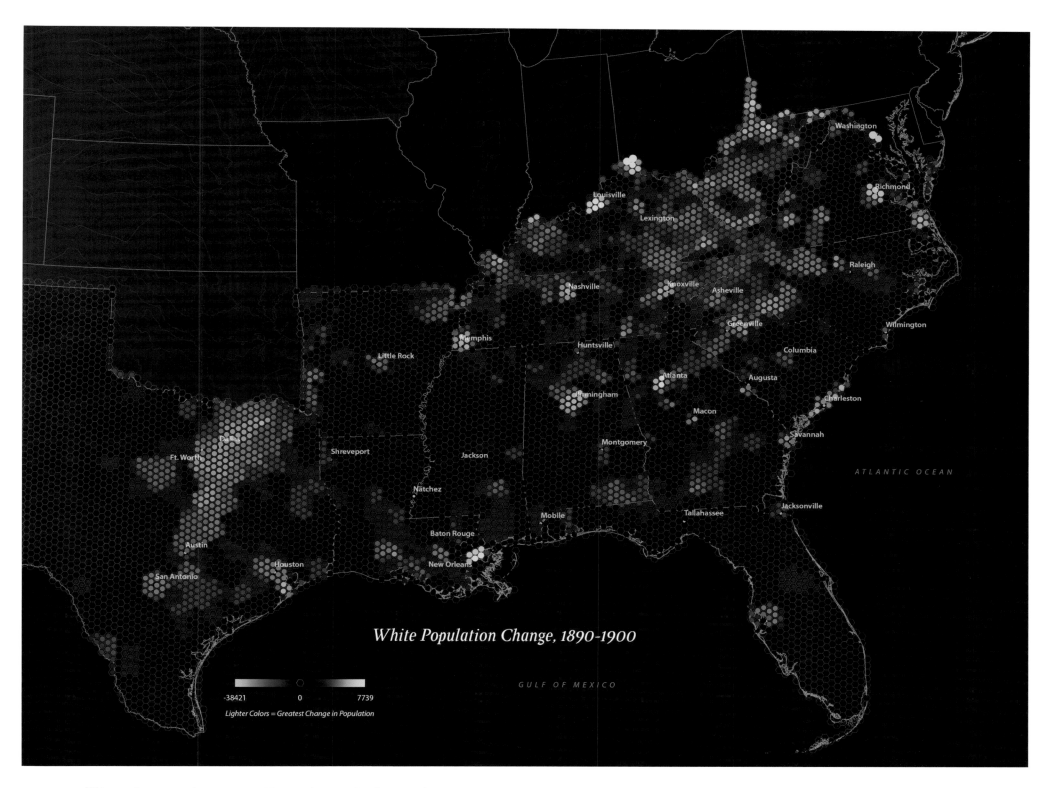

White Population Change, 1890-1900

-38421   0   7739

Lighter Colors = Greatest Change in Population

White southerners continue to move to Texas and to town, but they now also move to
parts of Appalachia, where lumbering and coalmining are accelerating.

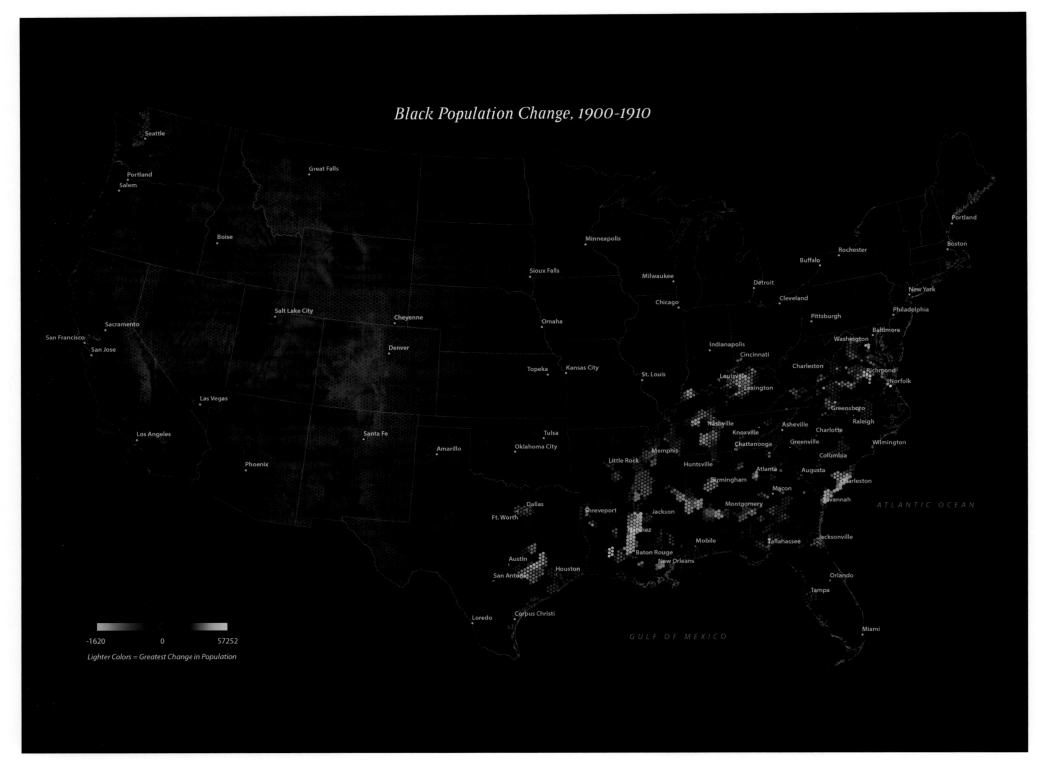

Black Population Change, 1900-1910

-1620   0   57252

Lighter Colors = Greatest Change in Population

Black southerners abandon large parts of the Black Belt, the Mississippi Valley, western Tennessee, and the plantation districts along the Atlantic in the decade before the Great Migration, moving to southern cities as well as the Mississippi-Yazoo Delta.

directly westward, showing no preference for northern or southern destinations. Those who moved from the Lower South moved farther west also but remained in the South.[28]

The native-born population of the South, despite standing outside the great currents of immigration from Europe in these decades, was no less mobile than the rest of the nation. Several southern states—West Virginia, Florida, Louisiana, and Texas—were among the few outside of the Far West that attracted many more people than left in the years around the turn of the century. Though Virginia lost population to other states in the 1890s, nine states in New England and the Midwest lost more.[29]

Black and white southerners faced a new threat when the boll weevil arrived in Texas from Mexico in 1892, the result of the spread of cotton farming on both sides of the border. Over the next thirty years, the weevil moved east in a path both inexorable and unpredictable, borne by the wind from one cotton field to another, ten or a hundred miles at a time all the way to the Atlantic Ocean. The insects multiplied in pestilential numbers. Weevil larvae, pupae, and adults consumed entire cotton plants with horrific efficiency, beginning with leaves and then moving to the buds and the boll of cotton fiber until the plant died or frost arrived to kill it. Adult weevils could survive winter in the remnants of the plants on the fields and in nearby trees and Spanish moss. A single pair could birth millions of offspring in one season.[30]

The weevils' cost was hard to measure as well as to predict. In counties hit hard by the insect, cotton production fell by half. Landowners and tenants suffered immediately and significantly. For the first twenty-five years after the weevil's arrival in the South, farmers could do little to stop its spread other than to clear their fields after the growing season and hope for favorable winds. Many in the infected areas quickly abandoned cotton in favor of corn, cutting their losses as well as their need for labor. Perversely, the weevil accelerated the growth and spread of cotton cultivation in unaffected areas as prices rose during the first decade of the twentieth century to levels not seen since the Civil War.

The boll weevil's effect on migration in the South was as unpredictable as the insect's spread. Its damage to crops arrived in slow-moving waves. Texas, Louisiana, and Mississippi were hit hard before 1915. Mississippi yielded a third less cotton than before the weevil, and Louisiana produced 40 percent less. Yet those states did not see a massive outmigration from their cotton districts, in part because cotton prices remained so high. The mobile tenant and laborer populations of the region surged into nearby counties, where planters rushed to get in a crop before the weevil arrived. Some tenants used the weevil to bargain with landowners desperate to grow as much cotton as they could while they could.

The number of people in counties adjacent to infestation grew by 50 percent and remained high until the weevil had done its damage over the next few years. Those newly affected counties then registered a 30 percent decline in population as laboring people moved to other unaffected counties, to southern towns and cities, or to Arkansas or Oklahoma. Black people moved, most notably, from the parts of Texas hit by the weevil to areas farther north, around Dallas, and from the lower Mississippi Valley to the Yazoo-Mississippi Delta, Memphis, and Little Rock.

The boll weevil, in other words, did not drive Black or white farmworkers out of the cotton South before 1915. Rather, the voracious insect led people to migrate within the South, in every direction, often in short and strategic moves. The boll weevil's most profound influence on migration would not occur for another decade and in places far from the site of its first arrival in the South.

The cotton-textile industry, long championed as the economic salvation of the older states, finally came into its own in the first decade of the twentieth century in the Piedmont, stretching from Virginia through the Carolinas and into Georgia. White people had been moving to the Piedmont since the end of the Civil War, attracted by expanding cotton farming, a predominantly white population, and the growth of towns and prosperous small cities. With water power abundant all along the fall line in the many rivers of the Piedmont, local consortia of investors funded the construction of hundreds of new mills. A large labor supply of white people—many of them women and children— proved eager to work for low but steady wages. The 17,000 textile hands in the South of 1880 grew to 98,000 by 1900, accounting for 30 percent of the nation's workers in the industry. About a third of those laborers lived in South Carolina, another third in North Carolina, and the rest were scattered across the Piedmont in Virginia, Georgia, and Alabama. Black people were precluded from working in the mills, places reserved for white women and children.

Many white southerners moved into unincorporated villages built by mill owners who provided, and controlled, housing, stores, and schools. The rapid increase in mills created a sudden labor shortage, and workers took advantage of the situation. With wages low and labor unions fiercely contested by the owners, mobility held out the best opportunity for resistance. Families could

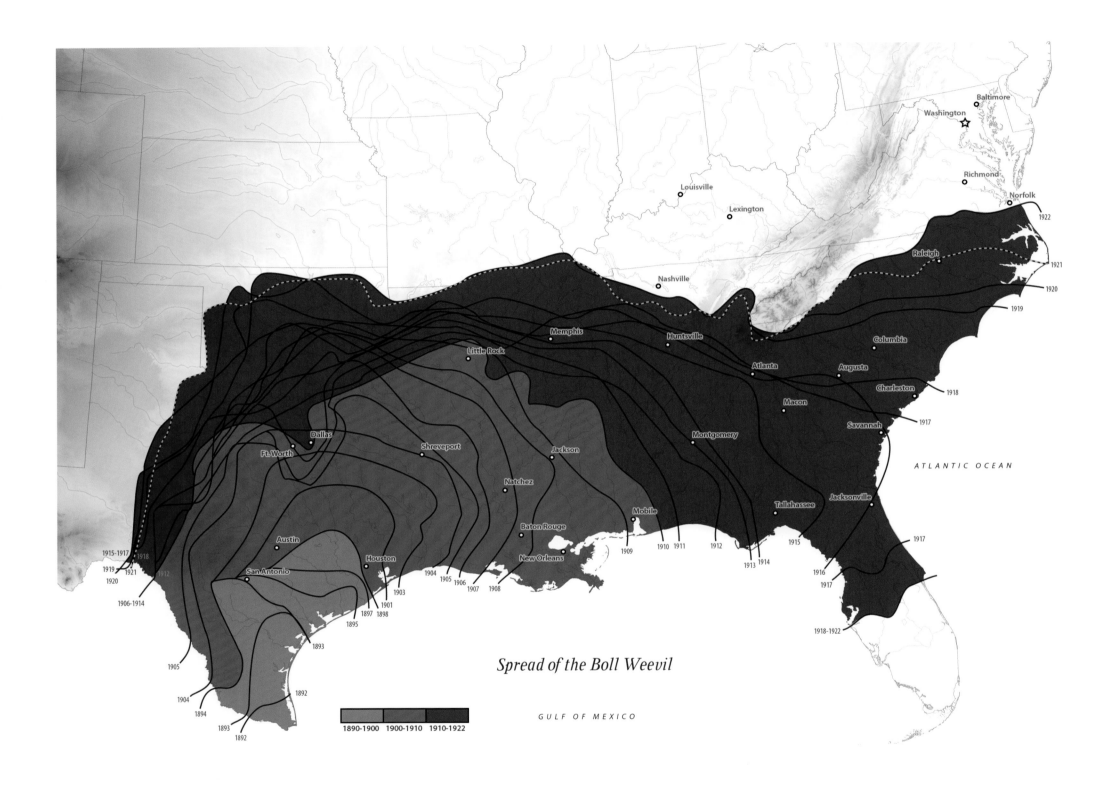

Spread of the Boll Weevil

| 1890–1900 | 1900–1910 | 1910–1922 |

GULF OF MEXICO

ATLANTIC OCEAN

Baltimore
Washington
Richmond
Norfolk
Louisville
Lexington
Nashville
Raleigh
Memphis
Huntsville
Columbia
Little Rock
Atlanta
Augusta
Charleston
Macon
Savannah
Dallas
Shreveport
Jackson
Montgomery
Ft. Worth
Natchez
Jacksonville
Tallahassee
Austin
Baton Rouge
Mobile
Houston
New Orleans
San Antonio

1922
1921
1920
1919
1918
1917
1917
1915
1916
1917
1918–1922
1909 1910 1911 1912 1913 1914
1904 1905 1906 1907 1908
1903
1901 1898
1897
1895
1893
1892
1905
1904
1894
1893
1892
1915–1917 1918
1919 1921
1920
1912
1906–1914

Entering Texas through Mexico, the boll weevil infests areas to the east with seemingly inexorable destruction. The insect's effect, though, varies greatly depending on the health of the farming regions where it arrives, causing greater economic damage in Georgia and South Carolina, near the end of its spread, than in Mississippi and Alabama, more than a decade earlier.

easily move from one mill village to another, finding jobs with which they were familiar. Agents traveled throughout the Piedmont, enticing workers with promises of better situations at competing mills. Some went into the mountains of North Carolina and Tennessee to recruit laborers and families willing to move to their mill towns. By 1907, the Piedmont had become "one long mill village," a journalist reported.[31]

A simultaneous transformation took place in the mountains of West Virginia, Kentucky, and Virginia. The southern Appalachians had long sustained high birthrates and shrinking farms. The arrival of railroads and logging crews provided new opportunities for men and women to supplement their farm income with what they called "public work," laboring in sawmills and supplying food to remote camps. By 1900, four major railroads had cut across the mountains, and feeder lines branched out into hollows throughout the region. Asheville and Knoxville grew rapidly, and smaller towns, more than six hundred of them company towns, sprung up along the rails.

Businessmen from outside the mountains controlled much of the hardwood forests and coal seams by 1910. At first, mountain farmers showed little interest in working the coal, then did so seasonally, and finally worked full time as their farms became ever smaller and less viable as land prices increased. Midwestern industries increasingly shifted to burning southern coal, the 40,000 tons from West Virginia in 1898 growing to 6 million tons in 1913. The demands of the mines soon outpaced the capacities of the local population, and labor agents went in search of new workers to bring into the region.

Unlike the textile mills, the heavy work at the coalmines was open to African Americans, most of them migrating from Virginia along the Norfolk and Western Railroad, which stretched all the way to the Atlantic coast. The Black population of central Appalachia grew from 4,800 to 40,000 people between 1880 and 1920. Black men built the railroads that made the transformation of the mountains possible; the legendary figure of John Henry stood for the thousands of men who suffered injury and death to cut tunnels and bridge rivers in the Appalachian Mountains.[32]

Immigrant workers also came in to the coal towns; by 1915, 32,000 miners from Italy, Hungary, and elsewhere in Europe lived in Appalachia, the only part of the South to attract immigrants in significant numbers. The overall population of the mountain regions shot up, from 200,000 in 1870 to 1,000,000 people in 1915.[33]

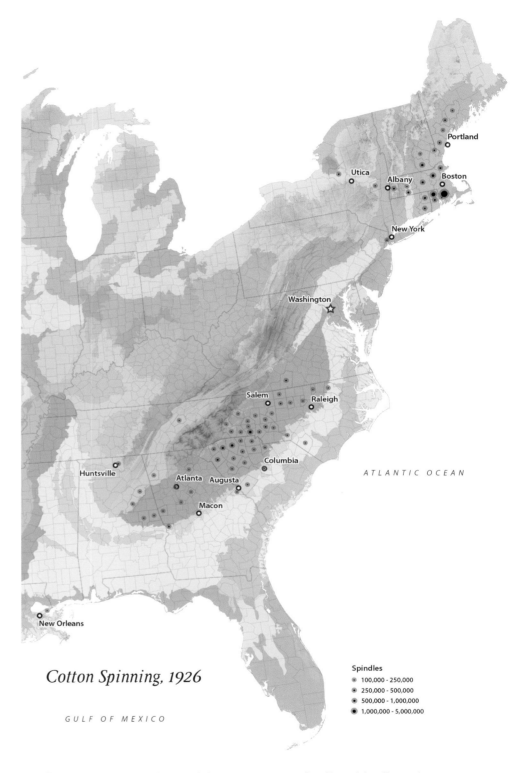

Cotton Spinning, 1926

Spindles
- 100,000 – 250,000
- 250,000 – 500,000
- 500,000 – 1,000,000
- 1,000,000 – 5,000,000

Over the first quarter of the twentieth century, cotton-textile mills and the villages that grow up around them transform the Piedmont, from southern Virginia through the Carolinas and northern Georgia to Alabama, creating an extensive belt of competition with the mills of New England.

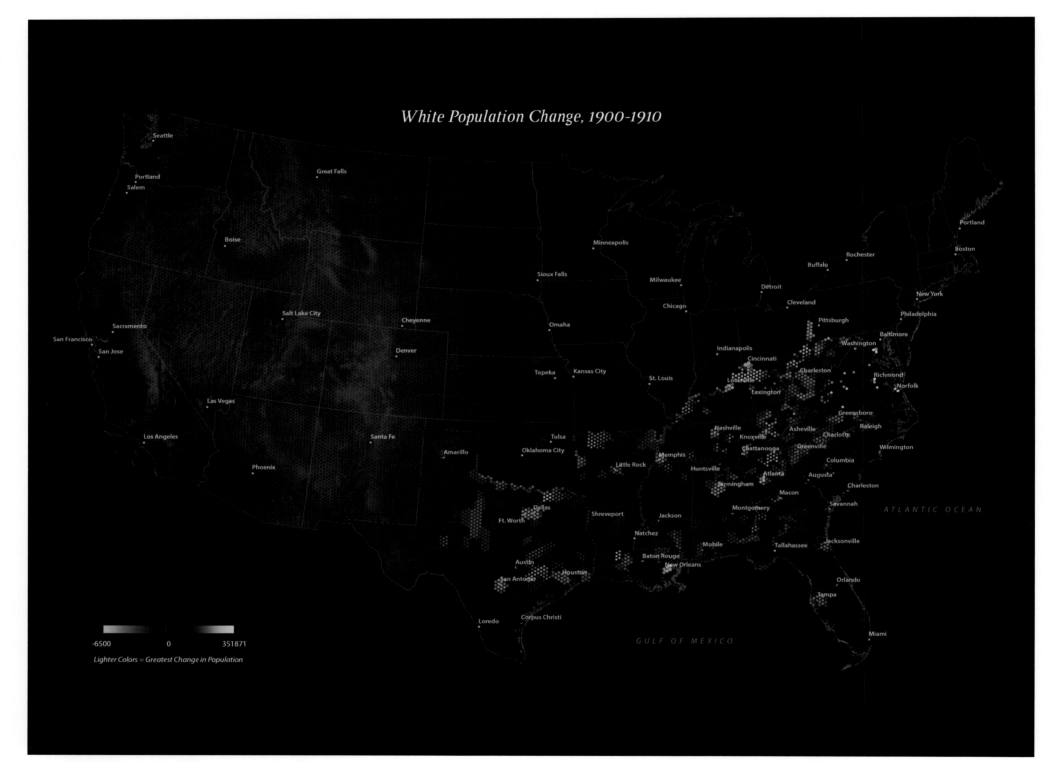

White Population Change, 1900-1910

-6500 0 351871

Lighter Colors = Greatest Change in Population

The relatively prosperous first decade of the new century sees white southerners moving to the largest cities of the region from the nearby countryside, even as many white people leave the South altogether.

By 1915, then, the South's population, always mobile, had branched out into new directions within the region. Tenants and sharecroppers, mill hands and coalminers, salesmen and agents, migrant laborers and timber workers—all had moved recently, and all were ready to move again.

THE FIRST GREAT MIGRATION

War in Europe suddenly upended the South's already restless population. Through the decades since the Civil War, millions of immigrants from Europe had filled the seemingly endless need for industrial labor in the North and Midwest. When that river of workers suddenly stopped with the outbreak of the Great War, employers immediately turned to the South. Pennsylvania railroads sent agents to recruit Black workers along the Atlantic coast in 1916, offering free transportation and food along the way, paying $1.80 a day when they arrived—far above the $1.00 a day many could earn in southern cities. Soon, hundreds and then thousands of Black people began to make the move northward, alone, in families, and in groups.[34]

The most intense movement came from places in the South that had already lost Black population in the preceding decade: the lower Mississippi River valley in Mississippi and Louisiana; across the Black Belt of Alabama and Georgia; through Tennessee, Kentucky, and Virginia; and along the Atlantic coast from Baltimore into Florida. The accelerated migration from these places radiated out and drew people from other regions that had been relatively stable before the Great War, especially northern Mississippi, southern Louisiana, and northern Florida.

White people blamed labor agents for the Black abandonment of the South, but after 1917, northern employers did not need to entice workers. Black migrants recruited one another with letters home, especially when they included cash and offers to help family and friends find their footing in the cities. One observer called early migrants "apostles of exodus" to those who followed. Those who stayed in the South used the departure of others as leverage for better wages and public schools at home.[35]

Nearly all of the migrants who left the South traveled to cities across the North. Those with more than 100,000 people—especially Chicago, New York, Philadelphia, and Detroit—attracted most of the southerners. Migrants tended to move directly northward, often the shortest distances by rail and thus the least expensive to travel. People from the Carolinas and Georgia migrated to New York and New Jersey; migrants from Alabama headed to-ward Ohio, Michigan, and Indiana; and those from Mississippi and Louisiana moved to Illinois and Missouri.

White employers and newspapers in the South panicked about the Black exodus, making it appear feverish and impulsive. Actually, however, the migration built due to ample information and careful planning. Black southerners knew from migrations within the South how to move, how to sustain themselves and their families through risk and loss, and how to persevere through dislocation and reestablishment. Many of those who went North had already relocated to the towns and cities of the South and had probably moved several times before. Most of them paid their own way on the trains that carried them to their new homes, showing that they had cash from wages rather than debits in a planters' ledger.

Literate people were more likely to leave than the illiterate. Most migrants were single and young, and men outnumbered women. Black newspapers, especially the *Chicago Defender,* spread the word. As one labor agent reported, "The migration became the theme of discussion in pulpits, lodges, barbershops, pool rooms, on the street; in fact, everywhere." White leaders tried to persuade Black leaders, often ministers, to slow the flight from the region, but those Black men had little power to stop the exodus.[36]

"The more one learns of the migration of Negroes from the southern States to the North during the years 1916–17," a government official wrote after surveying reports from across the South, "the more convinced he must become of the great variety of occasions and causes which led to the movement, of the great variety of motives and conditions among those who moved, and of the great variety of satisfaction or dissatisfaction which the movement caused both in the South and in the North and among the migrants themselves." The Great Migration built on and accelerated broader and more diverse relocations that had been working within the South since emancipation.[37]

One white observer in 1917 differentiated the "beckoning" forces from the "driving" forces. The beckoning came in the form of "high wages, little or no unemployment, a shorter working day than on the farm, less political and social discrimination than in the South, better educational facilities, and the lure of the city." The driving forces were "the relatively low wages paid farm labor, an unsatisfactory tenant or crop-sharing system, the boll weevil, the crop failures of 1916, lynching, disfranchisement, segregation, poor schools, and the monotony, isolation, and drudgery of farm life." The driving forces had grown more intense in recent decades; the beckoning forces appeared suddenly.[38]

Black Population Change, 1910-1920

-27224   0   76936

Lighter Colors = Greatest Change in Population

This, the Great Migration, pulls Black southerners from every locality where they had lived in large numbers except for the Mississippi-Yazoo Delta, where cotton brings high prices during the Great War. The Mississippi Valley and Black Belt see the greatest exodus, as Black people move to the northern and midwestern cities most directly connected by railroad to their southern homelands.

A quest for freedom drove the migrants, a freedom that combined "rights, opportunities, dignity, and pride," a student of Chicago's migration has written. Black people in the North did not "have to truckle to whites," and they could vote, send their children to decent schools, and work in factories where promotion and unionization stood as real possibilities. Migrants could, of course, see the limits of their new freedom as they confronted a shortage of public services, increasing residential segregation, and discrimination by employers, coworkers, and unions, but the benefits of migration outweighed these costs. The sudden shift to the North of nearly half a million people marked a revolutionary change for Black Americans, for northern cities, and for the United States in general.[39]

African American women had long been migrants within the South, and they moved quickly and in large numbers, both with their families and on their own, when war and immigration restrictions opened new opportunities in the North. Black women knew they would likely continue to work as domestics after the journey, for factories and other businesses were largely closed to them, but they moved to gain freedom in other parts of their lives. They usually traveled north with a clear destination in mind, a relative or trusted friend waiting, without pausing along the way. Some women on their own left children with relatives until they could become established and receive their sons and daughters with money for school, decent clothes, and security. These women sustained the connections between the North and the South that would shape life in both places for generations to come.[40]

The South did not become a mere backdrop for the Great Migration. Despite the drama and excitement of the migration to the North, nine out of ten Black Americans remained in the South during the war decade. During the twenty years between 1900 and 1920, in fact, more Black people moved to southern cities than to northern cities. African Americans often preferred shorter migrations that allowed them to stay in contact with relatives and home communities to sustain churches, schools, and self-help organizations.

The war years, moreover, offered unaccustomed opportunity in the South. The Yazoo-Mississippi Delta, directly adjacent to places so many African Americans left, attracted workers due to high cotton prices. The Birmingham area boomed as it produced iron and steel for the war, having grown by nearly a hundred thousand people in the preceding decade and adding another fifty thousand during the war decade. Nearby, the cities of Chattanooga, Atlanta, and Macon grew quickly as well. Texas cities expanded their Black populations, as did Tulsa, Little Rock, and Memphis. Those along the Atlantic coast flourished with war production; Charleston, Savannah, and Jacksonville all grew their Black and white populations, with Norfolk outpacing them all. The broad arc of the Piedmont from Greensboro and Raleigh through Columbia and Augusta saw the arrival of many Black migrants. The coalfields of West Virginia and Kentucky continued to attract Black miners and their families.[41]

The migration of white southerners in the war decade—893,000 people— was twice as large in sheer numbers as Black migrants from the South, even though that movement constituted a smaller share of the total white population. Like their Black counterparts, these southerners often moved to cities where the largest factories and businesses operated, but they easily found new homes in smaller places as well, enjoying the passport of skin color. While some northerners found the white-southern newcomers to be crude and comically unschooled in the ways of big cities, the new arrivals faced little overt discrimination. They blended quickly into the factories and schools of their new homes, even if they spoke with a drawl or twang that revealed their origins. White migration drew disproportionately from the educated and relatively well-to-do among southerners, and those migrants often found doors open to them. The white South showed more uniform movement and more dispersed urban growth than other regions during the war decade.

This massive but quiet movement went virtually unnoticed by the press at the time, unlike the Great Migration of African Americans. Similarly, white people moved to many places within the South without much notice and without markedly decreasing the overall white population in most of the places they left, thanks to high birthrates. Southern cities, as fast as they had grown, had plenty of room to expand when wartime urgency drove a new demand for labor. Many skilled, many retail, and almost all managerial jobs were reserved for white people, providing a range of opportunities closed to Black men and women.[42]

Places across the South saw their white population surge. Almost every southern city, interior or coastal, gained residents during the war decade. The hundreds of towns and cities of the textile Piedmont expanded until their populations blended into one another. The cities of Florida, including new ones such as Miami and Tampa, born of railroads, attracted white southerners as well as Cuban immigrants in large numbers. Appalachia grew rapidly from white migrants.[43]

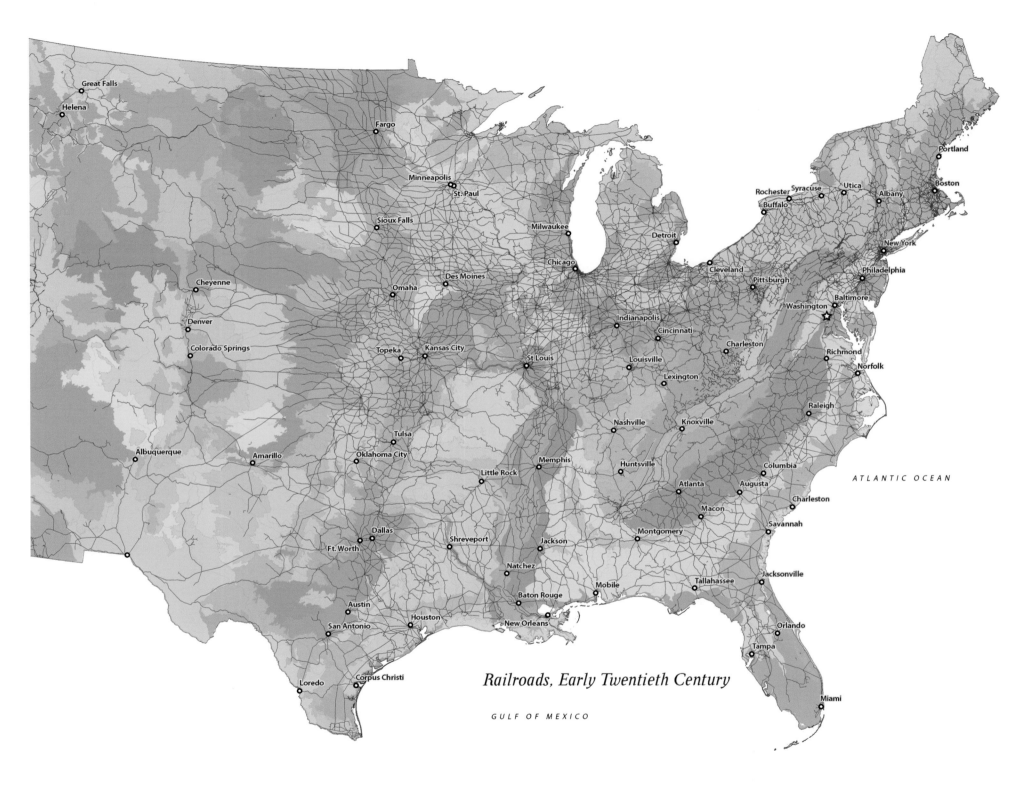

Great Falls

Helena

Fargo

Minneapolis
St. Paul

Sioux Falls

Cheyenne

Milwaukee

Detroit

Portland

Rochester Syracuse Utica
Buffalo Albany Boston

New York

Chicago

Cleveland

Philadelphia

Pittsburgh

Baltimore

Denver

Omaha

Des Moines

Indianapolis

Washington

Colorado Springs

Topeka

Kansas City

Cincinnati

Charleston

Richmond
Norfolk

St Louis

Louisville

Lexington

Raleigh

Tulsa

Nashville

Knoxville

ATLANTIC OCEAN

Albuquerque

Amarillo

Oklahoma City

Little Rock

Memphis

Huntsville

Columbia

Atlanta

Augusta

Charleston

Macon

Savannah

Dallas

Shreveport

Jackson

Montgomery

Ft. Worth

Natchez

Tallahassee

Jacksonville

Austin

Mobile

Baton Rouge

San Antonio

Houston

New Orleans

Orlando

Tampa

Railroads, Early Twentieth Century

Loredo

Corpus Christi

Miami

GULF OF MEXICO

By the early twentieth century, the South is laced throughout by an elaborate system of
railroads that shape transportation in the region even as gasoline automobiles and trucks begin
to spread. The railroads create modern Florida, running along both coasts and connecting its
new cities. Rail lines also push into previously isolated parts of the Appalachian Mountains,
transporting coal to the cities of the Midwest and creating mining towns wherever they reach.

White Population Change, 1910-1920

-782879   0   1103000

Lighter Colors = Greatest Change in Population

More than a million white residents leave the South even as the cities of the region grow
and as high fertility prevents absolute population decline in all but a few places, except along
the border with the Midwest.

The Great War and the Great Migration accelerated movements already underway in the South. The region stood not as a static contrast to striving elsewhere but embodied striving within itself. Rather than a sudden start from stagnation, the Great Migration was part of a much longer continuum of migration, and it was not the end of Black movement within the South. The Great Migration was echoed by white movement, overlapping in time but diverging in space, as it had been for decades before and would continue to do for generations.

THE 1920S

Many observers expected the migration of Black southerners to the North to stop when the war ended and the flow of immigrants from Europe resumed. Congressional acts in 1917 and 1924, however, radically slowed immigration, especially among Italians, Jews, Greeks, and Poles. The restrictions were so strong that more people from those countries left the United States than arrived. As factories shifted to peacetime production for a new consumer economy, Black and white southerners took jobs that European newcomers had filled just a few years before.

African American migration from the South actually accelerated during the 1920s. More than 810,000 Black southerners moved away from their native region during this time, twice as many as in the war decade. Far more than before, Black people fled Georgia and South Carolina. While large corporate-owned plantations to the west produced ever more cotton on rich soil with mobile day laborers, Georgia and South Carolina held smaller and more marginal farms. White and Black tenants working the exhausted, gullied land could barely survive on the low cotton prices of the postwar era. When the long-dreaded boll weevil, inexorably moving east, finally arrived soon after the armistice, Georgia and South Carolina farmers could not weather the resulting losses as their western counterparts had.

With the routes out of the region and into the North and Midwest clearly marked by their predecessors, Black Georgians and South Carolinians abandoned the countryside as the boll weevil devastated the cotton fields during the early 1920s, consuming nearly half the crop even as prices dropped sharply and remained low. In 1922 and 1923, factories in Detroit, Pittsburgh, and Chicago that had not hired many Black migrants during the war now turned to African American labor. Black Georgians and Carolinians boarded trains to take those jobs and others that emerged in industrial regions. Once

this migration began, it did not stop: Georgia lost more Black people than any other southern state over the coming decades.[44]

More concentrated in its arrival and its effects than the boll weevil, the Mississippi River flood of 1927 devastated lives and farms. After weeks of rain, a levee broke, and a wall of water a hundred feet high washed over farmlands, covering an area more than thirty miles wide and a hundred miles long. As one white resident wrote, the flood was "a torrent ten feet deep the size of Rhode Island; it was thirty-six hours coming and four months going; it was deep enough to drown a man, swift enough to upset a boat, and lasting enough to cancel a crop year." After other breaches in the levees, more than sixteen million acres lay underwater. As many as five hundred people died, and more than seven hundred thousand became homeless. If Black people in Mississippi needed another reason to leave for the North, the flood provided it: half the African American population left the Delta in the wake of the deluge.[45]

The homes of white families, too, were devastated by the Great Flood of 1927, but no similar exodus followed. That was because, in part, not many white people lived in the plantation districts along the river, and, in part, the planters and town dwellers who did live there benefited from wealth, transportation, and savings, all of which Black people did not have. White residents began rebuilding their homes and the levees, for they knew that the wealth of the Delta would endure after the floods had receded.

Across the South in the 1920s, in fact, the white population showed almost no signs of the disruptions that affected Black communities. While white people continued to avoid the Black Belt, pockets of actual decline appeared only in rural areas of northern Texas, where people moved into booming Dallas and Oklahoma City. Whites continued to leave the countryside of central Kentucky, Middle Tennessee, and northern Alabama for the Midwest and for nearby southern cities. Birmingham grew to 431,000 residents by 1930, and Knoxville and Nashville had passed 200,000 in population. White tenants from the cotton belt of Georgia, an area hit by the boll weevil in the 1920s, moved to Atlanta—whose surrounding region claimed nearly 750,000 people by 1930—and other cities of the Piedmont.

Florida grew faster than any other southern state between 1880 and 1930—and twice as fast as the nation as a whole. The railroads drove everything, reaching first to Jacksonville, then to Tampa, and then, after the draining of the Everglades and the dredging of swamplands, to Miami Beach, Palm

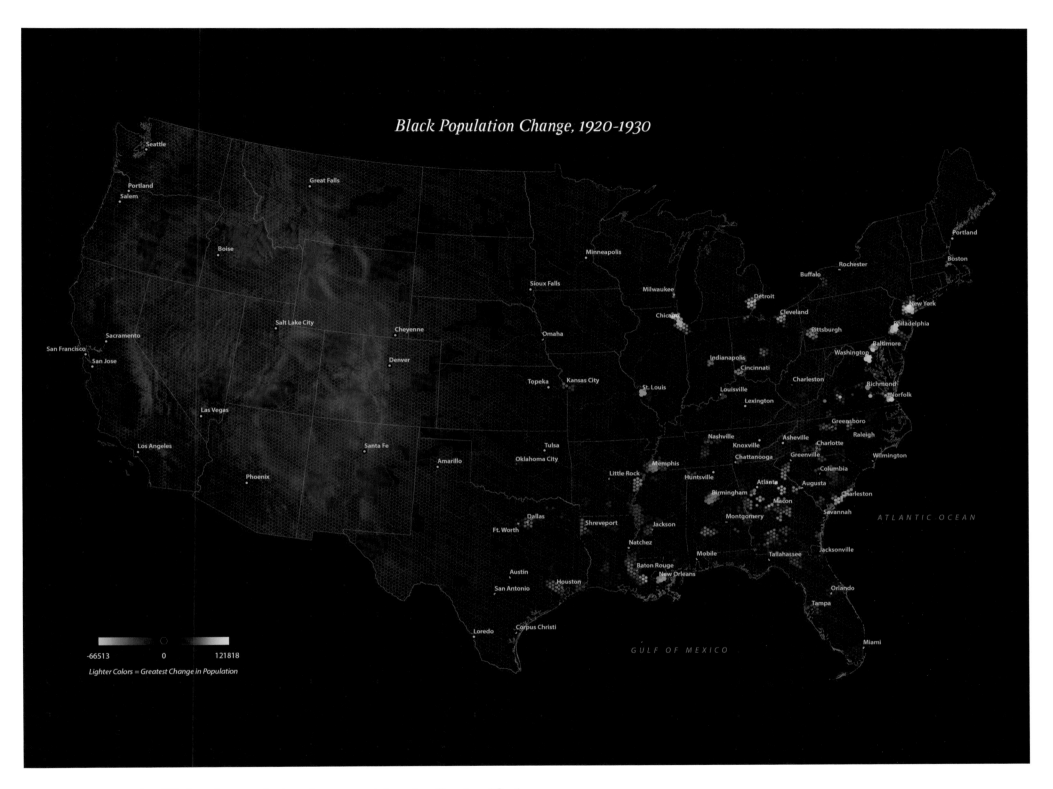

Black Population Change, 1920-1930

Seattle
Portland
Salem
Great Falls
Boise
Salt Lake City
Cheyenne
Sacramento
San Francisco
San Jose
Denver
Las Vegas
Los Angeles
Santa Fe
Phoenix
Amarillo
Minneapolis
Sioux Falls
Milwaukee
Omaha
Topeka
Kansas City
Tulsa
Oklahoma City
St. Louis
Chicago
Detroit
Cleveland
Pittsburgh
Indianapolis
Cincinnati
Louisville
Lexington
Charleston
Buffalo
Rochester
New York
Philadelphia
Baltimore
Washington
Richmond
Norfolk
Greensboro
Nashville
Knoxville
Asheville
Charlotte
Raleigh
Chattanooga
Greenville
Wilmington
Little Rock
Memphis
Huntsville
Columbia
Dallas
Ft. Worth
Shreveport
Jackson
Birmingham
Atlanta
Augusta
Macon
Charleston
Montgomery
Savannah
Natchez
Mobile
Tallahassee
Jacksonville
Austin
San Antonio
Houston
Baton Rouge
New Orleans
Orlando
Tampa
Loredo
Corpus Christi
Miami

ATLANTIC OCEAN
GULF OF MEXICO

-66513   0   121818

Lighter Colors = Greatest Change in Population

As the exodus of Black southerners gains force, far more people leave from Georgia and South
Carolina—both states ravaged by the boll weevil. The Yazoo Delta, relatively immune to Black
outmigration during the decade of the Great War, now sees massive departures as cotton prices
again decline.

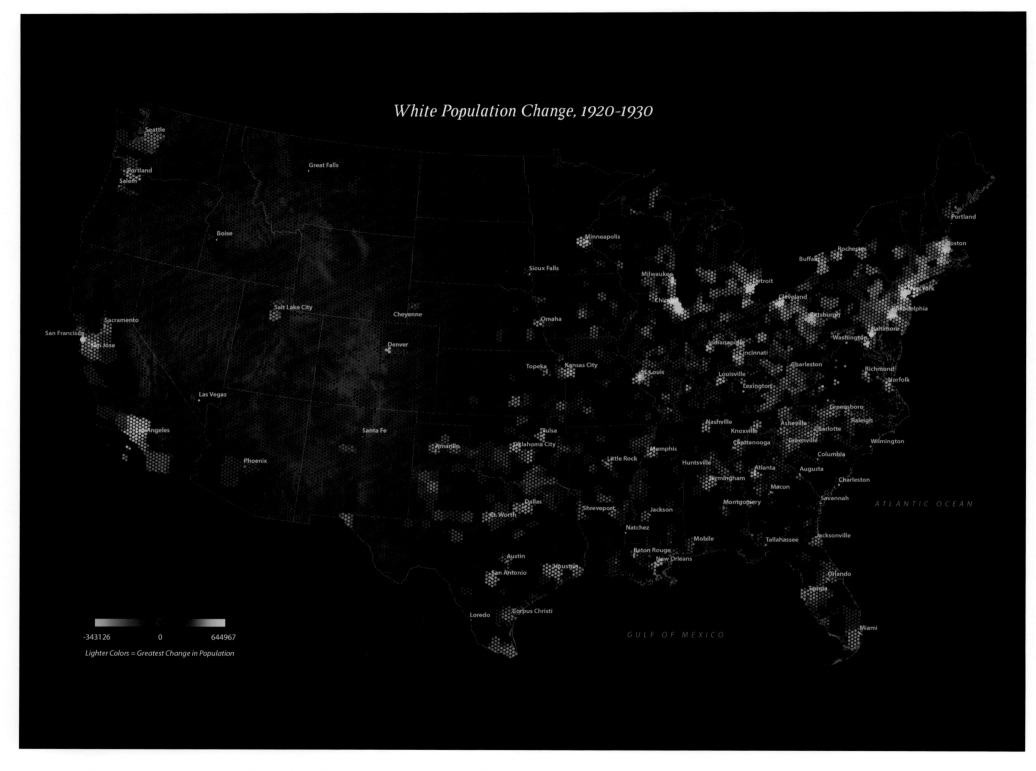

White southerners move to Appalachia, Florida, and Texas, while many leave the Upper South
states of Arkansas, Tennessee, and Kentucky along with weevil-damaged Georgia.

Beach, and Key West. Lumbering, phosphate mining, and vegetable farming flourished, along with the arrival of tourists from the Northeast and Midwest. World War I energized the state's economy with new army and submarine bases.

Florida's one thousand miles of paved roads in 1920 grew to three thousand a decade later. Tourist camps for motorists cropped up along the way, fostering a new kind of traveling. Three hundred thousand people moved to Florida in the mid-1920s, and a frantic real-estate fever rose and crashed by 1925. The next year, a hurricane killed four hundred people and left fifty thousand without homes. Tourists soon returned, however, and the real-estate market stabilized. By 1930, in excess of a million white people lived in Florida, along with more than four hundred thousand Black people.[46]

White population growth and density in other parts of the South did not always indicate prosperity. The mill towns of the Piedmont, the showcase for southern energy and ingenuity at the beginning of the century, fell into a prolonged crisis during the 1920s. Competition among the southern mills and with northern rivals drove down wages and drove up hours, even as the South claimed an ever-greater share of mills and more than two-thirds of all American textile workers. Overproduction and strikes by increasingly angry and active workers roiled the industry.[47]

The coalmines of Appalachia, after years of growth and boom, also faced serious struggles during the 1920s. Immigrants and Black southerners left the coalfields for midwestern or northeastern factories, and many white people did the same, especially from eastern Kentucky. In West Virginia, though, not enough white people migrated to reduce the population there, given the large size of families. Despite the widespread poverty of the coalfields, the state's population grew by almost 20 percent during the 1920s. In fact, the state would reach its all-time peak of population during these years. White people pieced together a living from working in the mines and on the remnants of family farms.

The signs of adaptation, progress, and stagnation in the white South masked the departure of 1.4 million people during the 1920s—600,000 more than the Black southerners who continued the Great Migration into that decade. As in the war years, white southerners continued to go where they pleased. Workers found eager employers in the auto factories of the Midwest, the timberlands of the Pacific Northwest, and the construction crews of booming cities across the country. White-collar workers and professionals found great opportunities during the expansive and enthusiastic twenties. White southerners with money and expertise to invest began to transform California and Arizona into cotton-producing regions with long-staple cotton, far away from the destructive reach of the boll weevil and with far-reaching consequences in the decades to come.[48]

THE 1930S

The Great Depression of the 1930s descended on a rural South already in distress. After several years of suffering, ad hoc relief efforts, and grudging aid during the first years of the 1930s, the arrival of the New Deal in 1933 changed the South in important ways, not all of them apparent at the time.

Less than half as many Black people left the region during the 1930s as had departed during the 1920s, their numbers falling to 392,000 migrants. Half a million fewer white people left the South than in the 1920s, their numbers declining to 986,000. Facing hard times everywhere in the nation, with no jobs beckoning in distant factories, many southerners, Black and white, wandered from one place to another, no one eager to see them. Many families fed themselves by taking whatever work they could find. Tourism, real-estate booms, car dealerships, and department stores, so promising only a few years earlier, now slowed and often failed.[49]

About a quarter of all southerners in the 1930s lived in tenant families, accounting for more than five million white people and three million Black people. Migratory workers—Black, white, and Mexican—followed the seasons for fruits, vegetables, and cotton. The nation became increasingly aware of the poverty and disease of the cotton fields, "a miserable panorama," one bitter commentator put it, "of unpainted shacks, rain-gullied fields, straggling fences, rattle-trap Fords, dirt, poverty, disease, drudgery, and monotony that stretches for a thousand miles across the cotton belt."

The New Deal struggled with inequities and injustices generations in the making. It reduced suffering in some places, giving people work and moments of dignity, while leaving unmet the needs of the poorest southerners in other places. Some people, including sharecroppers, joined unions and strikes to bring redress from landlords and mill owners. Nothing brought success. Cotton, largely as a result of global markets and the competition of new synthetic fibers such as rayon, began to loosen its hold on the South. The forty-five million acres of cotton planted in 1929 shrunk to twenty-three million ten years later, while corn, livestock, and feed crops expanded.

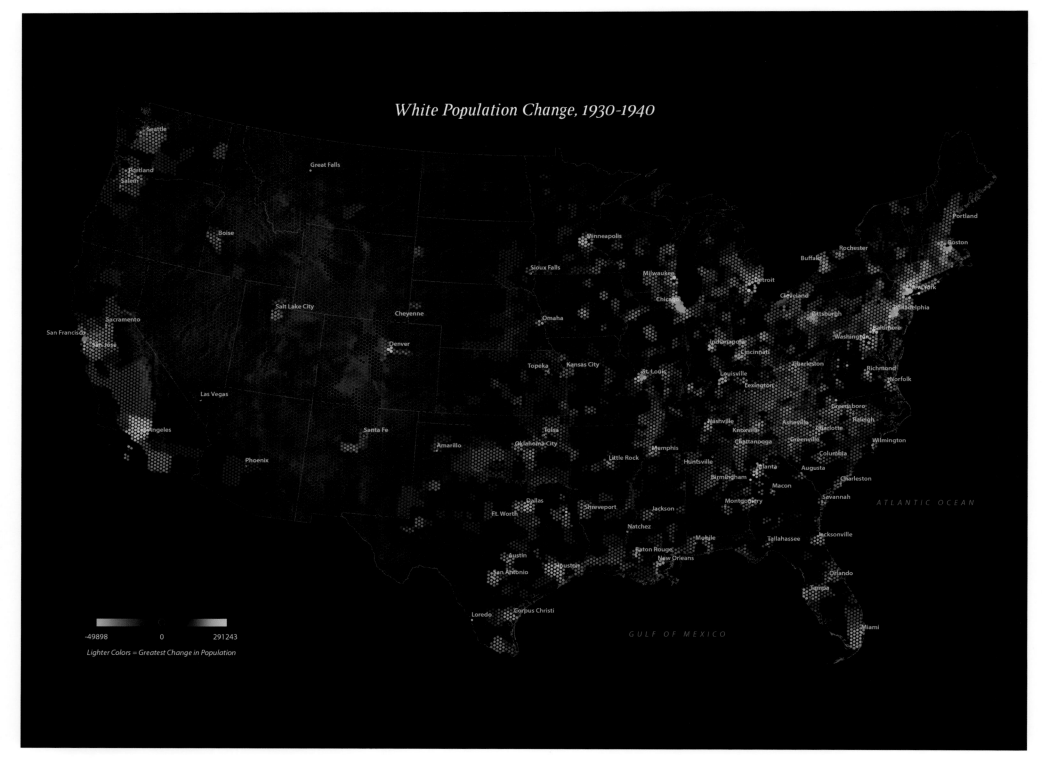

White Population Change, 1930-1940

Seattle
Portland
Salem
Boise
Great Falls
Minneapolis
Sioux Falls
Milwaukee
Detroit
Chicago
Cleveland
Rochester
Buffalo
Portland
Boston
New York
Philadelphia
Pittsburgh
Baltimore
Washington
Sacramento
San Francisco
San Jose
Salt Lake City
Cheyenne
Omaha
Denver
Topeka
Kansas City
St. Louis
Indianapolis
Cincinnati
Louisville
Lexington
Charleston
Richmond
Norfolk
Las Vegas
Los Angeles
Santa Fe
Amarillo
Oklahoma City
Tulsa
Memphis
Little Rock
Huntsville
Nashville
Knoxville
Chattanooga
Asheville
Greenville
Charlotte
Raleigh
Greensboro
Columbia
Wilmington
Phoenix
Birmingham
Atlanta
Augusta
Macon
Charleston
Savannah
Dallas
Ft. Worth
Shreveport
Jackson
Montgomery
ATLANTIC OCEAN
Natchez
Mobile
Tallahassee
Jacksonville
Austin
Houston
Baton Rouge
New Orleans
San Antonio
Orlando
Tampa
Loredo
Corpus Christi
GULF OF MEXICO
Miami

-49898   0   291243

Lighter Colors = Greatest Change in Population

In a decade that became famous for its images of migrant white families, relatively few white
southerners move except from the western reaches of the region in Oklahoma and Texas.
Farms offer more secure havens than the cities during the Great Depression, and few employers
outside the region offer opportunities in manufacturing. Appalachia continues to grow, both from
high birthrates and from few alternative places to move.

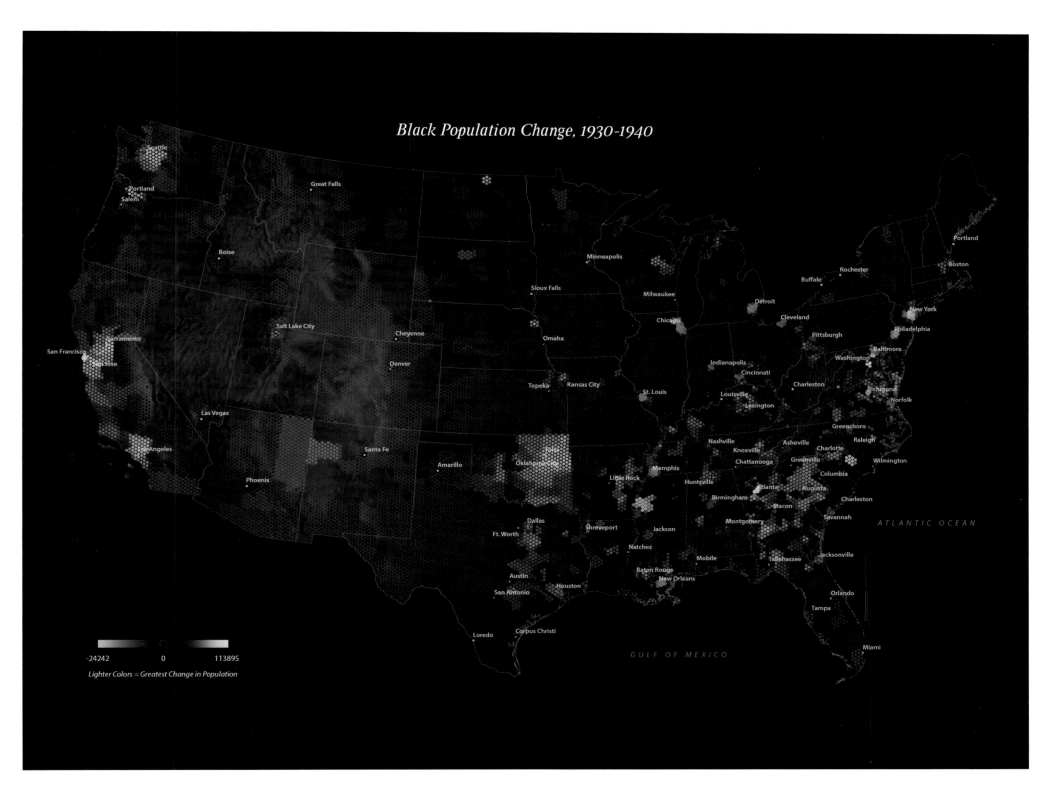

Black Population Change, 1930-1940

Large parts of South Carolina, Georgia, and northern Florida suffer an ongoing Black exodus driven by the boll weevil and the Great Depression. Black people flee Oklahoma and Texas, too, along with their white neighbors.

The small, scattered, and often hilly farms and plantations of Georgia, South Carolina, and the panhandle of Florida witnessed massive Black abandonment during the 1930s, as they had in the preceding decade when the boll weevil arrived. Rural areas across Virginia, Kentucky, and Tennessee, far from cotton fields, also saw their Black residents leave for cities in the Midwest and Northeast, where African American populations continued to grow despite the crisis in manufacturing.

Acreage reduction in the New Deal tackled fundamental problems of overproduction, paying farmers not to grow as much cotton, rice, or tobacco as they had grown before so that prices would rise. As one observer noted in 1934, however, "With one hand the cotton landlord takes agricultural subsidies and rental benefits from his government, with the other he pushes his tenant on relief."

Planters on larger plantations, especially in Mississippi, Arkansas, and Texas, took advantage of federal payments to reduce acreage and to purchase new gasoline-powered tractors to reduce their need for labor. The number of tractors in cotton states doubled during the 1920s, and again during the 1930s, to nearly a quarter of a million vehicles. Planters in the Mississippi and Arkansas Delta, with its flat land and large plantations, turned to machines with great enthusiasm: one planter purchased twenty-two tractors and thirteen cultivators. Together, these devices, driven by wage laborers, could do the work of 130 tenant families. Planters elsewhere in the Delta—where the largest landowners reaped especially large harvests of government bounty—spent hundreds of thousands of dollars buying tractors.[50]

Those who owned tractors no longer wanted to work with sharecroppers, who made a claim on part of the crop and required housing. Wage laborers were cheaper, more convenient, and more efficient. One observer in Arkansas (where in one county the number of tractors grew from 151 to 1,052 during the 1930s) reported that on a Saturday morning in the summer of 1937, trucks picked up as many as 1,500 laborers in Memphis and carried them to plantations in Arkansas, dozens of miles away. Where planters introduced tractors, farm size increased, the number of wage hands grew, and sharecropping families found fewer places to go.[51]

The people in the mountains of Appalachia struggled desperately, especially after a drought hit the region in 1930 and 1931. A Red Cross worker reported "almost unbelievable" suffering in that crisis and "a growing army of itinerants travelling on foot" to find food. Patching together work in the mines and on small parcels of mountain land, families raised more children to have more hands to help. One relief worker reported in 1933 that "cold, hunger, and disease" devastated the coal camps "to an extent almost without parallel in any group in this country." Children died from malnutrition and smallpox, scarlet fever, diphtheria, and typhoid. The New Deal proved more helpful to mountain people—most of them white—than it did to sharecroppers, bringing up their wages to a level higher than during the 1920s. By 1936, nearly half of all mountain families received relief from the federal government. The Civilian Conservation Corps and Works Progress Administration provided jobs, while price supports for tobacco allowed farmers to adopt a labor-intensive cash crop well suited for small farms and large families.[52]

Mine owners—like their planter counterparts in the cotton districts—turned to machines, especially after the United Mine Workers organized laborers to bargain collectively and raise wages. Mechanizing the loading of coal into mine cars on conveyor belts allowed companies to reduce their need for laborers: while only 2 percent of West Virginia coal had been loaded by machines in 1935, that amount had increased to 21 percent by 1938, a proportion that would continue to increase.[53]

Southerners, most of them white, migrated to California during the 1930s, though not in particularly large numbers compared to other regions in the eastern half of the country. A disproportionate share of those westward travelers came from Oklahoma, as the generic name for poor white migrants—"Okie"—signaled. But several thousand came from neighboring Arkansas, especially from the hilly northwestern half of the state. That area, which includes the Ozark Mountains, suffered from the worsening poverty that afflicted other areas with marginal land. From other places in the South, however, almost all westward migrants came from the cities, especially Birmingham, Nashville, Memphis, Little Rock, and the major centers of Texas. In the California migration, as in the white migration to the rest of the United States from the South, relatively prosperous people possessed the means and the skills to undertake such an ambitious relocation. Most bore little resemblance to the images of the impoverished migrant mother—of partial American Indian descent—that has proliferated through popular culture then and since.[54]

The South witnessed massive migrations in the four generations after the Civil War—probably, in total, the largest the nation has ever seen. Yet the fundamental patterns of racial division established by slavery endured through the cataclysmic changes of war, emancipation, the Great Migration, and the Great Depression. Despite all the journeys, most Black Americans still lived where they had lived before freedom: in the Black Belt that arced across the Lower South and in the plantation districts that lined the Mississippi River.

The ideals of a settler society still shaped white southerners' understanding of themselves, of African Americans, and of their place in the nation.

Even as the South changed around them, white southerners defended the principles of small government, lax regulation, and low taxes forged in the days of first settlement. Even as people worked for other people, they proclaimed themselves independent. Even as the South relied on the federal government for sustenance, it resented the power of that government. Even as Blacks left the South by the millions, segregation grew ever more entrenched.

The South would soon change abruptly, on a massive scale, and in profound ways. Whether people's minds would change was not clear.

THREE

ARRIVAL AND RETURN, 1940–2020

Events unimaginable in 1940 transformed the American South over the next four generations. A global war, followed by massive preparations for others that might follow, pushed billions of federal dollars into the South. A struggle of Black southerners to free themselves from segregation and disfranchisement changed the entire nation. Immigration laws enabled millions of people previously excluded to seek new lives in the United States, and many of them chose the South. Expansive cities, fed by federally funded interstate highways and subsidized mortgages, absorbed vast hinterlands into their orbits, suburbs changing their residents and their social consequences with each decade.

Swirling patterns of migration enabled and embodied these sudden and profound changes, bringing unprecedented prosperity to some places and abandoning others to perpetual poverty. White people, Black people, and immigrants followed distinct paths across the new southern landscape. Powerful currents reversed direction suddenly and unexpectedly, gaining ever greater force in the twenty-first century, carrying the South with them.

WAR AGAIN

From the moment World War II began, federal money, purpose, and power energized the South. The war felt like a strange deliverance, bringing long-awaited change to these states. Communities across the region prospered, while Black and white southerners, women and men, fought around the world. Like the United States as a whole, the South found itself stronger after the Armageddon than before.[1]

The rural South presented disheartening scenes of decline and crisis at the end of the 1930s. Farm families labored on diminished and struggling farms. Children suffered from malnutrition as parents pieced together bare livings from day labor. Black women performed domestic service for white families for wages that could not sustain them. Migrant workers, including Mexican immigrants, traveled up and down the Atlantic coast and across the South, from Florida to Texas, following the harvest and taking whatever work they could get. Federal officials paid farmers to plow under their cotton crops to raise prices, but that money went to landowners who then turned tenants off the land, leaving them homeless and helpless.

On the other hand, progress during the 1930s opened the way for rapid change when war came. Towns and cities had grown throughout the Great Depression, fed by metropolitan ambition and rural desperation. Roads and electric lines had spread during the hard times, advanced by the federal government. Debilitating diseases—pellagra, hookworm, tuberculosis, and malaria—had been eradicated by determined public-health campaigns. The Civilian Conservation Corps had carved national parks out of forests, and the Works Progress Administration had put up new public buildings across the South, employing people otherwise without work or income.

Military mobilization came with startling speed to the United States, fed by the overwhelming urgency of fighting simultaneous wars in Europe and across the Pacific. As officials struggled to build military capacity, it seemed at first that the South would be left behind. Massive factories in the North and Midwest previously devoted to automobiles and heavy machinery converted to tanks, airplanes, ships, armaments, and ordnance. The entire nation surged into motion as people moved to new construction and manufacturing jobs: fifteen million people moved, half of them over state lines, often toward the cities of the Northeast, Midwest, or Pacific coast.

Crowded rural districts of the South began emptying in 1941 as families uprooted themselves to travel to places they had never seen. At first, factory owners and public officials in the North and Midwest told migrants from the South to stay away, to leave the new opportunities for local people. Soon, though, an apparently limitless need for labor opened the door to strangers, including southerners. War production and workforces expanded as American soldiers and sailors fought on the far sides of the world.

Black southerners moved in hope that the nation's needs would open doors even for them. Drawing on information, encouragement, and support exchanged among themselves, Black southerners moved in even greater numbers during the 1940s than they had during the Great Migration. From the Upper South, from the Mississippi Valley, from the Black Belt, and from East Texas and Oklahoma, African Americans migrated to industrial and construction jobs in the North and West.

The war years created scenes of unfamiliar promise for Black Americans. The federal government worked to guarantee fair treatment for them in plants funded by public money. Unions welcomed the new workers, who in turn bolstered the unions. African American families cheered the contributions of their sons and daughters in the fight against racism abroad and urged the nation to achieve a double victory by vanquishing racism at home. Soldiers and their families saved to buy homes when they returned to what they hoped would be a better America.

Nearly 1.5 million African Americans left the South during the 1940s—200,000 more than during the previous twenty years. Most migrants moved to the major cities of the Atlantic coast and the upper Midwest. Others chose smaller places closer to home and family, such as Louisville, Cincinnati, Indianapolis, and Saint Louis. Hundreds of thousands made their way to the cities of California and the Pacific coast—to Los Angeles, San Francisco, Portland, and Seattle. California's Black population almost tripled, to more than 460,000 people, during the decade of the war.

White southerners, too, seized the chance to make new lives for themselves. More than 2.6 million white people left the South over the decade after 1940, more than in the preceding twenty years combined. As in the prewar decades, white people from Kentucky and Tennessee headed directly north to the factories of the Midwest. Rural Texas and Oklahoma, ravaged by agricultural crisis during the 1930s, saw massive migration, often to California, whose population grew by more than 3.5 million people. As in every decade since emancipation, those whites who lived in areas dominated by cotton plantations and impoverished Black workers left these places, where hopelessness hovered over the landscape.

Despite the departures of millions of Black and white southerners, migration within the South was even larger and more momentous. Four and a half million people moved within the region, often within the first years of mobilization for the war. Federal officials and state political leaders made sure that the South received its share of defense industries and military bases. While they did not enjoy the mature industrial foundation of the Great Lakes region, southern states did have plenty of inexpensive land, cooperative weather, and people eager to work. As a result, almost two-thirds of the army and navy bases within the United States were established in the South, often in remote areas. Of the nine largest camps in the nation, each able to house 50,000 personnel, the South claimed all but one. War-manufacturing projects brought Texas $1.4 billion, followed by Louisiana with $519 million and Alabama with about $500 million. Even the states with the least expansion—the Carolinas and Mississippi—saw manufacturing grow by $50 million during the five years of war.

The federal government's bulldozers transformed farmland to military use. "In two weeks," John Dos Passos observed with awe and sadness, "a back country settlement with its shacks and barns and outhouses and horsetroughs and fences, all the frail machinery of production built up on over the years by

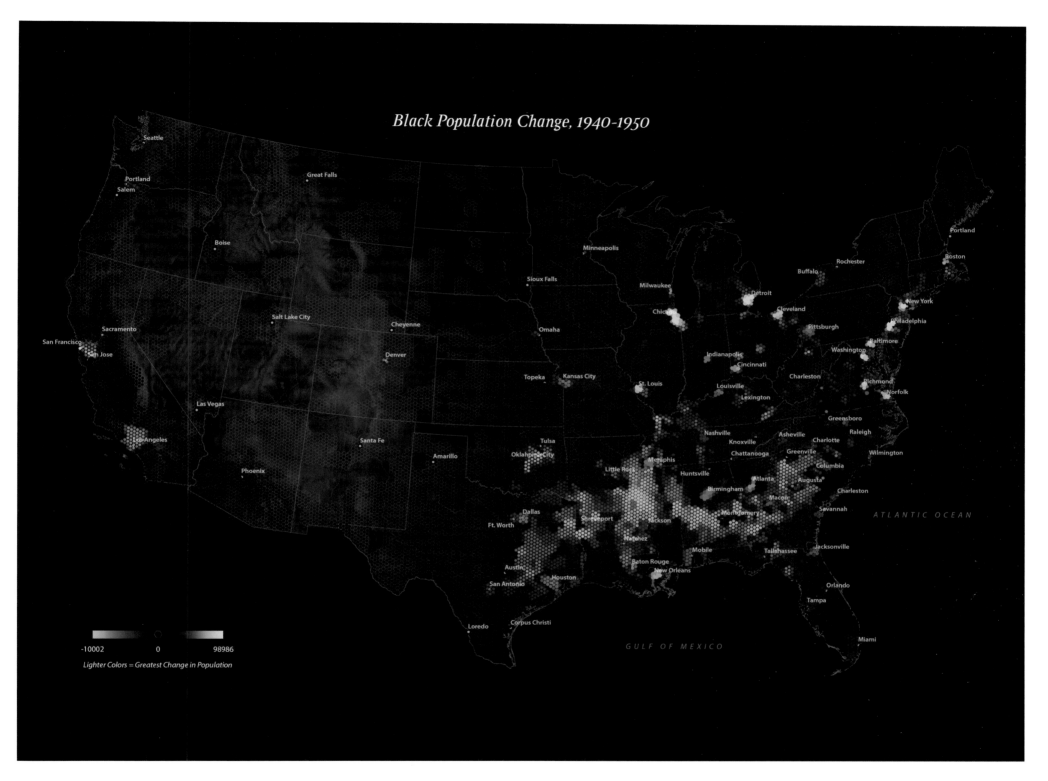

Black Population Change, 1940-1950

-10002   0   98986

Lighter Colors = Greatest Change in Population

The years of World War II and its aftermath see Black southerners leave not only the Black Belt and Delta, from which they had long been fleeing, but also rural Texas, Arkansas, Oklahoma, and the Piedmont, which had held out promise not long before.

White Population Change, 1940-1950

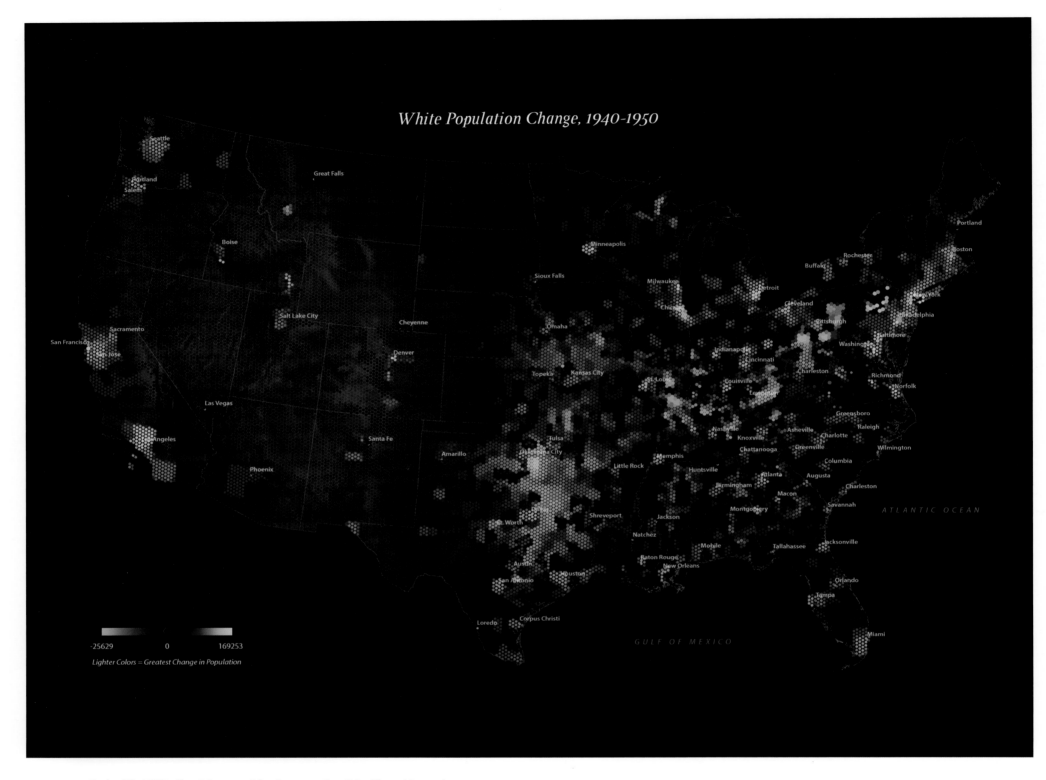

-25629   0   169253

Lighter Colors = Greatest Change in Population

During World War II and the years following, more than 2.5 million white southerners
leave the South for defense industries across the nation. Others pour into the burgeoning
cities of the South.

the plans and hopes and failures of generations of country people will have vanished utterly." In the place of that "frail machinery" of rural life emerged "the long runways of an airfield" or "the white concrete and glass tile oblongs of a war factory." Black landowners often lost the work of a lifetime in such expansion under eminent domain, compensated with a few dollars per acre.[2]

Hundreds of thousands of southerners went to work in the new defense plants and military bases in the South. White people took most of the new jobs in the factories, as federal efforts to prevent discrimination against African Americans did not offer effective protection in the segregated South. The sudden infusion of regular wages, paid at a higher level than workers had known before, sent money surging throughout southern communities. By 1944, more people received income from manufacturing than from agriculture in the South.

The South's urban population grew by 30 percent during the war, faster than the cities of the nation as a whole. Across the region, people rushed to boomtowns. Arriving in numbers greater than the facilities could absorb, migrants lived in tents and shantytowns in hopes they would be hired. Such camps appeared in North Carolina at Fort Bragg, in Florida at Camp Blanding, in Georgia at Fort Stewart and Fort Benning, in Alabama at Craig Army Air Force Base, in Mississippi at Camp Shelby, in Louisiana at Camp Beauregard and Camp Claiborne, and in Texas at Corpus Christi Naval Air Base. Ship-building, synthetic-rubber, and petroleum facilities attracted tens of thousands of workers to the Gulf coast. Texas gained 1.2 million people during the war decade. Newport News and Norfolk in Virginia grew at astounding rates. Oak Ridge, in East Tennessee, required more than a hundred thousand workers as the instant city raced to produced uranium for weapons of unprecedented power.[3]

The better jobs created by this feverish growth, such as welders and electricians, and the training and experience that accompanied them went to white men. White women found employment in ordnance plants, where their work resembled that of textile mills, and increasingly in other kinds of factories where labor demands outstripped the male population, but they were told not to expect to stay on the job at war's end. Though Black people found most public opportunities closed to them by state and local discrimination, private employers such as railroads and lumber companies, racing to take advantage of wartime demands, stole each other's labor force whenever they could.

Landowners watched as workers left farms for southern factories, where they could make in a day what they had earned in a week laboring on the land. Wages rose for even the poorest workers. Mexican Americans in Texas, driven by limitless demands for labor, saw their daily wage increase from one dollar to three dollars. Their population increased to more than a million people, surpassing that of African Americans in that state.

THE TRANSFORMATION OF THE RURAL SOUTH

Even during the war, people worried about what would follow in the southern countryside afterward. "I want to sound a warning against any belief that there can be any sizeable back-to-the-land movement after this war," a national official cautioned in 1944. Farming would "offer no large-scale possibilities. . . . We cannot afford again to think of agriculture as a refuge or national poorhouse." Though many southern soldiers fighting abroad dreamed of returning to the farms where they had grown up, they were destined not to stay there. The farm population of the South declined by three million people during the war years, and the decline accelerated thereafter. The South would no longer be dominated by "little farms for little people."[4]

Landowners used government subsidies to purchase new kinds of machinery—combines, balers, harvesters, and milking machines—radically and immediately reducing the need for laborers. Tractors and cotton-picking machines worked with powerful efficiency on broad flat fields stripped of fences, gardens, and buildings. Agricultural acreage expanded through the force of federal policy, expensive chemicals, and displacement of tenants and laborers. Planters began to replace cotton with other crops and with livestock. Landowning farmers, benefiting from government payments that subsidized 90 percent of southern croplands, saw their incomes more than double. Those landowners encouraged sharecroppers to leave when it suited the landlord's purposes and sought to stop migration when employers needed the cheap labor.

Faced with decline in traditional, small-scale farming, some entrepreneurial growers in hard-pressed areas created, step by step, innovations that would transform southern agriculture. Some began even before the wartime crisis. In hilly northwestern Arkansas and northern Georgia in the late 1930s, small landowners began to raise and market chickens in new ways. National feed producers encouraged local merchants to extend credit to farmers to purchase baby chicks and feed; poultry buyers traveled from one to farm to the next to purchase live chickens to transport to Saint Louis, Memphis, Atlanta, and even to Miami and Tampa. The electrification programs of the New Deal made it possible for farmers to light their chicken sheds, to pump in water, and to keep the temperature constant so that birds ate more and grew faster. Programs instructed poultry farmers how to counteract nutritional deficiencies and diseases that developed when thousands of birds were confined to heated buildings.[5]

Wartime demand for chicken surged as the government rationed red meat and began to buy poultry. In northern Georgia, the five thousand chickens sold in all of 1935 grew to thirty million per year at the end of the war and to nearly fifty million by 1949. By 1951, Georgia had become the leading poultry-producing state in the nation. This industry would spread across the South, attract workers to massive factories in remote communities, and trigger some of the most contentious scenes of labor and immigration conflict the South had ever seen. In northwestern Arkansas, John Tyson's business grew into the world's largest meat producer.[6]

Across the South, soybeans pushed aside the ragged monarch, King Cotton. Grown in China since 3000 BC, soybeans arrived in the United States at the beginning of the nineteenth century, used as forage for animals and a natural fertilizer rich in nitrogen for a few places in the South. When scientists found ways to remove the unpleasant smell and taste from soybeans in the 1930s, the crop found additional uses in margarine and shortening. World War II created new demand for soybeans, which could also be used for oils and for protein meals. While an acre of cotton required 184 hours of labor, an acre of soybeans required only 10 hours. The once-exotic plant became the South's "miracle crop," and by 1950, three million acres from Virginia to Texas produced soybeans. That number would double over the next decade and then multiply many times over as the South produced hundreds of millions of bushels every year.

Cotton underwent its own transformation. The center of production moved ever farther west, now to Texas, Oklahoma, New Mexico, Arizona, and California, watered through irrigation, harvested by machine, and weeded by herbicides. In 1930, about half the counties in the South grew cotton; by the end of the 1950s, only eleven counties produced cotton as their principal crop. Tenants found themselves so rapidly replaced by day labor, machinery, and chemicals that the federal census stopped counting tenants as a category soon after World War II.[7]

The wartime South, then, saw massive changes in manufacturing and agriculture, in the city and in the countryside, and in the interior and along the coasts. Millions of people deserted rural districts and headed for uncertain destinations, hoping for a kind of prosperity most had never known. Many succeeded in establishing new lives for themselves, but many hopes went unfulfilled. At war's end, white working women lost jobs they had recently won. Black southerners had been denied access to wartime training and skilled jobs that would have sustained them in peacetime. Small farms had fallen into neglect and would never recover. Cities had become overcrowded with temporary housing and precarious jobs. Soldiers and sailors returned to a South changed abruptly and profoundly.

EXODUS

"The South, by whatever comparative test, will emerge from this war with more social change and more unfinished business than any other section of the country," a southern white man observed. The postwar era provided a hard test for the region. As young southern men and women returned from camps and ships around the world, it was not clear what work might remain for them as wartime factories closed or tried to convert to peacetime uses. The farming communities they had left held out few prospects that could compete with what they had seen as they traveled far from home. Machines took jobs that people had performed just a few years earlier, leaving few opportunities for unskilled workers.[8]

Appalachia, as it had for the last several decades, suffered particularly hard blows from these changes. By 1950, two-thirds of the nation's coal was loaded mechanically, up from only 13 percent in 1935. The price of coal, temporarily increased by the war, declined as electricity and petroleum displaced the sooty mineral. Coal towns, abandoned by the companies that had built them, fell into ever-greater decay and despair. Unions grew weaker. Roads built under the New Deal offered easy escape to more promising locales, places that people in the mountains knew about because family and neighbors had moved there already.[9]

More than 3 million people left Appalachia over the three decades after 1940. West Virginia's population barely grew during the war, peaked in 1950, and then lost 400,000 people by 1960. Eastern Kentucky lost 250,000 people, a third of its population. Mountain areas where coalmining did not dominate the economy, such as East Tennessee and western North Carolina, also witnessed the departure of young people, with poverty haunting the hollows throughout the mountains. Four of every ten families lived below the poverty level in Appalachia, and half of the region's farmers and farm laborers left the land. By 1960, only 6 percent of mountain people worked full time in agriculture. The once-booming cities of Appalachia fell into decline, as Charleston, Knoxville, and Asheville lost people to Dayton and Cincinnati, to Akron and Cleveland.

While the South had prospered during the war, the rest of the nation had prospered, too. The cities in the Northeast, Midwest, and Far West held out prosperity and a fair chance for Black Americans that the South would not offer. The 1.1 million African Americans who moved away during the 1950s was exceeded only by the 1.4 million who left during the 1940s. Black southerners fled from places where farm labor had been replaced by farm machinery and herbicides, where communities had been abandoned, and where reasons to hope that things would get better had disappeared. White southerners sped the departure of Black laborers they no longer needed by restricting food-stamp distribution and spreading word of higher welfare payments in the cities of the North.[10]

White southern population loss during the 1950s—at 3.2 million, the greatest total number in one decade the South would ever know—reached ever deeper and more widely. The emptying of Appalachia, the continued losses of the Upper South, and the agricultural decline of northern Alabama, Mississippi, Louisiana, and Arkansas removed people from across large parts of the South. Arkansas claimed more people in 1940 than it would have again until 1980. Tennessee declared as its greatest social problem the loss of thousands of young people every year during the 1950s—and Kentucky lost even more residents than Tennessee.

Postwar Florida, by contrast, attracted millions of people, fed by rural decline and the ascent of the cities of Miami, Tampa, Jacksonville, Saint Petersburg, and Orlando. In 1940, Florida had been the most sparsely populated state in the South, but 172 military installations and massive training facilities sprang up during the war. The 1.9 million people in the state on the eve of the war grew to 2.8 million by 1950 and to 4.9 million by 1960. Florida's African American population almost doubled over those decades, as the state attracted more Black Georgians than any other destination, including northern states.[11]

During the 1940s and 1950s, too, Jewish Americans from the Northeast began to retire in Miami in ever-mounting numbers, while many white mid-westerners from other religious backgrounds chose Saint Petersburg. Starting in the 1950s and continuing for the next half century, a thousand retirees moved to Florida each week. The number of tourists to the state grew from one million a year in 1930 to five million in 1950. Immigrants also arrived from the Caribbean, the numbers foreshadowing massive migrations soon to come.

Florida stood as an extreme example of change across the South, especially in the spread of expansive cities. A new acronym emerged as demographers tried to describe cities that grew outward with remarkable speed: SMSA, or Standard Metropolitan Statistical Area, describing places that included both central cities and the suburbs spreading from them. Those metropolitan regions attracted people and businesses by concentrating transportation, business leadership, and financial and professional services. SMSAs contributed 84 percent of the South's growth during the 1940s and 90 percent during the 1950s, a remarkable pivot for a region dominated by rural growth for over a century.

Commentators found the future of the South hard to predict in the 1950s. The region enjoyed continued defense spending, enticing new consumer goods, a growing industrial sector, booming tourism, and rapidly expanding cities. Yet the South lost population every year because the rest of the United States was changing even more rapidly. The per-capita income of southerners grew faster than that of the nation as a whole through the 1950s, but the region could still claim only 76 percent of the national average of personal income in 1960. The wages, salaries, education, health care, and overall quality of life were simply higher in much of the rest of the nation than they were in the South. People of all descriptions left the region as a result.

The departure of so many residents, ironically, may have sped the South's economic and material change. The South exported millions of impoverished people from a countryside that held out few prospects of jobs. It was fortunate for them, for the region, and for the nation that the war and postwar prosperity created places for them to go that were, by and large, better than the places they left. Thanks to the enormous size and bounty of the United States, these millions of migrants, especially white people, benefited from relocation without having to leave their native country. They could enjoy opportunities that people from smaller, poorer, and less fortunate countries had to sacrifice so much to attain. There were no new languages to learn, no citizenship tests to take, no bureaucracies to satisfy, and no immigration officials or police to avoid.

White Population Change, 1950-1960

-266435 0 227211

Lighter Colors = Greatest Change in Population

In the greatest exodus of white southerners in the region's history—more than 3.2 million people—the 1950s see almost every rural district bleed population. Appalachia is hard hit, as are other areas on the edges of the South.

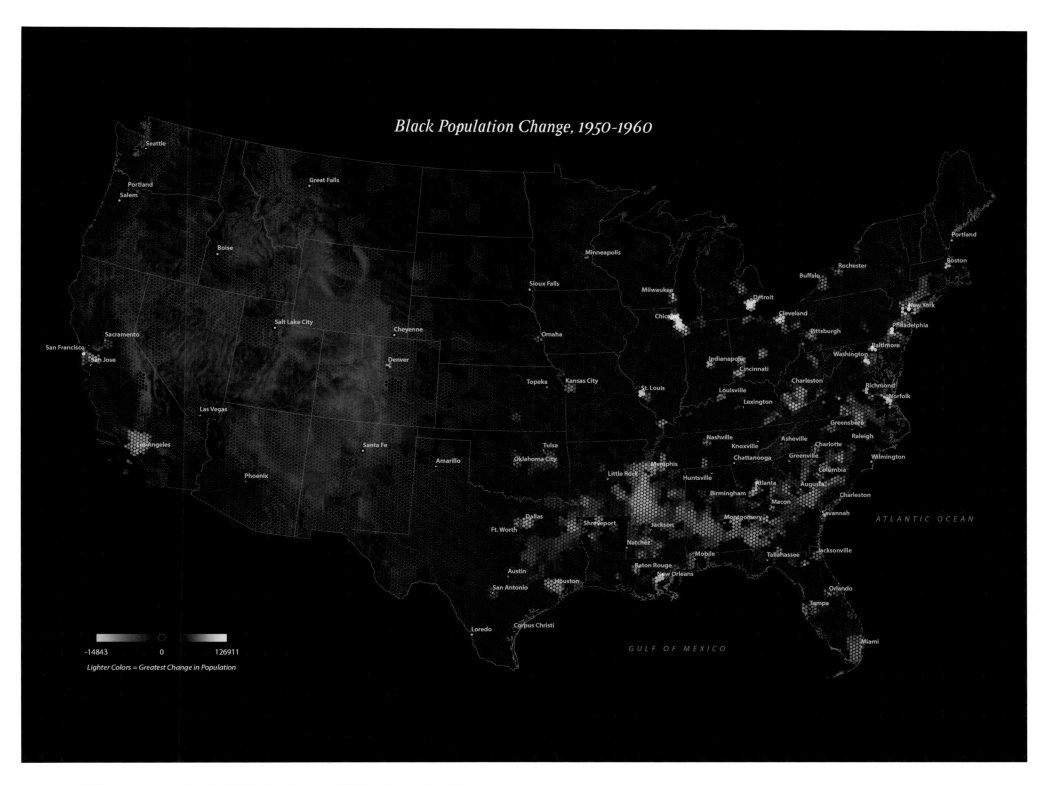

Black Population Change, 1950-1960

-14843   0   126911

Lighter Colors = Greatest Change in Population

While the momentum from the 1940s slows, the flow of Black southerners from the
hardest-hit rural areas of the region continues unbroken during the 1950s.

For Black people, leaving the South in the middle decades of the twentieth century brought great and immediate improvement in almost every facet of life. The cities of the North and West offered greater economic opportunity for them than even the most prosperous cities in the South. The North and West held out the opportunity to be full citizens, to be treated like other Americans in public spaces, and to have a chance to vote and to attend a decent school. Black migrants from the South were helped by people who had made the same journey not long before and shared familiar ways of talking and eating, of worshipping and celebrating. This Second Great Migration seemed a deliverance, a warmth under new suns.[12]

THE BLACK FREEDOM STRUGGLE

Black people who remained in the South—the majority of African Americans, it is important to remember—worked to create equity and justice where they lived. Wartime offered some new weapons in that struggle. The Fair Employment Practices Commission provided a basis for Black workers to demand and sometimes to acquire equal pay and treatment on the job. Some labor unions worked for greater racial justice. The National Association for the Advancement of Colored People had grown stronger during the war and collaborated with local advocates of equality, especially in the courts. A 1944 Supreme Court decision ended the white primary, one of the most powerful tools southern Democrats used to suppress the Black vote by bypassing general-election laws. Following the court's decision, Black southerners began to register to vote. In 1940, only 3 percent of African Americans had registered, but in 1947, the proportion increased to 12 percent, then to 20 percent by 1952. As Black veterans returned home to the South, they helped lead registration drives, and some even ran for office.[13]

Black migration strengthened efforts toward justice in the South. The growing Black population in cities offered more fertile ground for organizing than did scattered farms and tenant shacks. The churches, schools, newspapers, businesses, and civic organizations among urban African Americans stirred action. A growing number of Black families established a foothold in small businesses and property holdings. Southern Black migrants moved among towns and cities, often to larger places, gaining experience and finding potential allies. The exodus from the countryside meant that those who remained could bargain for higher wages and better working conditions.

Black migrants to northern cities aided their southern counterparts by forming a powerful new voting bloc. As those voters cemented their relationship to the Democratic Party, they pushed against the conservative white southerners who controlled much of that party's leadership and apparatus. The Democrats, struggling to placate both groups, broke apart as early as 1948, when the so-called Dixiecrats, furious with President Harry S. Truman's integration policies in the military, ran Senator Strom Thurmond for president and won electoral votes in several states of the Deep South. They failed to check federal authority, but their strident calls for segregation and states' rights struck notes that defenders of white supremacy would scream for the next two decades.

The struggle for the rights of Black southerners, then, gained force from several tributaries of migration and activism during the 1940s and 1950s. African American leaders searched for the most effective combination of legal, political, and direct-action strategies, working on all fronts simultaneously. The famous *Brown v. Board of Education* victory before the Supreme Court in 1954, declaring the "separate but equal" policy of school segregation illegal, grew out of brave efforts of isolated individuals to achieve fair education in their own communities. The defiance of school integration by the governor of Arkansas in 1957 forced President Dwight D. Eisenhower to invoke the power of the federal government against segregation. The Freedom Rides and lunch-counter sit-ins of 1960 used new interstate bus travel, chain franchises, and rapidly spreading televisions to challenge local injustice.[14]

Migration and prosperity did not automatically empower Black southerners or liberalize the white South. Years elapsed between rare victories in the freedom struggle. White southerners launched efforts of massive resistance against the schools, moved to all-white parts of metropolitan areas, created academies to avoid integrated schools, voted for defenders of segregation, encouraged Black people to leave, and even abandoned the South themselves by the millions. Black southerners with successful businesses or large congregations sometimes refused to support the movement for civil rights. While television networks sometimes broadcast southern injustice and violence to national audiences, local radio and newspapers supported segregation day in and day out.

And yet, the deep structural changes in the South brought by migration laid the groundwork for political change that appeared suddenly. The assassination of President John F. Kennedy triggered a wave of national remorse that Lyndon Johnson of Texas, building on generations of struggle and accomplishment by Black southerners, converted into the two most crucial events in the post–World War II South: the Civil Rights Act of 1964 and the Voting Rights Act of 1965. Passed by large majorities of the U.S. Congress, the first act outlawed discrimination based on race, color, religion, sex, or national origin—and thus racial segregation—while the latter outlawed racial discrimination in elections.

Riots broke out in cities from Detroit to Los Angeles because the new laws offered little to Black Americans outside the South. For many, the promise of the Great Migrations collapsed almost as quickly as it arose. Cities in the North and West had become deeply segregated. Manufacturing provided fewer jobs. Housing had become both dilapidated and expensive. Schools in Black neighborhoods suffered from underfunding and neglect. Police hostility and brutality plagued the streets.

While generations of immigrants from Europe benefited from decades of industrial growth through which they could make places for themselves in the United States, African Americans had enjoyed only a brief window of opportunity, a window that began to close almost as soon as it opened. Those in the North and West, especially second-generation migrants, did better than their counterparts who stayed in the South, but these differences faded after the 1960s. The South, at long last, began to develop in ways that attracted migrants—including African Americans—to a region that had experienced generations of loss.[15]

THE END OF STATE-ENFORCED SEGREGATION

The turning point in the South's economic development came in the mid-1960s. The Great Migrations, the massive federal spending of the New Deal and World War II, the abandonment of cotton, and the growth of manufacturing and cities had changed the lives of millions of southerners, improving them for most and narrowing the gap in the standard of living with the rest of the nation. Yet the South remained behind the national average in every major index. The economic transformation of the region that had been growing in different ways since emancipation and that had surged forward during World War II slowed in the 1950s.[16]

No white leaders of the South identified the African American exodus as a problem. Indeed, as one Black leader put it, "They wished we'd go back to Africa, but Chicago was close enough." No white politician put forward a plan to take advantage of southern Black talent and energy to transform the South. The Civil Rights Act and the Voting Rights Act, the products of unanticipated historical events and alignments, triumphed despite the venomous opposition of southern senators and representatives, despite ugly and empty acts of defiance by southern governors and local leaders, and despite votes by white southerners for those who vowed to defy the law of the land. Predictions of chaos, violence, and decline did not come to pass, but neither did immediate change in schools, neighborhoods, and workplaces. White backlash was increasingly couched in language that claimed to have nothing to do with race, language about neighborhood schools, property rights, and law and order. The white South voted for presidential candidates who played to resentment of such changes.[17]

Yet it soon became evident that the Civil Rights and Voting Rights Acts had begun to advance the southern economy in ways white beneficiaries of segregation had not expected. A modicum of justice accomplished what no amount of boosting by chambers of commerce or tax breaks by governors desperate for economic development could bring. Southern business leaders, large and small, had shown little resistance to segregation; indeed, many businessmen led efforts to slow or stop integration, claiming that it would damage fragile commercial growth. Northern-owned businesses, for their part, had easily adapted themselves to the segregated South.

The calculus began to change with the Black freedom struggle, for it became clear that businesses operating in the South paid a kind of moral tariff when camera crews and reporters chronicled their complicity. Early national retail chains, such as Woolworth's, found themselves boycotted nationally in the 1950s and early 1960s when their franchises in the South refused to seat Black customers at integrated lunch counters or allow them to try on clothes. International companies tempted by the incentives of low taxes and cheap labor might fear they would pay a different kind of tax by operating in the Jim Crow South, just as municipalities feared being forever branded by incidents of violence and disruption. The end of segregation did not come through the efforts of white business or civic leaders, but they benefited from that end nevertheless.

After the end of legal segregation, investors from beyond the region or the nation could build factories or branches in the South without such reputational risks. Textile factories, the earliest, largest, and most segregated southern industry, changed quickly after 1965 by hiring Black workers, reluctantly at first and then with greater confidence as time-worn stereotypes about their inability to work in factories or in supervisory roles turned out to be mythical. The chance of employment in the plants immediately affected Black migration. "There is a marked difference now," an African American employment manager told an interviewer, "and people who couldn't get away from here fast enough are coming back comfortably."[18]

The cities of the South served as examples to the rest of the region. Atlanta declared itself too busy to hate and reaped rewards—sometimes in surprising ways. The South, though fervent in its devotion to sports, had never had a major-league franchise in any sport until 1965, when the Milwaukee Braves became the Atlanta Braves. Their star player—Hank Aaron, an African American southerner—admitted that he was unhappy with the announcement but was persuaded by Atlanta's leaders that the city would offer a congenial home for him and his teammates. Teams in other sports emerged in New Orleans and Dallas soon thereafter, beginning a rush to the growing markets of a South freed from the stigma of legal segregation. These cities and others built coalitions across racial lines to construct airports and health facilities.[19]

The federal legislation of the mid-1960s did not immediately stop the ongoing flight from the South by Black people, but the outmigration slowed. While more than 800,000 Black southerners left the region during the 1960s, from the same places others had left during the 1950s, 300,000 fewer African Americans left than over the earlier decade. By the 1970s, Black people left only the distressed areas of the Upper South and along the Mississippi River. During the 1980s, the migration focused mainly from the Mississippi River westward through Louisiana and Arkansas and from southern Mississippi and southern Virginia. By the 1990s, only a few scattered counties across the South registered net losses of Black people.

White population net loss also slowed and then reversed as people began to come to the South from other places. During the 1960s, only Appalachia and heavily Black areas along the Mississippi River showed much decline. Virtually no counties showed net loss during the 1970s, though the Black Belt was stagnant for white migration. Then during the 1980s, white decline focused on the Mississippi River valley, Appalachia, and the Black Belt. But the white population increased during the 1990s everywhere except the Black Belt.

At the same time, the cities of the North, Midwest, and West faltered. The manufacturing that had provided the foundations for Black employment declined in the face of global competition. Nearly three-quarters of Black northerners and westerners lived in majority-Black neighborhoods in 1970, the residential segregation growing more extreme as white people left the central cities to which African Americans had moved. The differential between the South and the rest of the nation faded as the South finally began to offer opportunities for Black residents.[20]

The lives of American Indians with roots in the South changed as well. The New Deal offered some opportunities for some Native peoples, especially the Cherokees, as the Civilian Conservation Corps and the building of the Blue Ridge Parkway brought tourists to see what they took to be authentic dance and crafts. The outdoor drama *Unto These Hills* attracted hundreds of thousands of white visitors over several decades of performance. World War II saw more than 25,000 Native people fight for the United States, gaining a measure of recognition and gratitude even as laws in the 1950s pushed American Indians off tribal lands. By 1970, about half of all Native people lived in urban places.

As tribal identity became increasingly disconnected from allotments or reservations, American Indians, including those with ancestral ties to the South, became more determined to maintain their ties to one another. The Civil Rights Act and the Black freedom struggle inspired activism among Native peoples. A law in 1988 gave some American Indian tribes the opportunity to open gambling casinos on their remaining lands. Native peoples sought federal recognition to share in that opportunity, to protect their tribal lands, and to declare their pride in their ancestry. Tribes across the South turned to a broad array of strategies to determine who belonged to their people, depending on their own histories and situations. Native southerners became ever more visible and active in places where their ancestors had lived.[21]

THE NEW LANDSCAPE OF THE RURAL SOUTH

During the 1960s, the farm population of the South declined by almost half. Farm families that had accounted for 43 percent of the southern people in 1940 composed only 7 percent by 1970. A massive but silent migration of white and Black rural people unfolded year after year, little noticed by commentators. "Despite all the talk about government help, the transition out of agriculture for most people was unplanned and unassisted. Private economic forces commanded the decisions," one historian has explained. Farming became ever-more expensive, demanding "machinery, fertilizer, gasoline and

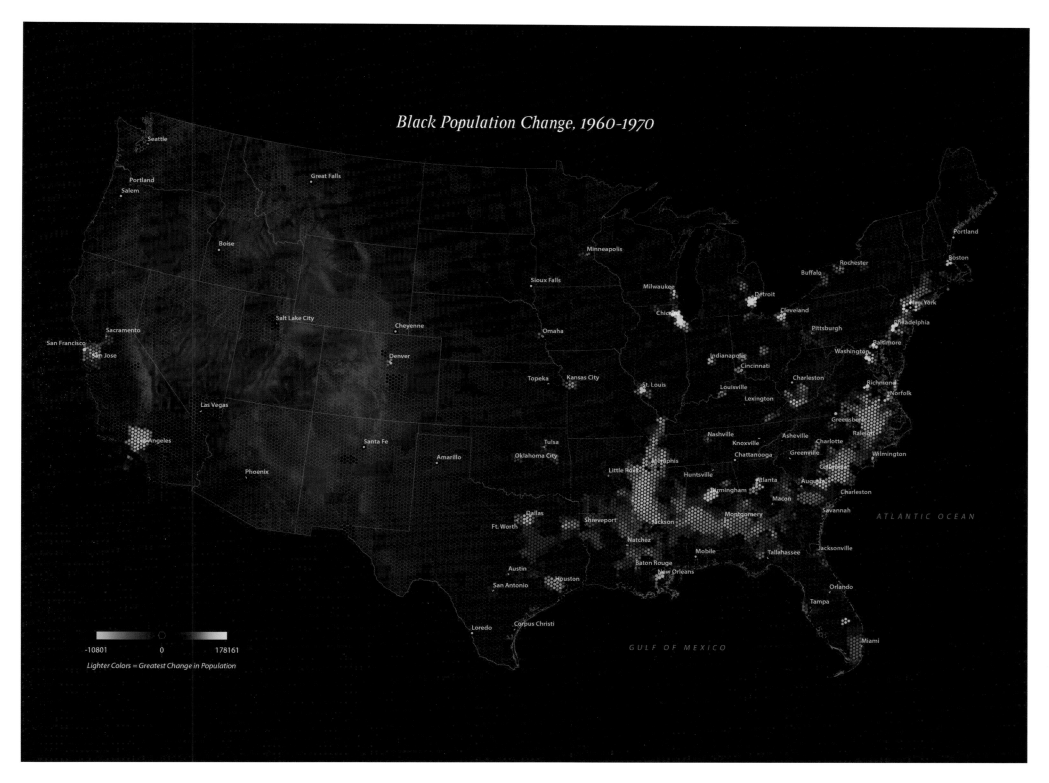

Black Population Change, 1960-1970

-10801   0   178161

Lighter Colors = Greatest Change in Population

The patterns of the preceding half century, as Black people continue to leave counties where they account for a large share of the population, slow in the decade of the Civil Rights Act and Voting Rights Act.

White Population Change, 1960-1970

-199176   0   82720

Lighter Colors = Greatest Change in Population

Appalachia continues to lose population in large numbers, while the rest of the white South sees
a demographic stabilization. Florida accelerates the rapid growth of its white population.

diesel fuel, insecticides and fungicides, hybrid seed, and other inputs." In the early 1990s, the U.S. Census Bureau simply stopped counting the number of Americans living on farms. Corporations, wealthy partnerships, and private-equity firms bought up old plantations for lumber and hunting, restoring those parts of the South to uses they had sustained before the cotton revolution of the early nineteenth century.[22]

Rural areas experienced widespread change as many manufacturers built small factories in the twenty years after World War II. Almost 40 percent of those southern factories were located in the countryside or small towns, where large numbers of underemployed farmworkers were glad to have the steady, if low, pay of a factory. Unions found it difficult to organize workers in these remote places, and local officials did all they could to keep the employees out of unions.

Increasingly, though, these firms had to compete in a global market for labor in which costs were even lower than in the rural South. Factories began to leave in the 1970s, and the abandonment continued into the twenty-first century, leaving behind former workers with few skills, with little education, and now in middle age. The South did not create robust social-welfare and health programs to protect vulnerable members of the community, nor had it invested in schools to develop native talent, rendering itself open to competition from even less fortunate places. Rural families suffered in the absence of support and often moved to towns and cities if they could.

The rural exodus dislocated more Black than white southerners. While white farms decreased by 58 percent after 1940—to 61,000 people—in 1970, the number of Black farmers in ten southern states had declined 88 percent, from 132,000 to only 16,000 people. The U.S. Department of Agriculture sped the decline of African American farmers through its promotion of capital-intensive and scientific farming, often accompanied with prejudicial loan policies and allotments. A 1999 Supreme Court decision secured compensation for injustices against Black farmers incurred before 1981, but by then, many more Black families had lost their farms. Similar discrimination damaged the efforts of Native Americans, women, and Latinx people to sustain farms.[23]

The rural South fell quiet. Schools and churches closed. Elderly people lived alone, far from medical care. Local stores and businesses gave up, as dollar stores and "big box" chains monopolized retail for items small and large. Young people barely paused after high school before leaving. White people continued to leave Appalachia, perpetuating a decades-old migration. Across the South, in a band widening and deepening as it stretched from Virginia to Louisiana, rural counties endured the loss of white populations at the turn of the twenty-first century, often in areas with large Black populations. This loss, for its part, concentrated in places where Black people still outnumbered white people and where rural economies struggled: southern Virginia, eastern North Carolina, Piedmont South Carolina and Georgia, the Black Belt of Alabama, the Mississippi River valley, and large parts of Louisiana, Arkansas, and Texas.[24]

Departure and movement sped along the growing interstate-highway system. The network of divided four-lane roads began with a presidential act in 1956, and its consequences unfolded for the rest of the twentieth century, one exit at a time. In 1960, the first highways in the region ran north and south through Alabama and Mississippi and diagonally across Tennessee. By 1965, the number of miles had almost doubled as the interstates radiated from Atlanta, Birmingham, Memphis, Little Rock, and the cities of Texas. By 1970, the roads had reached the length of Florida and extended from the North Carolina coast west through the mountains of southern Appalachia and across Tennessee. By 1975, the highways ran the extent of the Shenandoah Valley—the site of the first expansion of the South by white settlers and enslaved people two hundred years before. By 1980, an interstate crossed Florida from the Atlantic to the Gulf and stretched almost the full length of the Gulf coast. By 1985, the southern part of the great artery of I-95 had been completed through the Carolinas and Georgia, while northern Virginia, Atlanta, and the Dallas–Fort Worth area had grown into powerful highway hubs. By 1990, a network of more than forty thousand miles of uniform roads connected the South internally and with the rest of the nation.[25]

The interstate-highway system did not expand easily and smoothly. The massive roads, expensive to build and maintain while offering relatively infrequent entrances and exits, cut through rural and urban areas despite the wishes of the people who lived there. The future of rural communities depended not only on whether the interstate passed through their county but also on whether travelers would be able to descend from the rivers of traffic into a new roadside outpost of chain gas stations and fast-food restaurants. Signs implored travelers to visit downtowns rendered "historic" by the commerce of the interstate, but few did. Rural communities seldom benefited from the arrival of the highway except to enjoy quicker travel to somewhere larger with chain stores and restaurants.

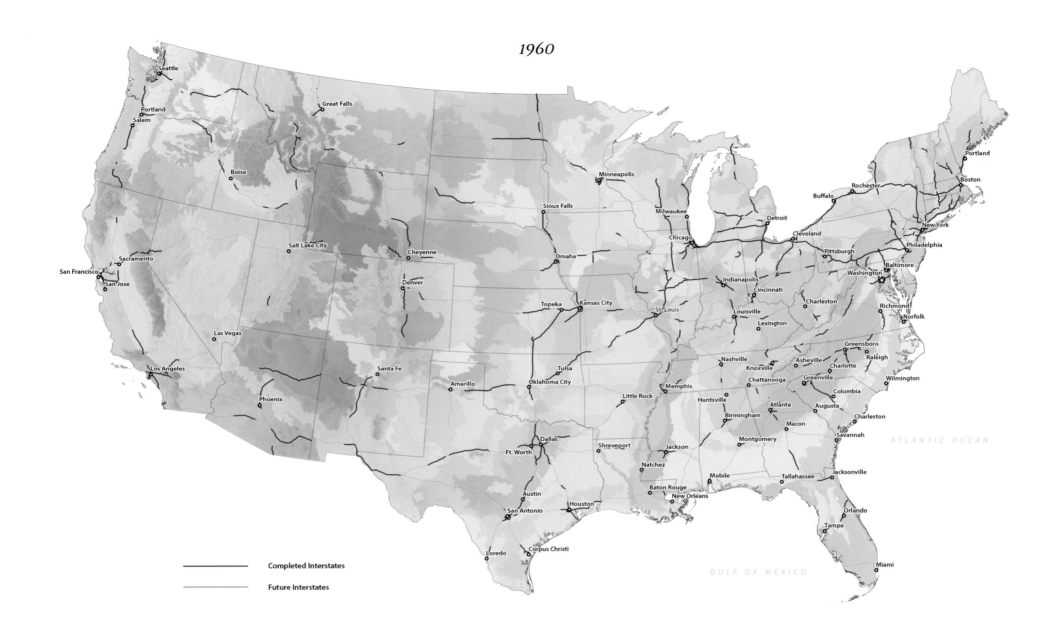

1960

Completed Interstates

Future Interstates

With each passing year, the interstate-highway network integrates the South
internally and with the rest of the nation.

1965

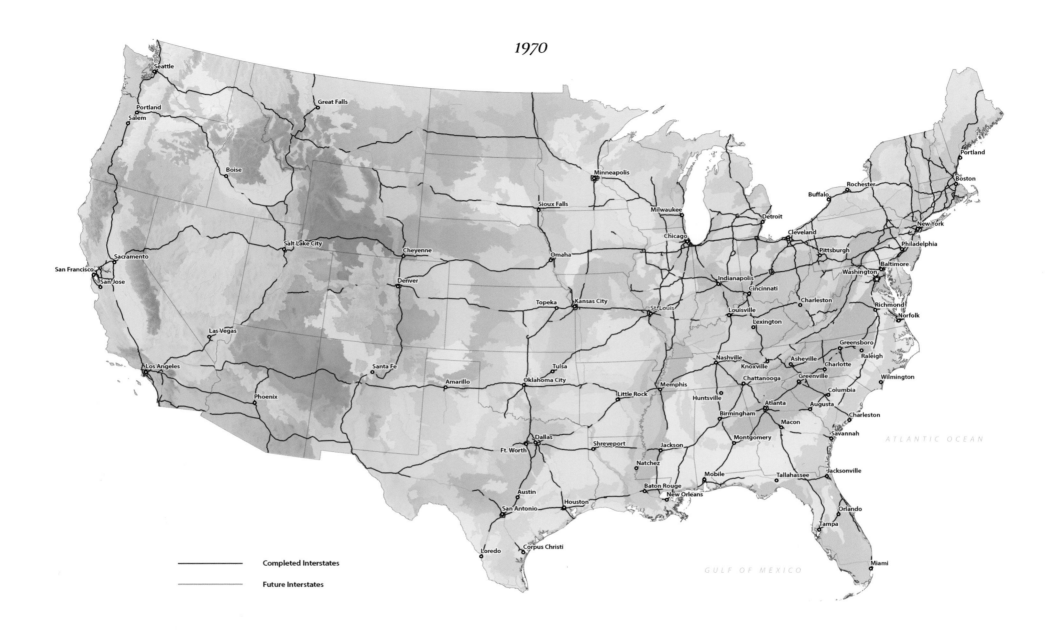

1970

Seattle
Portland
Salem
Great Falls
Boise
Minneapolis
Rochester
Buffalo
Portland
Boston
Sioux Falls
Milwaukee
Detroit
New York
Salt Lake City
Cheyenne
Omaha
Chicago
Cleveland
Pittsburgh
Philadelphia
Sacramento
Denver
Indianapolis
Washington
Baltimore
San Francisco
San Jose
Topeka
Kansas City
St. Louis
Cincinnati
Charleston
Richmond
Norfolk
Louisville
Lexington
Las Vegas
Greensboro
Santa Fe
Tulsa
Nashville
Asheville
Raleigh
Los Angeles
Amarillo
Oklahoma City
Memphis
Knoxville
Charlotte
Wilmington
Phoenix
Little Rock
Chattanooga
Greenville
Huntsville
Atlanta
Columbia
Birmingham
Augusta
Charleston
Dallas
Macon
Savannah
ATLANTIC OCEAN
Ft. Worth
Shreveport
Jackson
Montgomery
Natchez
Austin
Baton Rouge
Mobile
Tallahassee
Jacksonville
Houston
New Orleans
San Antonio
Orlando
Loredo
Corpus Christi
Tampa
GULF OF MEXICO
Miami

Completed Interstates

Future Interstates

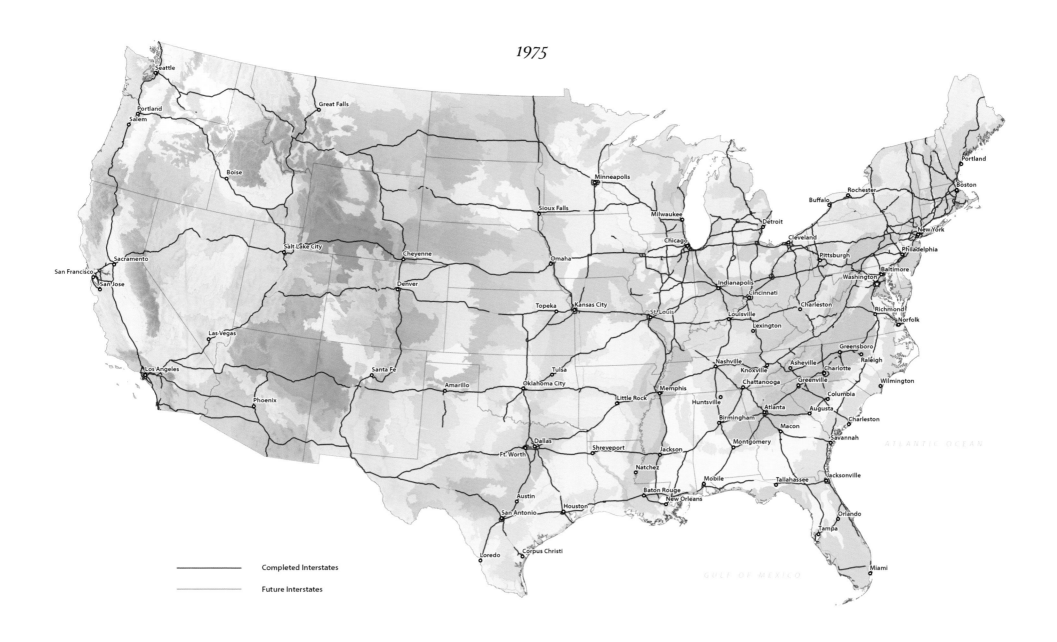

1975

Seattle
Portland
Salem
Great Falls
Boise
Minneapolis
Sioux Falls
Milwaukee
Detroit
Buffalo
Rochester
Portland
Boston
New York
Cleveland
Chicago
Pittsburgh
Philadelphia
Salt Lake City
Cheyenne
Omaha
Indianapolis
Baltimore
Sacramento
Denver
Cincinnati
Washington
San Francisco
Topeka
Kansas City
St. Louis
Charleston
Richmond
San Jose
Louisville
Norfolk
Lexington
Las Vegas
Greensboro
Tulsa
Nashville
Asheville
Charlotte
Raleigh
Santa Fe
Knoxville
Los Angeles
Oklahoma City
Memphis
Chattanooga
Greenville
Wilmington
Amarillo
Little Rock
Huntsville
Columbia
Phoenix
Birmingham
Atlanta
Augusta
Macon
Charleston
Dallas
Shreveport
Montgomery
Savannah
Ft. Worth
Jackson
ATLANTIC OCEAN
Natchez
Austin
Mobile
Tallahassee
Jacksonville
San Antonio
Baton Rouge
New Orleans
Houston
Orlando
Tampa
Loredo
Corpus Christi
GULF OF MEXICO
Miami

——— Completed Interstates

——— Future Interstates

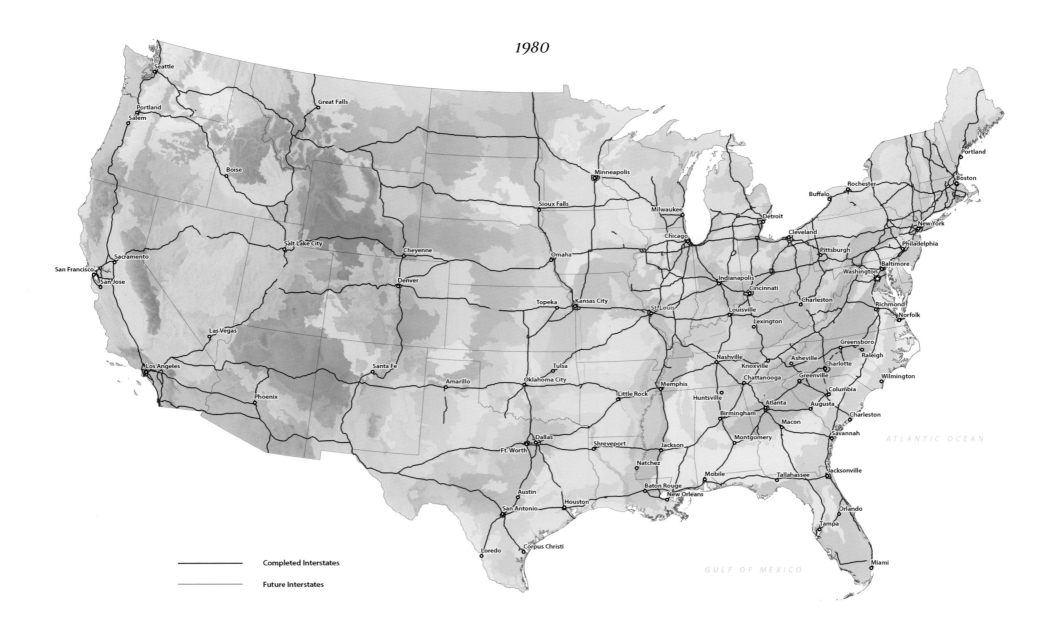

1980

Completed Interstates

Future Interstates

Much of the rural South skipped generations of gradual development when they found their communities bisected by the interstate. Areas of farms and hamlets gathered around general stores and gas stations turned almost instantly into suburbs feeding shopping centers. Many southerners welcomed these changes, finding that they could now commute to a better-paying job or shop at a store with better prices and selection. Some took advantage of the opportunity provided by this new kind of settlement to create vast businesses. Sam Walton of Bentonville, Arkansas, built the largest retail empire in the world on this grid.

For many places, though, economic decline and population loss fed one another in a mounting cycle. Counties caught in the vortex desperately competed for any jobs they could attract. One industry combined the profits of industrialized agriculture with those of low-cost factory work and the speed of the interstate highways. The southern poultry business, which had grown rapidly during the postwar years, now grew even faster as companies integrated all facets of the industry, aided by the federal government and an American public harboring an apparently boundless hunger for chicken. Men such as Georgia's Jesse Dixon Jewell and John Tyson of Arkansas consolidated the business, selling precooked chicken to restaurants and inventing new cuts. The breakthrough with chicken nuggets came with the introduction of dipping sauces, based on high fructose corn syrup, that varied the taste of the sodium- and fat-filled breaded pieces of chicken.[26]

Growers in the poultry industry resembled tenants in the sharecropping system, producing a crop for the profits of those who owned the company, investing in chicken houses while falling into debt and working other jobs to cover the losses. Chicken farming exacted a cost on the landscape as well. "As the industry grew," one historian has written, "piles of dead chickens, manure, and offal could be found on farms, in fields, beside processing plants, and in municipal sewage systems." The industry also "unleashed pesticides, hormones, and antibiotics into the air and water." The price of chicken declined even as demand for it escalated, driving those producing it to ever greater extremes of cost-cutting and exploitation.[27]

When chicken processing began to take off in the postwar South, it employed mainly white women. As the work became ever more intense and dangerous, African Americans—again, mainly women—took the jobs. The poultry industry did all it could to prevent organized labor in the plants and to remove any constraints on its business. Abuse flourished in this environ-

ment, ranging from racial and sexual harassment to violations of health and safety laws. Worker turnover reached 100 percent a year in some plants. As demand for chicken continued to increase and plants ran twenty-four hours a day, employers complained of labor shortages. They began to look beyond the South to meet their need for ever more workers.

IMMIGRANTS COME TO THE SOUTH

Throughout its history, the South attracted far fewer immigrants than other regions of the United States. While some Irish and Germans migrated there before the Civil War, the former tended to cluster in cities and the latter on farms in Texas. After emancipation, planters and other employers dreamed of attracting "coolie" labor from China through the Caribbean, but those efforts failed after a few experiments. The South fell ever farther behind as the high tide of immigration brought people from eastern and southern Europe to the North and Midwest at the turn of the twentieth century. Most of the South became ever more homogenous and starkly divided between Black and white as the rest of the nation became ever more diverse.

Florida and Texas, on the other hand, saw immigrants and migrant laborers establish themselves and eventually grow into some of the largest immigrant populations in the United States. Cuban immigrants arrived in Florida as early as the 1870s, fleeing from war on their home island. They moved first to Key West and then to Tampa, where thousands built a vibrant community centered around cigar factories. Seasonal workers from Cuba also came to Florida to labor in construction and on plantations producing sugarcane, citrus, and vegetables. The Bahamas sent a large and steady stream of migrant workers, and that stream grew after the founding of Miami in 1896 and the opening of regular steamship travel. In the first two decades of the twentieth century, more than 10,000 people left the Bahamas, a fifth of the islands' population. The Bahamians and other immigrants from the West Indies established a strong and growing community in Miami.[28]

People from the Caribbean journeyed to Miami throughout the twentieth century. The numbers of Cubans soared after the revolution of 1959, arriving in waves as relations between Cuba and the United States shifted. In the fifty years after the revolution, more than a million Cubans came to Florida, supported by the American government, often prospering and sustaining a strong communal identity. The United States proved less welcoming to people from Haiti, often poor and desperate, who were restricted to unskilled jobs when they were not turned back entirely. Nicaraguans came, too, as their country fell into internal conflict, followed by Mexicans, Puerto Ricans, Dominicans, and others from throughout Latin America. In the early twenty-first century, Florida contained 3.7 million foreign-born people, almost 20 percent of its population. They distributed themselves throughout the state, often to rural areas, where they became the main labor force.[29]

Mexican immigrants came to the South throughout the twentieth century. In the years between the world wars, workers from Mexico migrated to New Orleans and the Mississippi Delta. They continued to move to the Arkansas Delta during and after World War II and to southern Georgia starting in the 1960s. These migrants came over multiple routes, with different purposes and destinations in mind. As both Mexico and the South changed, these immigrants altered their strategies to take advantage of what the South might offer. White southerners and Black southerners exhibited a broad array of reactions to the migrants, ranging from welcome to violence, depending on local circumstances and political contexts.[30]

Texas attracted the largest number of immigrants from Mexico. Mexican people had already grown into the largest minority in the state by World War II, and the increase continued in the following decades as the state required their labor to fuel its rampant growth. Migrants to Texas gathered in the rapidly growing cities and soon spread to small towns and rural areas, where they constituted a critical part of the labor population. The vibrant economy and growth of Texas allowed it to absorb immigrants in large numbers. In 2015, more than half of the 4.7 million foreign-born people in Texas had migrated from Mexico.[31]

Throughout the 1990s, Florida and Texas continued to account for much of the Latinx population growth in the South, but Mexican Americans and other Spanish-speaking peoples also established communities in northern Virginia, Piedmont North Carolina, and Atlanta, Nashville, and Memphis. In the first decade of the twentieth-first century, immigrants from Latin America, especially Mexico, began to move into many other parts of the South. Every major city saw rapid growth, as did many smaller town and rural counties, especially in a band in the Piedmont. A few hundred people arriving in a place where the rest of the population was not growing could quickly account for a large share of the local population.[32]

The Latinx migration to and movement within the South grew as belated and unintended consequences of changing immigration laws. With an eye on international perception of the United States in the Cold War and the escalating fighting in Vietnam, in 1965 Congress eliminated national origin, race, and ancestry as the bases of immigration. The Immigration and Nationality Act privileged relatives of U.S. citizens and people with professional training. But it granted the same number of visas each year to all nations in the Eastern Hemisphere while limiting, for the first time, immigration from the Western Hemisphere and thus from Mexico and other parts of Latin America. Advocates of the law, while proud of its provisions, did not expect it to have significant effects on the profile of the American population.[33]

Those advocates proved to be mistaken. The share of the population of the United States born abroad grew from 5 percent in 1965 to 14 percent by 2017. Although the Immigration and Nationality Act placed a cap on people from the Western Hemisphere entering the United States, a strong demand for workers in the American Southwest drew about half of the people who moved into the country between 1971 and 1991 from Latin America, about a quarter of them from Mexico. A 1986 measure attempted to slow undocumented migration by granting amnesty to nearly three million people already in the country and outlawing the hiring of undocumented immigrants, but this inadvertently encouraged many people who had moved to the United States without documentation to remain rather than risk returning. The border with Mexico increasingly became militarized, and critics began to equate Latinx immigrants with illegality. Undocumented immigrants began to look for places beyond California and other areas of immigrant concentration and surveillance.[34]

In such an environment, rural areas of the South held advantages. Most Latinx immigrants who came to Arkansas to work in the poultry plants in the 1990s and 2000s, for example, had lived elsewhere in the United States. Rural Arkansas offered opportunities these migrants had not found in the large cities, where greater numbers of other immigrants gathered. In Arkansas, they were told by industry recruiters or fellow countrymen who approached them, they would have year-round work. They would encounter few officials to demand their documents, especially because their new employers promised to shield them. The cost of living would be low, and they would even have a chance to earn enough to buy a home. Unlike some other places in the South, there were few African American people competing for the jobs in the parts of Arkansas where the plants operated. The new arrivals would live among other Spanish-speaking people from El Salvador and Puerto Rico.[35]

Population Change of Latin American Immigrants and Their Descendants, 1990-2000

-109   0   149211

Lighter Colors = Greatest Change in Population

People immigrating to the South from destinations in Latin America first settle in Florida
and Texas, but others choose the larger cities of the region as their destination.

Population Change of Latin American Immigrants and Their Descendants, 2000-2010

-543   0   115813

Lighter Colors = Greatest Change in Population

People of Latin descent spread throughout the South, radiating from the cities into the countryside. The Piedmont becomes a major site of Latinx settlement.

Migrants to Arkansas' chicken-processing plants, aided by people from their home countries, adapted to their new communities, schools, churches, shops, and apartment complexes. The migrants' integration into rural areas, ironically, was in some ways easier because of the lower educational level, agricultural labor, lower wages, and higher poverty shared by their white and Black neighbors. Immigrants imparted economic and social vitality to declining industries and communities, helping keep local schools open and giving new life and mission to local churches.

Despite these contributions, immigrants from Latin America found themselves under attack at the national, state, and local levels by the media and politicians. They had, in some ways, succeeded too well. Their white and Black neighbors began to focus less on the immigrants' strong work and savings ethic and more on their legal status. In fact, the identity of "illegal aliens" soon overrode any other identity, accomplishment, or ambition. The phrase washed out the distinctions between naturalized citizens and undocumented people, between temporary residents and permanent residents. The presence of immigrants went from seeming a boon to the community to a burden, even though there were no other Americans willing to take on the brutal work of disemboweling and dismembering chickens.[36]

Some places in the South, particularly Texas and its border with Mexico, became predictable flashpoints as the nation struggled with immigration. Poultry plants, too, became places of conflict as federal agents raided them to take undocumented workers into custody and perhaps to deport them. Southern politicians often joined national leaders who demonized Latin American immigrants as criminals, even though records showed that they were less likely than native-born Americans to break the law. Critics caricatured immigrants as drains on public resources, even though they paid taxes without representation. The South included seven out of ten states with the largest increase in undocumented migrants between 1990 and 2010. The majority of these were young, single Mexican men, though the presence of women rose as did migrants from other places in Latin America. They scattered across the region in a patchwork of rural, suburban, and metropolitan areas, following the job opportunities of a global economy.

Immigrants from Asia came in large numbers to the South at the same time as immigrants from Latin America. The 1965 law that had restricted immigration from the Western Hemisphere intentionally enabled immigration from Asia. At first, the new law did not bring many people to the South, although in the 1970s, refugees from war-ravaged Vietnam were distributed across the region by the federal government to diminish their burden on any one place. In the 1980s, a more generous refugee policy encouraged a rapid growth of a broader array of Asian immigrants to the South. By 2000, the region claimed two million of the seven million Asian immigrants in the United States.[37]

Protected by the federal government in the spirit of the Civil Rights Act of 1964, Asian immigrants to the South found new opportunities in employment, business creation, and education. Those with advanced education filled well-paying jobs in technology and banking. Those with medical training, especially immigrants from India and the Philippines, discovered strong demand for their skills after the creation of Medicare and Medicaid in 1965. Fed by these opportunities, the Asian American population of the South continued to grow rapidly into the twenty-first century, increasing 43 percent between 2000 and 2010. While they spread across large parts of the South in small numbers in many communities, most tended to concentrate in the larger cities. More Asian Americans lived in Texas than in Hawaii by 2010, more in Atlanta than in San Francisco.[38]

Asian Americans came to the South from a remarkable range of cultures and nations, with Asian Indians in the largest numbers, followed by Chinese, Vietnamese, and Filipinos. People from different backgrounds found widely varying degrees of success in their new homes. Most Asian Americans in the South enjoyed higher incomes than their counterparts elsewhere in the country, but people who came as refugees, such Hmong people, Cambodians, and Laotians, suffered high rates of poverty and isolation. Class divisions among Asian Americans troubled many in those communities as their populations grew in number and diversity.

The South at the beginning of the twenty-first century claimed four of the five states where immigrant families were growing most rapidly: Texas, California, Florida, Georgia, and North Carolina. More than a quarter of all immigrants in the United States lived in the region. The South became, virtually overnight, one of the most diverse areas of the United States.

THE METROPOLITAN SOUTH

Cities had always played a critical role in southern migration. During the slave regime, they served as nodes in the slave trade and ports that shipped

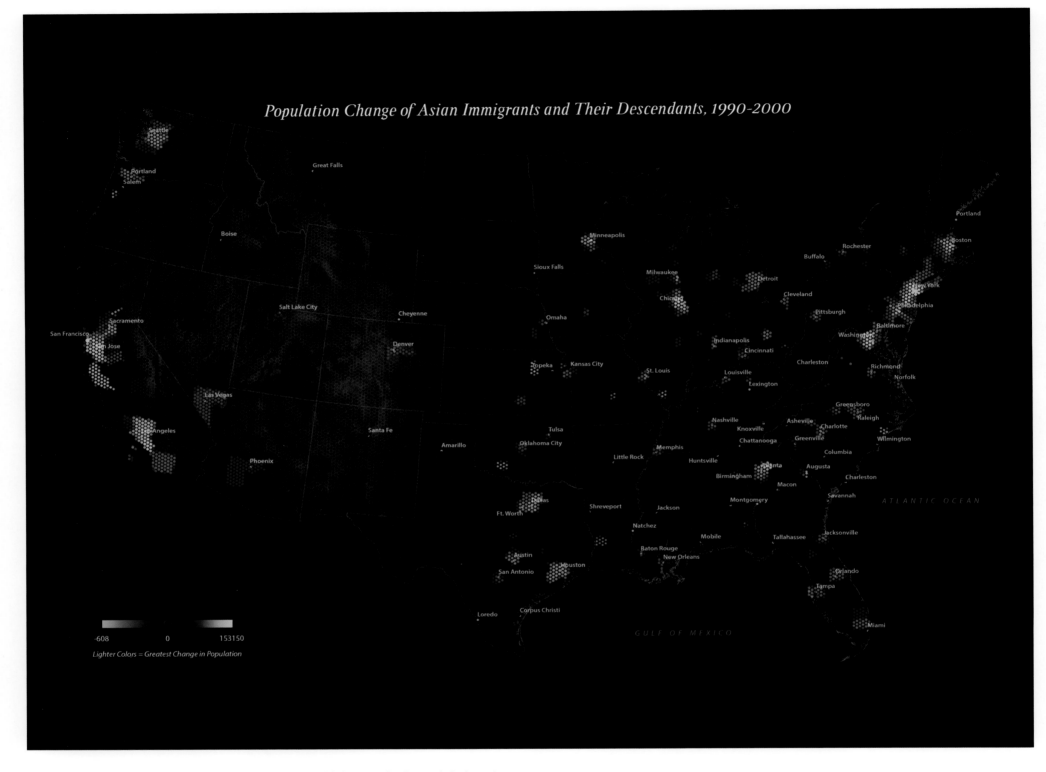

Population Change of Asian Immigrants and Their Descendants, 1990-2000

-608   0   153150

Lighter Colors = Greatest Change in Population

Immigrants and their children from a broad range of Asian countries first settle in the major
cities of the South, especially in Texas, Florida, Georgia, North Carolina, and Virginia.

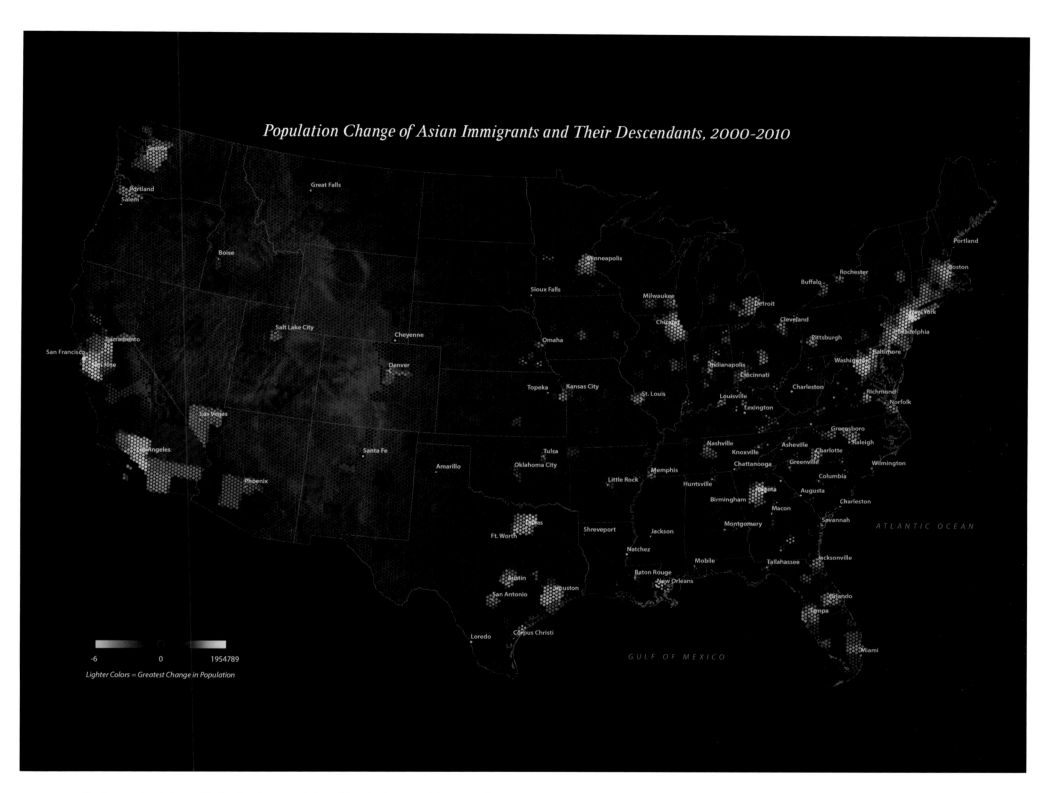

Population Change of Asian Immigrants and Their Descendants, 2000-2010

-6   0   1954789

Lighter Colors = Greatest Change in Population

The burgeoning Asian and Asian American population of the South concentrates around
the larger cities of the region.

the vast bounties of cotton, sugar, and rice enslaved people produced. During the New South era, cities old and new bridged the South with the North and West, integrating a new system of commerce and communication. During the first two-thirds of the twentieth century, they drew in rural people from across the South and energized the economies of large areas. Over the last third of the twentieth century and the early decades of the twenty-first century, southern cities emerged as the most dynamic metropolises in the entire United States, growing and diversifying at remarkable rates.[39]

Florida experienced in heightened form many of the changes transforming other parts of the South. Claiming ten of the top twenty-five national metropolitan areas during the 1970s, by the 1980s, Florida had nine of the top twelve. Only a "few hundred thousand of Florida's 15 million residents" lived outside a metropolitan area by the end of the century, observed one historian. Orlando, already growing rapidly, skyrocketed with the arrival of Disney World in 1971, "the world's most successful commercial attraction." In the early twenty-first century, it became the fifth-fastest-growing city in the United States and claimed more than 2.5 million people in its metropolitan area. The Sierra Club declared Orlando the leading embodiment of what it called "edgeless" urban sprawl: "low-density development that separates where people live from where they shop, work, recreate, and educate—thus requiring cars to move between zones." Tourism drove much of Florida's economy, with more than 126 million visitors in 2018 alone.[40]

The arrival of retirees in Florida from all over the nation, decade after decade, brought different benefits and costs. The state attracted more seniors during the second half of the twentieth century than any other, these older newcomers moving to new developments created in areas where few migrants had lived before. By 2015, migration had made Florida the "grayest" state in the nation, with nearly a fifth of its population over sixty-five years old.[41]

In other parts of the South, metropolitan areas connected into new kinds of regions. An urban and suburban arc stretched from northern Virginia, through Richmond, and on to Virginia Beach, accounting for much of that state's population growth and increasing diversity. Suburbs, cities, retailers, and factories lined the I-85 belt from the "Research Triangle" of North Carolina to Atlanta, blurring into one another along the interstate. Atlanta itself expanded exponentially, its borders radiating deep into the Georgia countryside along perpetually congested highways. Nashville boomed, producing

cars bearing Japanese names as well as proudly American country music. The cities of Texas developed into some of the largest in the nation, with Houston, San Antonio, Dallas, and Austin growing apparently without end.

Southern suburbs did not simply accrue around central cities, as they had earlier and elsewhere, but often grew independently, competing at their outset with the host city for people, capital, and political power. Bypasses and beltways connected suburbs to one another without passing through the core city itself. Neologisms sprouted to describe the new constellations of growth on the outer edges of metropolitan growth: "agriburbs, rurban settlements, rural fringes and borderlands, suburbscapes, penurbia, farm fringe streetcar suburbs, and wilderburbs."[42]

In all these changes, the South moved in the same directions as the rest of the nation, only more quickly and with greater contrast with what had come before. The region began with less of a capital investment in older cities and housing stock; for southern cities to grow, they would have to be new. The region began with a large and distressed rural population; southern cities would grow by tapping into the flight from the countryside. The South and the national era of interstates, franchise restaurants, expansive suburbs, and international immigration emerged together, suddenly, with little inertia. Airports connected to networks of national and global connections, and Atlanta boasted the busiest airport in the United States, serving more than 100 million passengers each year.

Southern cities expanded into a countryside ripe for such growth. Interstate highways pushed into undeveloped areas, where planned housing developments, enabled by inexpensive immigrant labor and preassembled components, emerged in a matter of months. Compliant local officials made it easy for developers to move in, glad for increased revenue even though new schools and roads often consumed more than the taxes the new neighborhoods generated. Lax regulations for septic systems and water sources plagued new homeowners, even as newer developments began nearby. International corporations built large factories in the South, with automotive companies in particular choosing the region for its relatively low labor costs and low levels of union organizing. Six southern states—Alabama, Florida, Louisiana, North Carolina, South Carolina, and Tennessee—won more than four billion dollars, more than half of all European investment in the United States, with enormous subsidies and tax breaks.[43]

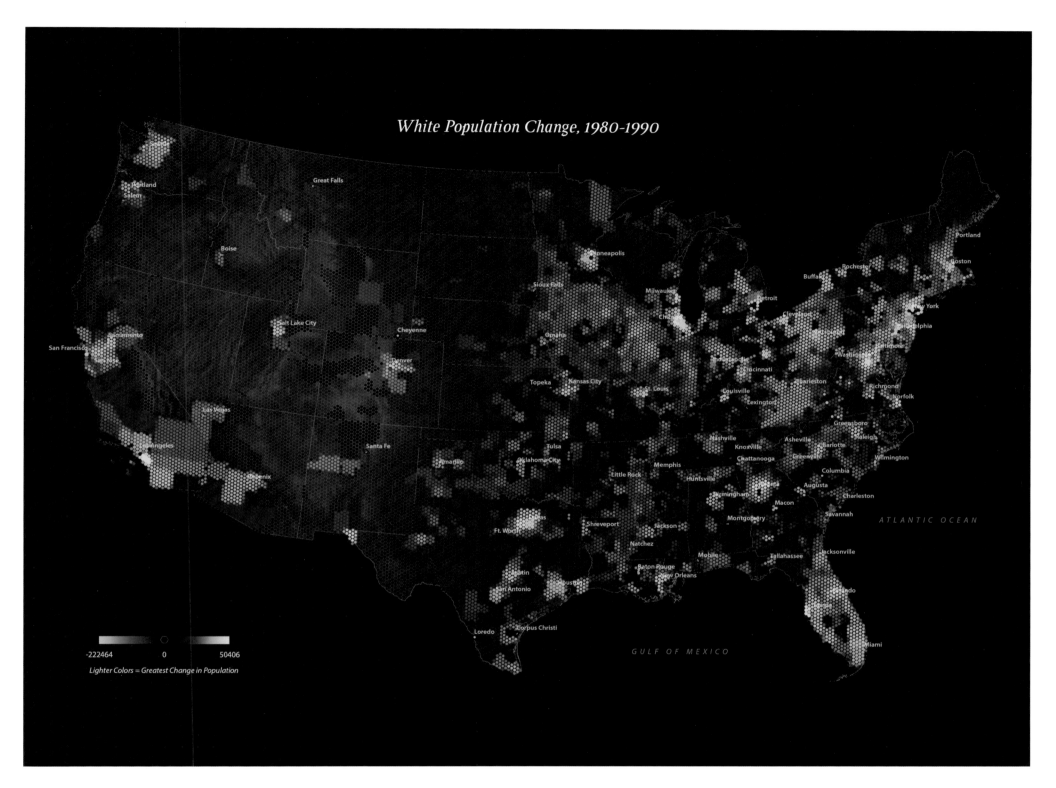

White Population Change, 1980-1990

-222464   0   50406

Lighter Colors = Greatest Change in Population

The flight from the rural South to the region's cities accelerates, with the Mississippi River valley, the Black Belt, and Appalachia particularly hard hit as Florida and the Upper South grow rapidly.

Black Population Change, 1980-1990

Seattle
Portland
Salem
Great Falls
Portland
Boise
Boston
Minneapolis
Rochester
Sioux Falls
Buffalo
Milwaukee
Detroit
New York
Chicago
Cleveland
Salt Lake City
Cheyenne
Pittsburgh
Philadelphia
Sacramento
Omaha
Denver
Indianapolis
Washington
Baltimore
San Francisco
Cincinnati
San Jose
Topeka
Kansas City
Charleston
Richmond
St. Louis
Louisville
Norfolk
Las Vegas
Lexington
Greensboro
Nashville
Asheville
Raleigh
Los Angeles
Tulsa
Knoxville
Charlotte
Santa Fe
Oklahoma City
Chattanooga
Greenville
Wilmington
Phoenix
Memphis
Columbia
Little Rock
Huntsville
Atlanta
Amarillo
Augusta
Birmingham
Macon
Charleston
Dallas
Montgomery
Savannah
ATLANTIC OCEAN
Ft. Worth
Shreveport
Jackson
Natchez
Mobile
Jacksonville
Tallahassee
Austin
Baton Rouge
Houston
New Orleans
San Antonio
Orlando
Tampa
Loredo
Corpus Christi
GULF OF MEXICO
Miami

-15491   0   101980

Lighter Colors = Greatest Change in Population

The tide of Black population growth spreads to southern cities and suburbs, with
every part of the South seeing expansion.

The demography of suburbs continually changed. In the era of segregation, some Black businessmen had worked with white officials to set aside areas for Black development in separate suburban neighborhoods. Those places morphed rapidly into areas where African American professionals could enjoy suburban living and neighbors who welcomed one another. These "Negro expansion areas" appeared in many southern cities, beginning in Atlanta but then spreading to Houston, Memphis, Miami, other locales across the region, often around African American colleges and universities. New suburbs dominated by Black people tended to be near older suburbs where African Americans had a large presence.

The new residents of emerging Black communities, often young families, had to fight against redlining, underfunded schools, and substandard services as they built their neighborhoods. Once-hopeful suburbs came to be considered ghettoes, while so-called urban renewal, triggered by highway building but drawing upon the agendas of many vested interests, destroyed traditional Black housing and created public housing in its place. Some African American businessmen and political leaders collaborated with white officials and commercial firms to build racial segregation into the plats of the booming cities of the South.[44]

White people, for their part, fled the inner city and Black suburbs, undermining the tax base and civic health of southern cities. These in turn annexed hundreds of square miles on their outskirts in which to expand, further building segregation into the fabric of real estate and daily life. Central cities experienced gentrification as people sought to live in places with a history and identity. That preference, often the luxury of white people with resources, raised tax rates and pushed poorer people out of neighborhoods where they had long lived.

As white people moved into new suburbs or rejuvenated urban neighborhoods, they left behind older suburbs that filled with new migrants. The first to arrive were African Americans eager to buy their own homes, especially after the Civil Rights Act provided Black homeowners leverage against those who violated equal-housing laws. By 2000, 6.8 million African Americans lived in southern suburbs, more than three times than in any other region and three-quarters of the 11.9 million African Americans who lived in the South. Many of those people had migrated to the South for just the kind of opportunity the new suburbs offered.

THE GREAT RETURN

Beginning in the late 1960s, more people started coming to the South than leaving it. Plenty did still leave, in roughly the same numbers as before—about 1.1 million Black southerners and about 4.5 million white southerners over the last two decades of the twentieth century—but twice as many people came to the South than left in those twenty years. African Americans began a net migration to the South for the first time in the nation's history. In the late 1960s, the South had lost 280,000 Black residents to other parts of the country; in the late 1970s, the region had gained 100,000 African Americans.

At the beginning of the twenty-first century, southern cities accounted for the top five in Black-population growth: Atlanta, Dallas, Houston, Miami, and Washington, D.C. Black Americans left New York City, Chicago, Los Angeles, Philadelphia, and Detroit. Atlanta attracted more Black migrants than any other American city from 1980 to 2010. In 1970, it stood thirteenth among national cities in African American population. In 2010, it was second only to New York.[45]

Every southern state, from Virginia through Texas, from Kentucky to Florida, claimed a metropolitan area that showed a net gain of African Americans at the beginning of the twenty-first century. Over two-thirds of Black migrants in the United States chose the South, while about half of white people did. Only 6 percent of Black migrants moved to the West when they left the Northeast, while about a quarter of white people did. College-educated African Americans moved to the South in especially large numbers, as did Black retirees, who selected Georgia, Texas, and North Carolina as their preferred destinations. The share of the total African American population who lived in the South grew to 57 percent in 2010 from its low of 53 percent in 1970. By 2010, 83 percent of Black southerners lived in metropolitan regions, and most of them lived in the largest of those.[46]

While African Americans moved to the South, white Americans moved much less than they had in earlier generations. When they did relocate, they moved in the same directions as Black and immigrant populations, southward and westward, but they chose smaller metropolitan regions and homes on the edges of those areas. White people moved for the same reasons as other Americans, to go to states with a lower cost of living, warmer weather, and appealing amenities. The states that dominated American migration for many generations—those of the Northeast, Midwest, and even the Pacific

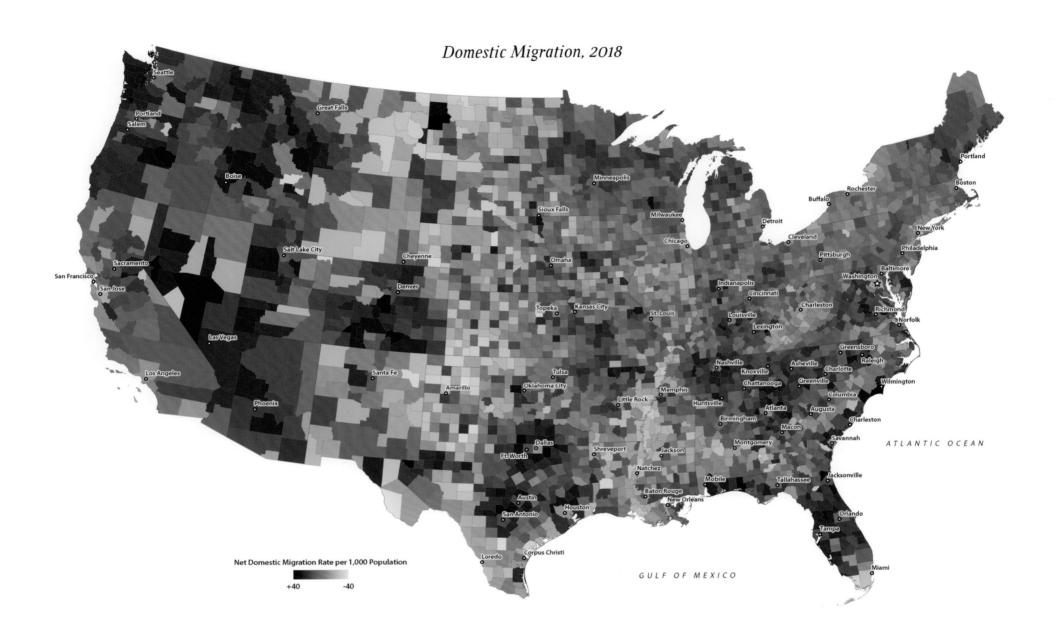

Domestic Migration, 2018

Net Domestic Migration Rate per 1,000 Population

+40   -40

Many parts of the South attract people during the second decade of the twenty-first century. The major exceptions are places that had long been losing population: the Mississippi River valley and the mountains of Appalachia.

coast—came to seem less appealing to Americans of many backgrounds. The concentration of industry and population that drove the first generations of growth no longer proved an advantage in an era of knowledge work and telecommuting. Those whites who remained where they were, particularly in rural communities across the nation, found themselves living in older, whiter, more isolated, and poorer communities.

In 2020, more than half of the babies born in the United States had parents currently in minority populations. Asian and Latinx populations, younger and more fertile than the white population, accounted for more than three-fourths of the overall growth of the United States. The Carolinas, Tennessee, and Georgia proved newly attractive to minorities, joining the longtime bastions of Florida and Texas as destinations for such migrants. Other southern states were less attractive to the newly diverse migration, as Alabama, Mississippi, Louisiana, Arkansas, Kentucky, and West Virginia saw only moderate growth.[47]

In a remarkable development, "American Indians" registered a 39 percent increase in the federal census between 2000 and 2010, growing twice as fast as the national population as a whole. The apparent resurgence was partly a product of definition, for in 2000, Americans were first presented the opportunity to self-identify with more than one race. Almost half of those who claimed "American Indian and Alaska Native" identity did so along with another racial identity. About two-thirds of these respondents identified their race in addition to Native as white, followed by about equal proportions who claimed Black and Native ancestry or who claimed white, Black, and Native ancestry. Of those Americans who claimed Native backgrounds in combination with other backgrounds, the South tied with the West at about a third of the population, nearly twice the proportion of the Midwest and nearly three times that of the Northeast.

The South's share of the self-identified Native population grew during the first decade of the twenty-first century relative to the rest of the country, advancing at 48 percent. The three states with the most rapid rate of growth were all southern: Texas, North Carolina, and Florida. The tribe with the largest self-identified population was the Cherokee, with 819,000 people. Two hundred years after the displacement of American Indians across the South, after generations of their predicted disappearance, many Americans declared their identity with indigenous peoples.[48]

Maps of people who self-identify as Native with roots in the South show patterns of great mobility. Those maps, based on the 2010 census, reflect migrations across several decades. Each bears the marks of the histories of particular tribes, suggesting the power of ancestral homelands, the effects of removal to Oklahoma, the persistence of Native peoples in lands from which many had been driven, and the determination of people from each Native tribe to find new opportunities despite the obstacles before them.

The claim of so many to Native ancestry is a strange turn in southern history, especially as people otherwise recognized as white are eager for a connection to a people who were persecuted and driven from their homes. On one hand, this is arguably a heartening change from most of American history. On the other hand, the claim of widespread self-identification is a major political problem for Native people themselves, who have established citizenship standards within their nations. While some claimants may express sincere beliefs in their ancestry, others seek to leverage that identity for material or social gain. The ironies are powerful and multiple.

NEW POLITICAL LANDSCAPES

Support for both major political parties in the early twenty-first century followed the contours of southern migration from generations before. The forced marches of domestic slavery and more hopeful post-emancipation migrations defined the long arc of African American population that stood as a bulwark for the Democratic Party. Black voters proved loyal supporters of the party from the Virginia Tidewater to the Gulf of Mexico, in the countryside and in cities.

Southern suburbs shifted their loyalties. In the decades following desegregation, white residents abandoned the Democratic Party for the Republican, a party that declared its devotion to property rights, low taxes, unobtrusive government, and local choice in schools, claiming race-neutral purposes even as it separated Black and white people. In the twenty-first century, Democrats' emphasis on the rights of women, improved health care, and investment in education appealed to college-educated white people, especially women, moving to the rapidly growing suburbs across the region. As migrants from other regions moved to the South, they sometimes brought liberal politics with them as well, their presence evident in the cities and suburbs of Virginia, Florida, the Piedmont of the Carolinas, Atlanta, and Texas.[49]

Population of American Indians, 2010

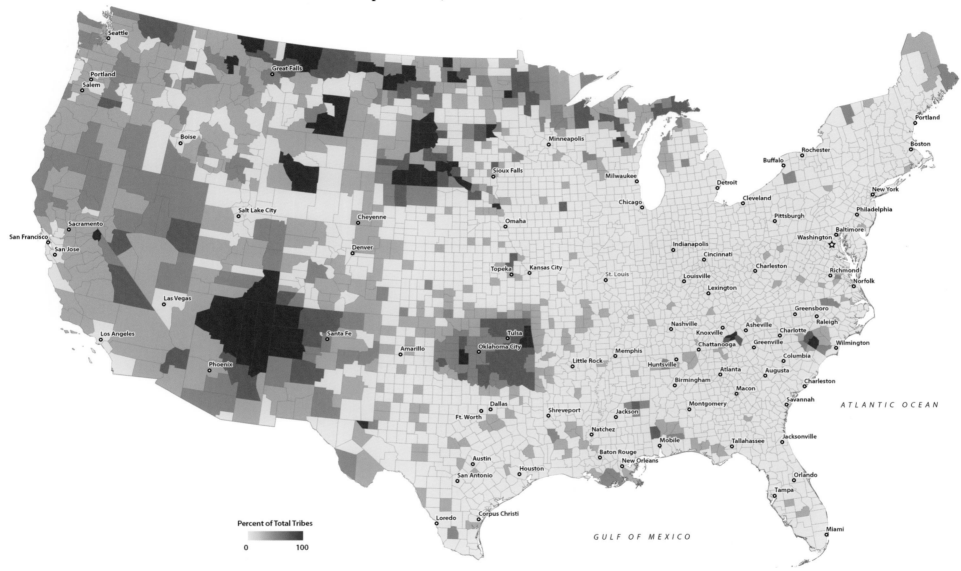

Seattle · Portland · Salem · Great Falls · Boise · Sacramento · San Francisco · San Jose · Salt Lake City · Cheyenne · Las Vegas · Los Angeles · Denver · Santa Fe · Phoenix · Amarillo · Topeka · Kansas City · Dallas · Ft. Worth · Shreveport · Loredo · Corpus Christi · Austin · San Antonio · Houston · Natchez · Baton Rouge · New Orleans · Mobile

Minneapolis · Sioux Falls · Milwaukee · Chicago · Omaha · St. Louis · Tulsa · Oklahoma City · Little Rock · Memphis · Jackson · Huntsville · Birmingham · Montgomery

Detroit · Buffalo · Rochester · Cleveland · Pittsburgh · Indianapolis · Cincinnati · Louisville · Lexington · Nashville · Knoxville · Chattanooga · Atlanta · Macon · Tallahassee · Jacksonville · Orlando · Tampa · Miami

Portland · Boston · New York · Philadelphia · Baltimore · Washington · Charleston · Richmond · Norfolk · Greensboro · Raleigh · Asheville · Charlotte · Greenville · Columbia · Augusta · Charleston · Savannah · Wilmington

ATLANTIC OCEAN

GULF OF MEXICO

Percent of Total Tribes
0 — 100

Despite centuries of dispossession and forced removal, people of Native ancestry live
across the South, often anchored in the places they occupied before white settlement.

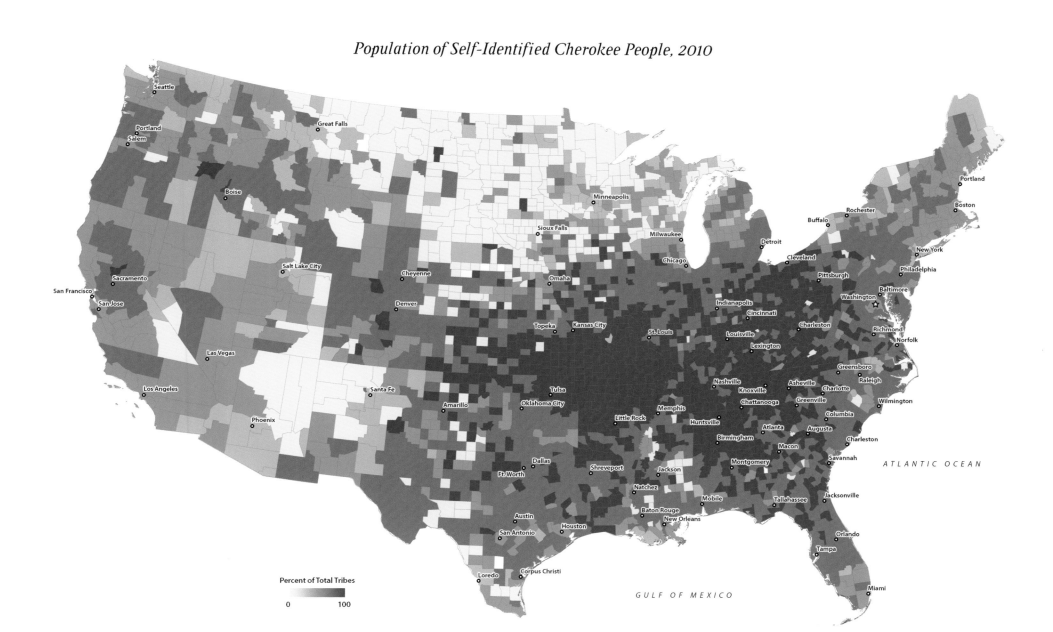

Population of Self-Identified Cherokee People, 2010

Percent of Total Tribes

0   100

Population of Self-Identified Seminole People, 2010

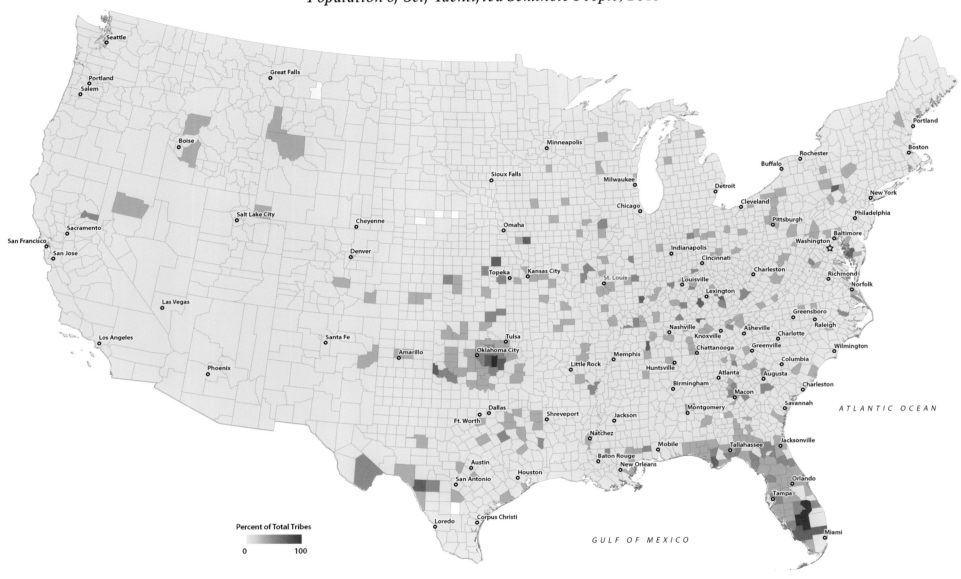

Percent of Total Tribes

0   100

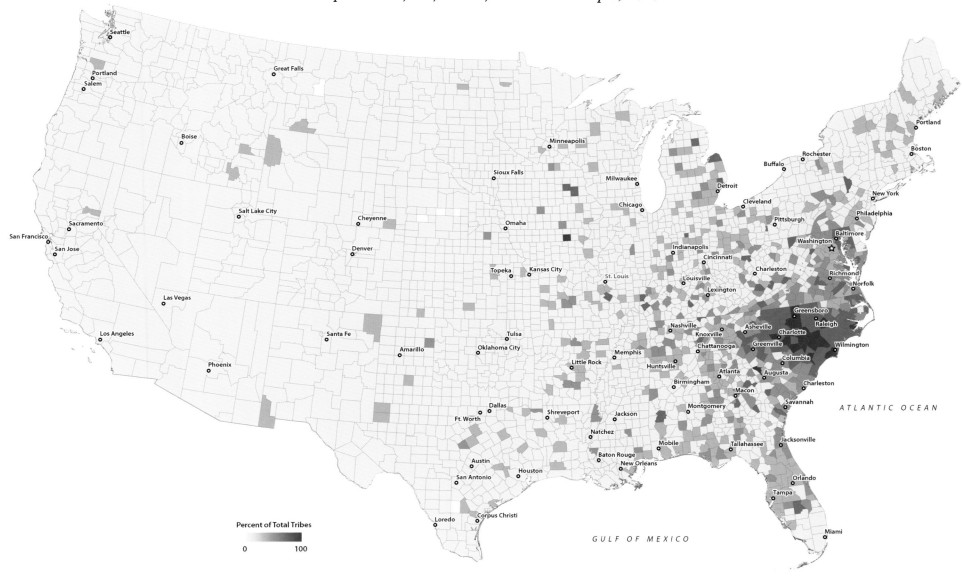

Population of Self-Identified Lumbee People, 2010

Percent of Total Tribes

0   100

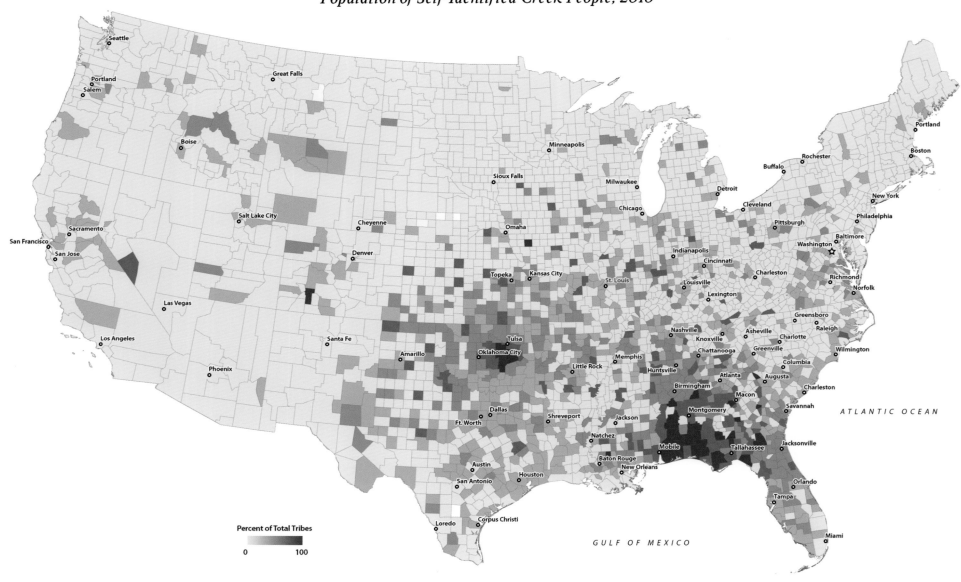

Population of Self-Identified Creek People, 2010

Seattle
Portland
Salem
Great Falls
Boise
Minneapolis
Portland
Boston
Sioux Falls
Buffalo
Rochester
New York
Milwaukee
Detroit
Cleveland
Philadelphia
Sacramento
Salt Lake City
Chicago
Pittsburgh
Baltimore
San Francisco
Cheyenne
Omaha
Indianapolis
Washington
San Jose
Denver
Cincinnati
Richmond
Topeka
Kansas City
Louisville
Charleston
Norfolk
Las Vegas
St. Louis
Lexington
Greensboro
Santa Fe
Nashville
Asheville
Raleigh
Los Angeles
Tulsa
Knoxville
Charlotte
Amarillo
Oklahoma City
Chattanooga
Greenville
Wilmington
Phoenix
Memphis
Huntsville
Columbia
Little Rock
Atlanta
Augusta
Charleston
Birmingham
Macon
Dallas
Savannah
ATLANTIC OCEAN
Ft. Worth
Shreveport
Jackson
Montgomery
Natchez
Mobile
Tallahassee
Jacksonville
Austin
Baton Rouge
New Orleans
San Antonio
Houston
Orlando
Loredo
Tampa
Corpus Christi
GULF OF MEXICO
Miami

Percent of Total Tribes
0   100

120

Population of Self-Identified Choctaw People, 2010

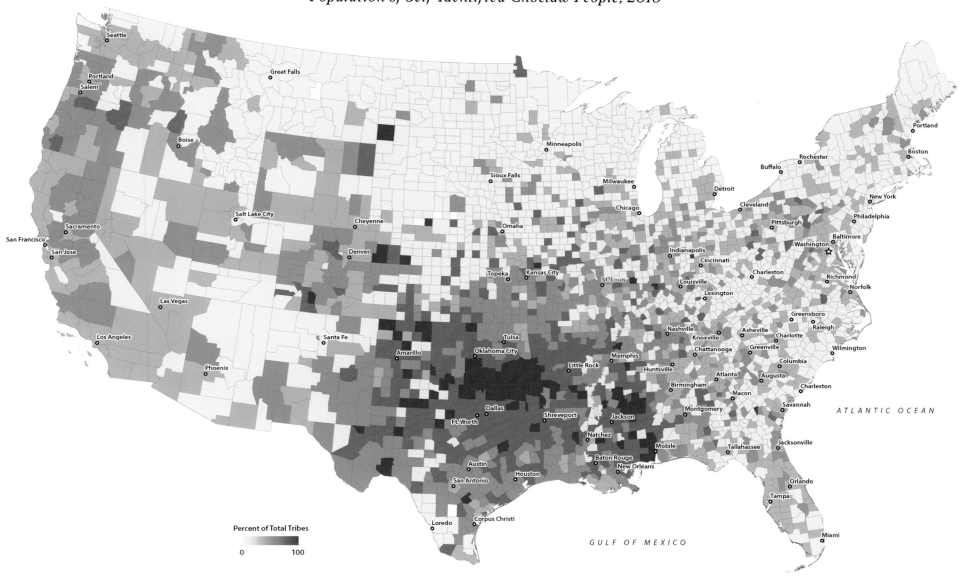

Percent of Total Tribes

0   100

ATLANTIC OCEAN

GULF OF MEXICO

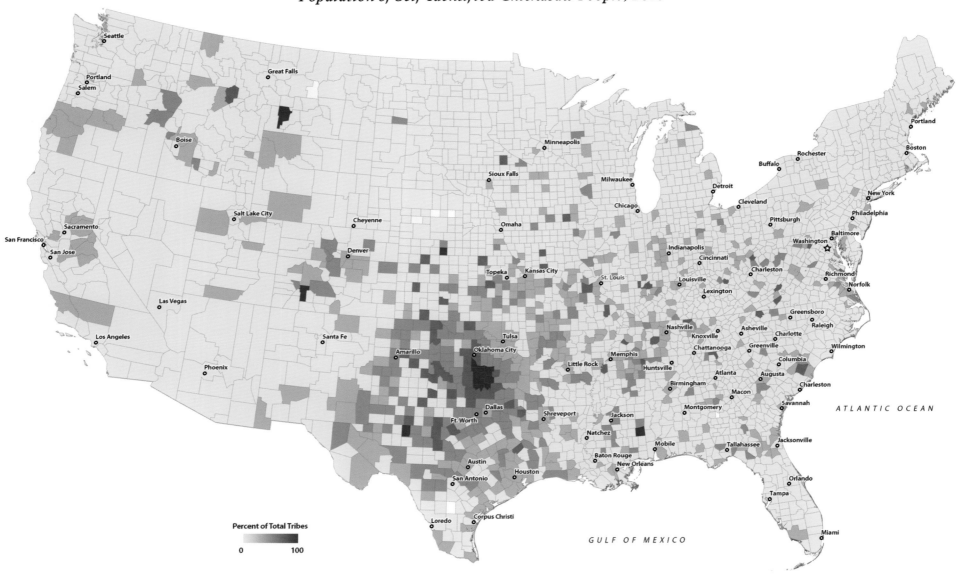

Population of Self-Identified Chickasaw People, 2010

Percent of Total Tribes

0   100

Election of 2016

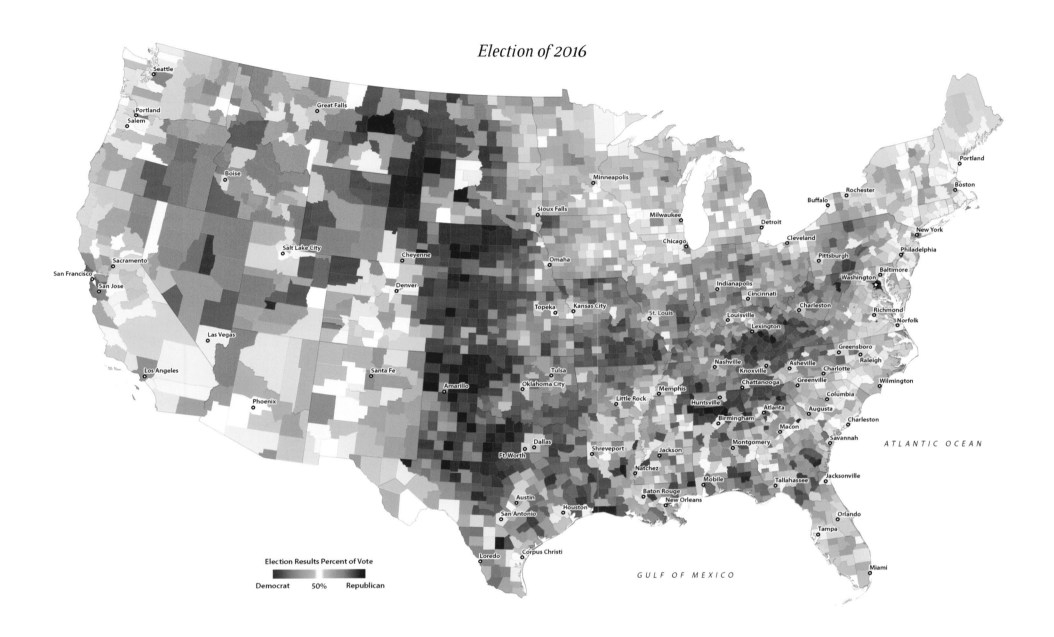

Election Results Percent of Vote

Democrat   50%   Republican

The familiar red-and-blue map of the partisan divisions of the United States in the early twenty-first century shows the legacy of more than two centuries of migration. African Americans of the Black Belt, from Washington, D.C., to the Mississippi River, vote for the Democrats, as do the cities of the North and Midwest where Black southerners migrated. Cities and more diverse suburbs also vote for the Democrats. Most of the rural South, though, is resolutely Republican, especially Appalachia, the piney woods of the Atlantic and Gulf coasts, and most of Texas.

The growing Latinx populations of the South searched for security and possibility in older suburbs abandoned by white residents. Those immigrants turned to the Democrats, especially after the Republicans opposed immigration and the advancement of children born of undocumented immigrants. In some parts of the South, particularly South Texas, Latinx immigrants developed enough numbers to turn rural counties to the Democrats. Diverse immigrant communities from Asia divided their votes between the parties. Indian-American Republican governors from Louisiana and South Carolina—Bobby Jindal and Nikki Haley—assumed national visibility.

In the rural areas that still covered much of the southern landscape in the early twenty-first century, the great majority of white southerners supported the Republican Party, upholding ideals from the white settler society that first shaped the South: low taxes, rights to gun ownership, conservative evangelical Christianity, and defiance of urban values and dictates. Counties that had long been dominated by conservative Democrats switched to the Republicans in the early 1970s and stayed there despite temporary support of native sons Jimmy Carter and Bill Clinton. Those counties proved steadfast supporters of Ronald Reagan, George W. Bush, and Donald Trump.[50]

Favorable districting and the bias of the Electoral College provide the South's rural white counties with power disproportionate to their numbers, but urban, suburban, and immigrant migration make the South more politically volatile with each election.

REVELATIONS

The COVID-19 pandemic of 2020 revealed the vulnerabilities of the changing South. As in other parts of the country, distressed neighborhoods in large cities suffered high rates of infection and death. In the South, moreover, the coronavirus quickly spread far beyond cities into the countryside, into places already enduring poor health and deep poverty made worse by out-migration. These rural areas possessed few hospitals, and even fewer intensive care units, to confront the infection.[51]

In both city and countryside, multigenerational housing, inadequate health care, and racial discrimination exacerbated the chronic heart disease, asthma, emphysema, diabetes, and high blood pressure that afflicted poor communities. Meatpacking and poultry-processing facilities suffered devastating attacks of the virus. Communities near prisons confronted virulent spread of the disease. Nursing homes, where large numbers of older people concentrated, proved early and persistent sources of contagion.[52]

Black southerners and immigrants and their children from Latin America stood at particular risk because of their work, their neighborhoods, and their poverty. Across the South, Black and Latinx people, working in food service and health care jobs deemed essential to the economy, contracted the virus out of proportion to their percentages of the population. Death rates from the coronavirus skewed even more than infection rates, as people of color died at twice the rate of white people carrying the disease.[53]

While such sharp ethnic disparities appeared elsewhere in the United States, including among Native peoples on reservations in the West, the South witnessed a particularly widespread dispersion of the virus because of political and policy decisions. Several southern governors refused to acknowledge the threat of the infections, downplaying its consequences and imposing few restrictions. Many white southerners demonstrated their contempt for government edicts and expert advice by defiantly gathering at parties and bars, at churches and in restaurants, refusing to wear masks and practice distancing. Within weeks, faced with skyrocketing numbers of infections, public opinion forced governors to impose rigorous rules. Their delay, the result of political convictions born in the long-ago era of settlement, allowed sickness and death to spread in the South.

The Black Lives Matter protests of 2020 testified to disparities in justice during the same weeks that the coronavirus revealed disparities in social health. The brutal killing of George Floyd, a Black man, by Minneapolis police in May triggered massive demonstrations across the United States. Every state in the nation, and many countries beyond, saw weeks of peaceful protests of police violence and in support of Black humanity. The cities and towns of the South registered their share of demonstrations against the injustice and inequality that had followed Black migrants from the South throughout the nation.[54]

Protestors, as part of their campaign for historical as well as contemporary reckoning, brought down statues of Confederate generals. The ground beneath the monuments' pedestals had eroded and grown unstable, it turned out, with the constant shifting of people in the South. The monuments of granite and bronze claimed permanence and dominion, but they fell suddenly and forever as the South moved on without them.

Family Income Below Poverty Level, 2016

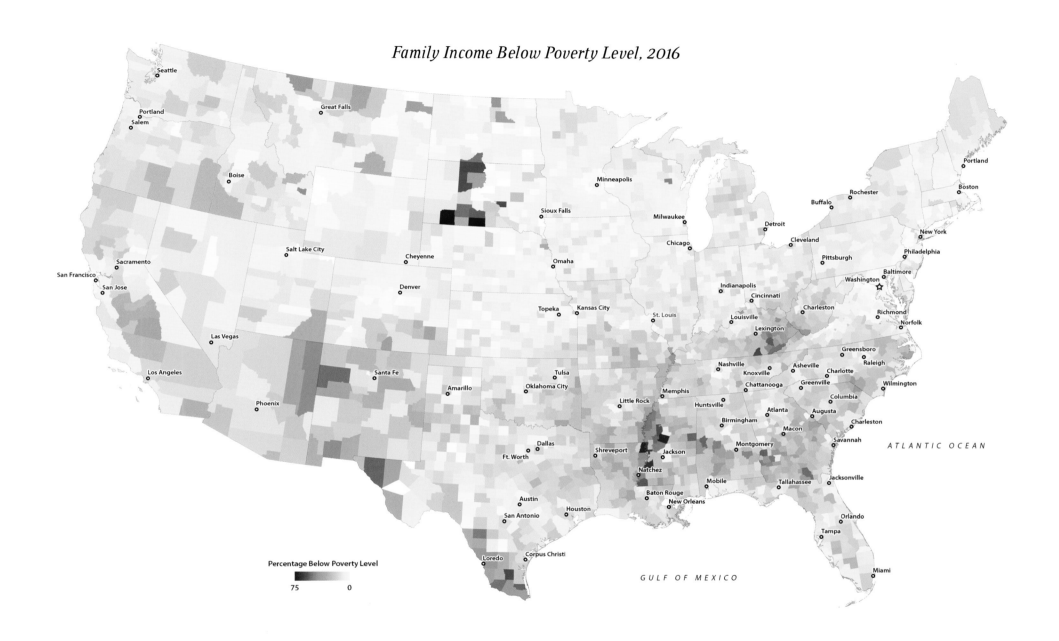

Percentage Below Poverty Level

75   0

In a dispiriting and familiar pattern, the Black Belt of the Lower South and the mountains of the Upper South contain especially large proportions of families living in poverty. The entire rural South holds many people who endure low incomes, including places close to and including the region's cities.

Patterns of Poor Health, 2016

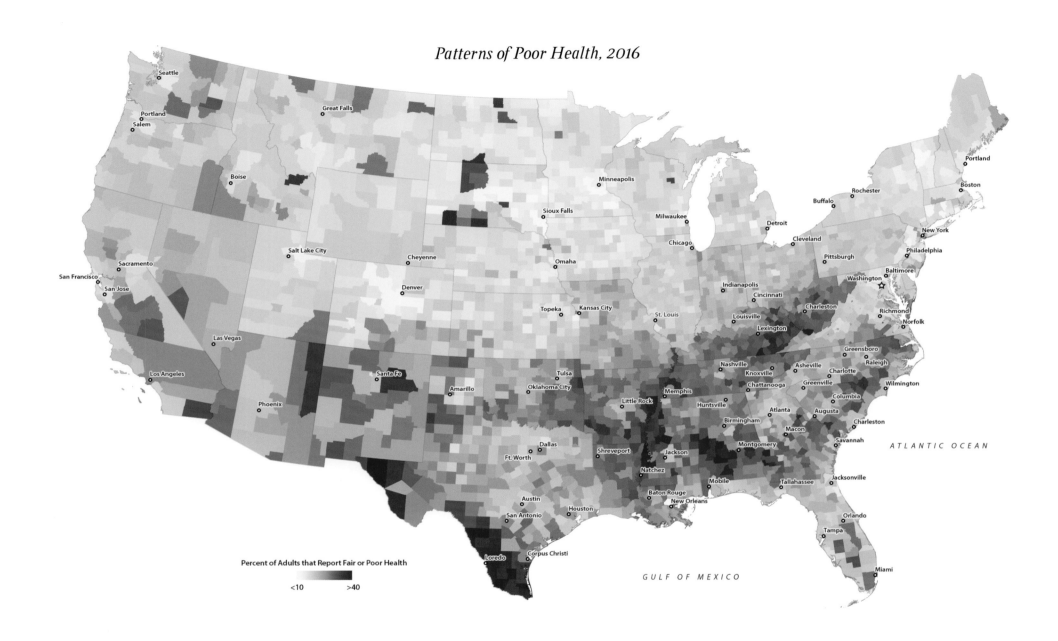

Percent of Adults that Report Fair or Poor Health

<10   >40

Much of the South suffers disproportionately with illness and disability, though some
states take greater responsibility for the health of their residents than others.

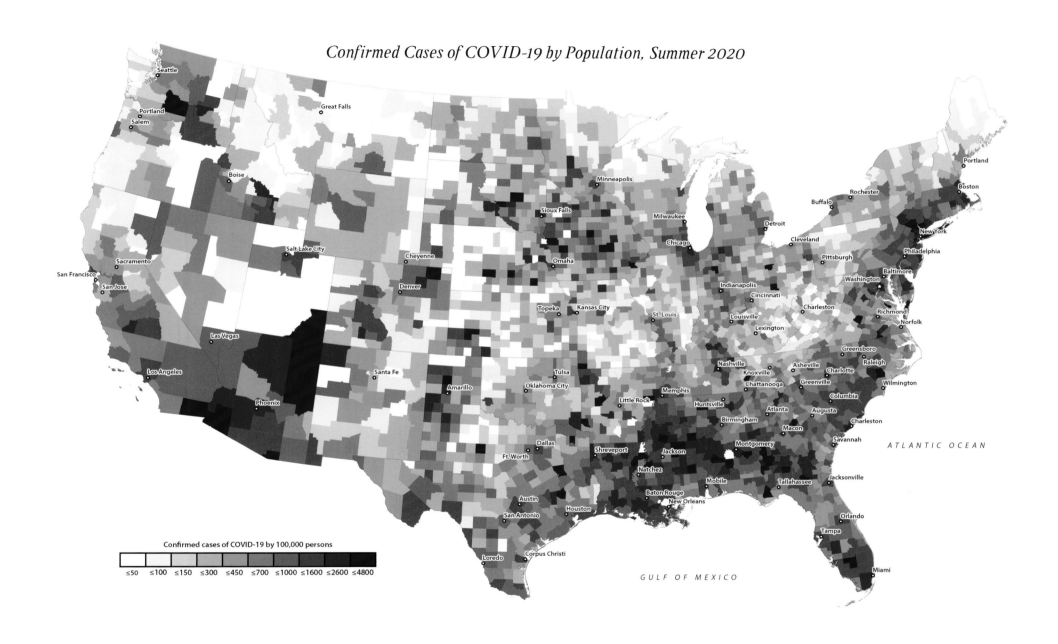

Confirmed Cases of COVID-19 by Population, Summer 2020

Confirmed cases of COVID-19 by 100,000 persons

≤50 ≤100 ≤150 ≤300 ≤450 ≤700 ≤1000 ≤1600 ≤2600 ≤4800

The coronavirus that arrived in the United States in early 2020 quickly spread across the entire South, infecting and killing Black and Latinx people with particular severity.

ACKNOWLEDGMENTS

This book would have been impossible—indeed unimaginable—without the vision, skill, and patience of my collaborators, Justin Madron and Nathaniel Ayers. Their work, along with their colleague at the University of Richmond's Digital Scholarship Lab, Robert Nelson, gave me the idea for this book in the first place. When I saw how they had mapped the forced migration of enslaved people in the South, using a version of methods employed here, it occurred to me that we could map everyone in the South across all its history. That was easier imagined than accomplished, of course, and so it fell to Justin and Nate to figure out how to turn massive data sets into the maps that form the core of this book.

I needed such an idea because I was invited to give the Walter J. Fleming Lectures at Louisiana State University in 2018. I was delighted to receive the invitation from Victor Stater and expert coordination by Alice Wolfe. It was wonderful to see old friends Aaron Sheehan-Dean, who cooked up vats of delicious gumbo at a big party at his house, and Andrew Burstein, who lent me his office for last-minute revisions to my last lecture. I enjoyed meeting LSU graduate students and faculty and hearing about their work. The audience offered excellent questions that helped me shape the book in new and helpful ways.

Pulling together the lectures required reacquainting myself with the vast historical literature of the American South and discovering much I had missed. The ratio of footnotes to text in the book measures my debt to those who have come before me.

I'm particularly grateful to my allies at Louisiana State University Press. Rand Dotson eagerly accepted the challenge of producing such a complex book, and Catherine Kadair expertly steered it through production. Kevin Brock edited it with great skill and sensitivity. The design expertise of Barbara Bourgoyne has created a beautiful volume.

Several friends gave an earlier version of this book a rigorous and friendly reading. Joshua Rothman and Susan Schulten read a more ragged manuscript with generosity and honesty, making it considerably better. William Cronon shared his enthusiasm and expertise in characteristic ways, helping us clarify the assumptions of our mapping and much else besides. Gregory Smithers shared his understanding of Native history, and Gavin Wright and James Cobb helped me better understand recent decades of the South's history.

The book is dedicated to the graduate students with whom I worked over nearly three decades at the University of Virginia. Laboring over this book, I realized that many of them had explored problems and topics I explore here, offering interpretations I have adopted and credited. I cite their work with particular pride and gratitude.

As always, Abby has been an ideal traveling companion at every step of a journey we have shared for a lifetime.

APPENDIX THE METHOD OF MAPPING MIGRATIONS

Justin Madron and Nathaniel Ayers

It is no small challenge to map population change over time in the United States, given how often and how dramatically county boundaries have been redrawn. In order to compare population and other patterns across decades, we overlay a honeycomb of hexagon-shaped spaces, or hexbins, on our maps.

To apply data to the hexbins, we first create what a Geographic Information System (GIS) calls a "union" of county boundaries across subsequent decades with tessellated hexbins.[1] We use an areal-interpolation technique to remap county boundaries to those hexbins using the area-weighted algorithm, well suited for showing broad patterns of population change over long periods of time. The output of this union process creates a feature that has attributes of both the data source (population by county) and the target feature (the constant hex identification). We can then distribute the population into those areas proportional to their area and calculate migrations over the decade using the weighted areal-interpolation algorithm detailed in the formulas below.[2]

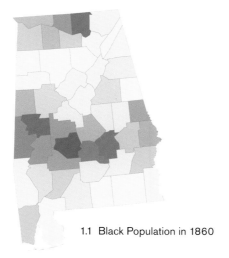

1.1 Black Population in 1860

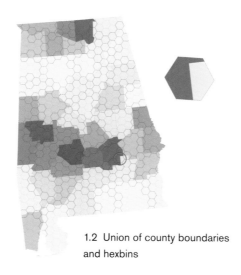

1.2 Union of county boundaries and hexbins

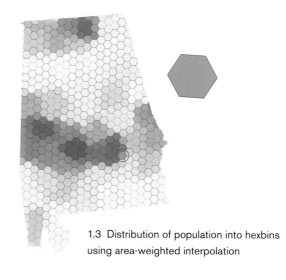

1.3 Distribution of population into hexbins using area-weighted interpolation

We start by creating a union of the county boundaries (source) and hex-bins (target). (See figure 1.2.) Then we calculate an areal weight for each intersected feature. Let:

- W_i = areal weight for intersected feature i
- A_i = area of intersected feature i
- A_j = total area of source feature j

$W_i = A_i/A_j$

Next, we need to estimate the share of the population value for each decade that occupies the intersected feature. Let:

- E_i = estimated value for intersected feature i
- W_i = areal weight for intersected feature i
- V_j = population value for source feature j

$E_i = V_j * W_i$

Next, we summarize the data based on the target identification number. Let:

- G_k = sum of all estimated values for target feature k
- E_{ik} = estimated values from intersected features in i within target

$G_k = \sum E_{ik}$

Finally, we estimate net increase and decrease from the target features of each decade (figures 2.1 and 2.2). Let:

- C_k = net increase or decrease from target features k
- N_i = estimated values from target features from earlier decade in i within target
- N_k = estimated values from target features from later decade in k within target

$C_k = (N_i - N_k)$

Additionally, centroids are calculated for each hexbin with the appropriate aggregated census data (figure 2.3), giving us the following results.

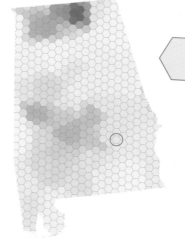

2.1 Distributed population into hexbins for Black population in 1830

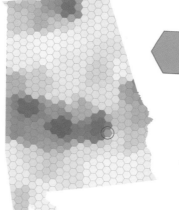

2.2 Distributed population into hexbins for Black population in 1840

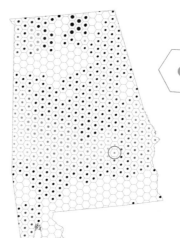

2.3 Centroids showing Black population change from 1840 to 1850

CARTOGRAPHY METHOD

The maps use a multivariate proportional symbology method to visualize two variables.[3] The circumference of the dot represents population size (figure 3.1), and the color gradient signifies population change, which is either increasing (shades of brown) or decreasing (shades of blue) (figure 3.2). While we use a consistent color scheme across maps, the scale each uses must vary. We, of course, cannot use the same scale to visualize population and population change in a nation of 309 million people in 2010 that we use for a nation of 3.9 million in 1790. Cities with larger populations are represented by larger symbols (12 point) and places with smaller populations by smaller symbols (9 point).

Our data sets, which we will share, of course enable other kinds of analysis of these complex patterns.

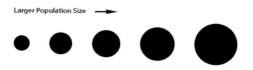

3.1 Original population size reported by the census count of the first year

3.2 Increasing and decreasing population from one decade to another

NOTES

HOW TO READ THIS BOOK

1. Paul Schor, *Counting Americans: How the U.S. Census Classified the Nation*, trans. Lys Ann Weiss (New York: Oxford University Press, 2017), offers a detailed analysis of the ways the census has reflected, created, and perpetuated notions of racial and ethnic identities. For a convenient overview of changing categories, see "What Census Calls Us: A Historical Timeline," Pew Research Center, June 10, 2015, https://www.pewsocialtrends.org/interactives/multiracial-timeline/.

The U.S. census did not record, in particular, the lives of North America's indigenous peoples in adequate detail or with attention to their identities, so we have relied on other, still inadequate, ways of representing their forced and constrained migrations until the very recent past.

1. CREATING THE SOUTH, 1790–1860

1. There is a remarkably rich literature on this complex history. Good places to start are the excellent overview in Gregory D. Smithers, *Native Southerners: Indigenous History from Origins to Removal* (Norman: University of Oklahoma Press, 2019), and Gregory A. Waselkov, Peter H. Wood, and M. Thomas Hatley, eds., *Powhatan's Mantle: Indians in the Colonial Southeast*, rev. ed. (Lincoln: University of Nebraska Press, 2006). Several chapters in the latter are especially helpful for our purposes: Helen Hornbeck Tanner, "The Land and Water Communication Systems of the Southeastern Indians"; Peter H. Wood, "The Changing Population of the Colonial South: An Overview by Race and Region, 1685–1790"; and Marvin T. Smith, "Aboriginal Population Movements in the Early Historic Period Interior Southeast." Also see Richard F. Brown, ed., *Coastal Encounters: The Transformation of the Gulf South in the Eighteenth Century* (Lincoln: University of Nebraska Press, 2007).

For helpful perspectives on the rapidly developing literature, see Andrew K. Rank and Kristofer Ray, "Indians as Southerners; Southerners as Indians: Rethinking the History of a Region," *Native South* 10 (2017): vii–xiv; and Angela Pulley Hudson, "Unsettling Histories of the South," *Southern Cultures* (Fall 2019): 30–45. See also Alan Gallay, *The Indian Slave Trade: The Rise of the*

English Empire in the American South, 1670–1717 (New Haven, CT: Yale University Press, 2002); Robbie Ethridge, *From Chicaza to Chickasaw: The European Invasion and the Transformation of the Mississippian World, 1540–1714* (Chapel Hill: University of North Carolina Press, 2010); Andrew K. Frank, *Before the Pioneers: Indians, Settlers, Slaves, and the Founding of Miami* (Gainesville: University Press of Florida, 2017); and Christina Snyder, *Slavery in Indian Country: The Changing Face of Captivity in Early America* (Cambridge, MA: Harvard University Press, 2012).

2. See Jeffrey Ostler, *Surviving Genocide: Native Nations and the United States from the American Revolution to Bleeding Kansas* (New Haven, CT: Yale University Press, 2019); Angela Pulley Hudson, *Creek Paths and Federal Roads: Indians, Settlers, and Slaves and the Making of the American South* (Chapel Hill: University of North Carolina Press, 2010); Gregory D. Smithers, *Native Diasporas: Indigenous Identities and Settler Colonialism in the Americas* (Lincoln: University of Nebraska Press, 2014); Katherine M. B. Osburn, *Choctaw Resurgence in Mississippi: Race, Class, and Nation Building in the Jim Crow South, 1830–1977* (Lincoln: University of Nebraska Press, 2014); Daniel H. Usner Jr., *Indians, Settlers, and Slaves in a Frontier Exchange Economy: The Lower Mississippi Valley before 1783* (Chapel Hill: University of North Carolina Press, 1992); James Merrell, *The Indians' New World: Catawbas and Their Neighbors from European Contact through the Era of Removal* (Chapel Hill: University of North Carolina Press, 1989); James Taylor Carson, *Searching for the Bright Path: The Mississippi Choctaws from Prehistory to Removal* (Lincoln: University of Nebraska Press, 1999); David W. Miller, *The Taking of American Indian Lands in the Southeast: A History of Territorial Cessions and Forced Relocations, 1607–1840* (Jefferson, NC: McFarland, 2011); and Charles C. Boyce, "Indian Land Cessions in the United States," in *Eighteenth Annual Report of the Bureau of American Ethnology, 1896–1897*, Smithsonian Institution (Washington, DC: U.S. Government Printing Office, 1899).

3. For a useful overview of South Carolina and Louisiana, see Richard Follett, Sven Beckert, Peter Coclanis, and Barbara Hahn, *Plantation Kingdom: The American South and Its Global Commodities* (Baltimore: Johns Hopkins University Press, 2016). Beckert and Hahn offer excellent surveys of cotton and tobacco, respectively. For a fascinating portrayal of Charleston's wealth and aspirations,

see Maurie D. McInnis, *The Politics of Taste in Antebellum Charleston* (Chapel Hill: University of North Carolina Press, 2005).

4. Scott P. Marler, *The Merchants' Capital: New Orleans and the Political Economy of the Nineteenth-Century South* (New York: Cambridge University Press, 2013).

5. See Brooks Blevins, *Cattle in the Cotton Fields: A History of Cattle Raising in Alabama* (Tuscaloosa: University of Alabama Press, 2014), 3–7.

6. On the determination of southerners to expand slavery from the outset of the new nation, see John Craig Hammond, *Slavery, Freedom, and Expansion in the Early American West* (Charlottesville: University of Virginia Press, 2009).

7. See the pioneering work by Allan Kulikoff, *Tobacco and Slaves: The Development of Southern Cultures in the Chesapeake, 1680–1800* (Chapel Hill: University of North Carolina Press, 1986), 77.

8. For the tension surrounding such decisions and migrations, see Joan F. Cashin, *A Family Venture: Men and Women on the Southern Frontier* (New York: Oxford University Press, 1991).

9. Stephen Aron, *How the West Was Lost: The Transformation of Kentucky from Daniel Boone to Henry Clay* (Baltimore: Johns Hopkins University Press, 1996). An influential account of white migration appears in Frank L. Owsley, "The Pattern of Migration and Settlement on the Southern Frontier," *Journal of Southern History* 11 (May 1945): 147–76.

10. Tiya Miles, *Ties That Bind: The Story of an Afro-Cherokee Family in Slavery and Freedom* (Berkeley: University of California Press, 2005).

11. See Stephen V. Ash, *Middle Tennessee Society Transformed, 1860–1870: War and Peace in the Upper South* (Baton Rouge: Louisiana State University Press, 1988).

12. Mary Beth Pudup, "The Limits of Subsistence: Agriculture and Industry in Central Appalachia," *Agricultural History* 64 (Winter 1990): 64–67.

13. The idea of settler societies has created a large literature. Especially helpful studies include James Belich, *Replenishing the Earth: The Settler Revolution and the Rise of the Anglo World, 1783–1939* (Oxford: Oxford University Press, 2009); Lisa Ford, *Settler Sovereignty Jurisdiction and Indigenous People in America and Australia, 1788–1836* (Cambridge, MA: Harvard University Press, 2010); Walter L. Hixson, *American Settler Colonialism: A History* (New York: Palgrave Macmillan, 2013); Angela Woollacott, *Settler Society in the Australian Colonies: Self-Government and Imperial Culture* (New York: Oxford University Press, 2015); and Edward Cavanagh and Lorenzo Veracini, eds., *Routledge Handbook of the History of Settler Colonialism* (New York: Routledge, 2017), esp. Matthew Crow, "Atlantic North America from Contact to the Late Nineteenth Century."

For a sophisticated consideration of settler colonialism in the American context, see Jeffrey Ostler, "Locating Settler Colonialism in Early American History," *William and Mary Quarterly* 76 (July 2019): 443–50. Ostler concludes: "Settler colonialism was not total, but the United States had to a significant degree achieved what it had intended at its founding: the replacement of Indians with its own citizens, many owning enslaved people. If a case can be made for the applicability of settler colonialism anywhere in early American history, it would have to be in the early republic and antebellum United States." Ibid., 445.

14. See Anthony E. Kaye, "The Second Slavery: Modernity in the Nineteenth-Century South," *Journal of Southern History* 75 (Aug. 2009): 627–50; and Erik Mathisen, "The Second Slavery, Capitalism, and Emancipation in Civil War America," *Journal of the Civil War Era* 8 (Dec. 2018): 677–99.

15. See Joyce E. Chaplin, *An Anxious Pursuit: Agricultural Innovation and Modernity in the Lower South, 1730–1815* (Chapel Hill: University of North Carolina Press, 1993), 328–29; and Angela Lakwete, *Inventing the Cotton Gin: Machine and Myth in Antebellum America* (Baltimore: Johns Hopkins University Press, 2003).

16. Daniel S. Dupre, *Transforming the Cotton Frontier: Madison County, Alabama, 1800–1840* (Baton Rouge: Louisiana State University Press, 1997).

17. See Christopher Morris, *Becoming Southern: The Evolution of a Way of Life, Warren County and Vicksburg, Mississippi, 1770–1860* (New York: Oxford University Press, 1995).

18. Jefferson quoted in a valuable overview of this entire era, Calvin Schermerhorn, *Unrequited Toil: A History of United States Slavery* (Cambridge: Cambridge University Press, 2018), 37. Also see Thomas D. Clark and John D. W. Guice, *Frontiers in Conflict: The Old Southwest, 1795–1830* (Albuquerque: University of New Mexico Press, 1989); Peter J. Kastor, *The Nation's Crucible: The Louisiana Purchase and the Creation of America* (New Haven, CT: Yale University Press, 2004); and Cameron B. Strang, *Frontiers of Science: Imperialism and Natural Knowledge in the Gulf South Borderlands, 1500–1850* (Chapel Hill: University of North Carolina Press, 2018).

19. Claudio Saunt, *A New Order of Things: Property, Power, and the Transformation of the Creek Indians, 1733–1816* (Cambridge: Cambridge University Press, 1999). See also C. S. Monaco, *The Second Seminole War and the Limits of American Aggression* (Baltimore: Johns Hopkins University Press, 2018); and Andrew K. Frank, "Red, Black, and Seminole: Community Convergence on the Florida Borderlands, 1780–1840," in *Borderland Narratives: Negotiation and Accommodation in North America's Contested Spaces, 1500–1850*, ed. Andrew K. Frank and A. Glenn Crothers (Gainesville: University of Florida Press, 2017), 46–67; Edward E. Baptist, *Creating an Old South: Middle Florida's Plantation Frontier before the Civil War* (Chapel Hill: University of North Carolina Press, 2002).

20. Quoted in James Oakes, *The Ruling Race: A History of American Slaveholders* (New York: Alfred A. Knopf, 1982), 77. Oakes was one of the first historians to focus on the importance of migration and mobility in the slave South. Gavin Wright, *Slavery and American Economic Development* (Baton Rouge: Louisiana State University Press, 2006), emphasizes the flexibility, including mobility, that came from slaveholders' property rights over their enslaved workforce.

21. See the excellent account in Steven F. Miller, "Plantation Labor Organization and Slave Life on the Cotton Frontier: The Alabama-Mississippi Black Belt, 1815–1840," in *Cultivation and Culture: Labor and the Shaping of Slave Life in the Americas,* ed. Ira Berlin and Philip D. Morgan (Charlottesville: University Press of Virginia, 1993), 155–69.

22. For powerful accounts of this struggle, see Christopher B. Haveman, *Rivers of Sand: Creek Indian Emigration, Relocation, and Ethnic Cleansing in the American South* (Lincoln: University of Nebraska Press, 2016); Barbara Krauthamer, *Black Slaves, Indian Masters: Slavery, Emancipation, and Citizenship in the Native American South* (Chapel Hill: University of North Carolina Press, 2013); Calvin Schermerhorn, "'The Time Is Now Just Arriving When Many Capitalists Will Make Fortunes': Indian Removal, Finance, and Slavery in the Making of the American Cotton South," in *Linking the Histories of Slavery in North America and Its Borderlands,* ed. James F. Brooks and Bonnie Martin (Santa Fe, NM: SAR, 2015), 151–70; David E. Wilkins, *Hollow Justice: A History of Indigenous Claims in the United States* (New Haven, CT: Yale University Press, 2013); and Osburn, *Choctaw Resurgence.*

23. Christina Snyder, *Great Crossings: Indians, Settlers, and Slaves in the Age of Jackson* (New York: Oxford University Press, 2017), 315.

24. See J. Mills Thornton III, *Politics and Power in a Slave Society: Alabama, 1800–1860* (Baton Rouge: Louisiana State University Press, 1978).

25. See Walter Johnson, *River of Dark Dreams: Slavery and Empire in the Cotton Kingdom* (Cambridge, MA: Harvard University Press, 2013).

26. This interpretation is that of Andrew J. Torget's excellent work *Seeds of Empire: Cotton, Slavery, and the Transformation of the Texas Borderlands, 1800–1850* (Chapel Hill: University of North Carolina Press, 2015).

27. This account draws from Watson Jennison's insightful interpretation in *Cultivating Race: The Expansion of Slavery in Georgia, 1750–1860* (Lexington: University of Kentucky Press, 2012).

28. See Haveman, *Rivers of Sand*; Gregory D. Smithers, *The Cherokee Diaspora: An Indigenous History of Migration, Resettlement, and Identity* (New Haven, CT: Yale University Press, 2015); and Tim Alan Garrison, "Inevitability and the Southern Opposition to Indian Removal," in *The Native South: New Histories and Enduring Legacies,* ed. Tim Alan Garrison and Greg O'Brien (Lincoln: University of Nebraska Press, 2017), 107–25. For the specifics regarding land, see Mary Elizabeth Young, *Redskins, Ruffleshirts, and Rednecks: Indian Allotments in Alabama and Mississippi* (Norman: University of Oklahoma Press, 1961).

29. "Statements from the Debate on Indian Removal," Columbia University, http://www.columbia.edu/~lmg21/BC3180/removal.html, accessed Mar. 21, 2014.

30. See Chaplin, *Anxious Pursuit.*

31. America's domestic slave trade has been the subject of excellent studies. See Frederic Bancroft, *Slave Trading in the Old South* (1931; repr., New York: Frederic Ungar, 1959); Michael Tadman, *Speculators and Slaves: Masters, Traders, and Slaves in the Old South* (Madison: University of Wisconsin Press, 1996); Walter Johnson, *Soul by Soul: Inside the Antebellum Slave Market* (Cambridge, MA: Harvard University Press, 1999); Ira Berlin, *Generations of Captivity: A History of African-American Slaves* (Cambridge, MA: Harvard University Press, 2003); Calvin Schermerhorn, *Money over Mastery, Family over Freedom: Slavery in the Antebellum Upper South* (Baltimore: Johns Hopkins University Press, 2011); Maurie D. McInnis, *Slaves Waiting for Sale: Abolitionist Art and the American Slave Trade* (Chicago: University of Chicago Press, 2013); Johnson, *River of Dark Dreams*; Joshua D. Rothman, "The Contours of Cotton Capitalism: Speculation, Slavery, and Economic Panic in Mississippi, 1832–1841," in *Slavery's Capitalism: A New History of American Economic Development,* ed. Sven Beckert and Seth Rockman (Philadelphia: University of Pennsylvania Press, 2016), 122–46; Calvin Schermerhorn, *The Business of Slavery and the Rise of American Capitalism, 1815–1860* (New Haven, CT: Yale University Press, 2015); and Schermerhorn, *Unrequited Toil.*

32. See Caitlin Rosenthal, *Accounting for Slavery: Masters and Management* (Cambridge, MA: Harvard University Press, 2018).

33. On the migrations of free Black people, see the classic work by Ira Berlin, *Slaves without Masters: The Free Negro in the Antebellum South* (New York: Random House, 1974), 170–75.

34. Carter G. Woodson, *A Century of Negro Migration* (Washington, DC: Association for the Study of Negro Life and History, 1918), 17.

35. For a useful overview of the shifting network of escape, see Eric Foner, *Gateway to Freedom: The Hidden History of the Underground Railroad* (New York: W. W. Norton, 2015).

36. See S. Charles Bolton, *Fugitivism: Escaping Slavery in the Lower Mississippi Valley, 1820–1860* (Fayetteville: University of Arkansas Press, 2019); John Hope Franklin and Loren Schweninger, *Runaway Slaves: Rebels on the Plantation* (New York: Oxford University Press, 1999); Larry Eugene Rivers, *Rebels and Runaways: Slave Resistance in Nineteenth-Century Florida* (Urbana: University of Illinois Press, 2012); Matthew Clavin, *Aiming for Pensacola: Fugitive Slaves on the Atlantic and Southern Frontier* (Cambridge, MA: Harvard University Press, 2015); David Celeski, *The Waterman's Song: Slavery and Freedom in Maritime North Carolina* (Chapel Hill: University of North Carolina Press, 2001); Sylviane A. Diouf, *Slavery's Exiles: The Story of American Maroons* (New York: New York University Press, 2014); and Thomas C. Buchanan, *Black Life on the Mississippi: Slaves, Free Blacks, and the Western Steamboat World* (Chapel Hill: University of North Carolina Press, 2004).

37. See Smithers, *Native Southerners*; Claudio Saunt, "Financing Dispossession: Stocks, Bonds, and the Deportation of Native Peoples in the Antebellum United States," *Journal of American History* (Sept. 2019): 315–37; Theda Perdue, *Slavery and the Evolution of Cherokee Society, 1540–1866* (Knoxville: University of Tennessee Press, 1979); Michael D. Green, *The Politics of Indian Removal: Creek Government and Society in Crisis* (Lincoln: University of Nebraska Press, 1982); Merrell, *Indians' New World*; Miller, *Taking of American Indian Lands in the Southeast*; Smithers, *Cherokee Diaspora*; Haveman, *Rivers of Sand*; and Garrison, "Inevitability and the Southern Opposition to Indian Removal."

38. See Krauthamer, *Black Slaves, Indian Masters*, 9–10, 43–45. Jeffrey Ostler provides full, and painful, accounts of each nation's removal. He points out that while American Indians were "removed" in the North as well as the South, more people and a larger proportion of people were driven out of the South—64,000 of 75,000 compared to 24,000 of 48,000 in the North. A higher percentage of displaced southern Native peoples died as well, about 20 percent compared to about 12 percent. Ostler, *Surviving Genocide*, 189–90, 212, 247–87, 361.

39. Monaco, *Second Seminole War.*

40. Gina Caison argues: "Indigenous land claims are not terminated when or just because non-Native southerners feel attached to their homes. . . . Native people exist as national citizens of their own spaces and . . . despite attempts at removal, Native people and nations still exist regardless of how much or how little they have in common culturally, politically, or individually." *Red States: Indigeneity, Settler Colonialism, and Southern Studies* (Athens: University of Georgia Press, 2018), 6. Caison also reminds us that the southern landscape was "dotted with a complex network of distinct and interconnected sovereign nations beholden to one another as partners in a web." Also see Malinda Maynor Lowery, *The Lumbee Indians: An American Struggle* (Chapel Hill: University of North Carolina Press, 2018); Frank, "Red, Black, and Seminole," 46–67; Claudio Saunt, *Black, White, and Indian: Race and the Unmaking of an American Family* (New York: Oxford University Press, 2005); and Osburn, *Choctaw Resurgence.*

41. The numbers who remained varied from one people to another, and those who did remain often avoided census takers. Estimates range from a few hundred to a thousand or more Creeks, Cherokees, Chickasaws, Choctaws, and Seminoles. Email from Greg D. Smithers, Dec. 9, 2019, citing the following sources: Grant Foreman, *The Five Civilized Tribes: Cherokee, Chickasaw, Choctaw, Creek, Seminole* (Norman: University of Oklahoma Press, 1934); Arrell M. Gibson, *The Chickasaws* (Norman: University of Oklahoma Press, 1971); Arthur H. DeRosier Jr., *The Removal of the Choctaw Indians* (Knoxville: University of Tennessee Press, 1970); Russell Thornton, *The Cherokees: A Population History* (Lincoln: University of Nebraska Press, 1990); Carson, *Searching for the Bright Path*; Amanda L. Paige, Fuller L. Bumpers, and Daniel F. Littlefield, *Chickasaw Removal* (Ada, OK: Chickasaw, 2010); Haveman, *Rivers of Sand.*

42. Barbara Krauthamer offers penetrating comments on these issues in *Black Slaves, Indian Masters*, 2–11. See also Jane F. Lancaster, *Removal Aftershock: The Seminoles' Struggles to Survive in the West, 1836–1866* (Knoxville: University of Tennessee Press, 1994).

43. Saunt, "Financing Dispossession"; Osburn, *Choctaw Resurgence*, 21–29.

44. Sven Beckert, *Empire of Cotton: A Global History* (New York: Alfred Knopf, 2014).

45. Richard Follett, *The Sugar Masters: Planters and Slaves in Louisiana's Cane World, 1820–1860* (Baton Rouge: Louisiana State University Press, 2005).

46. The same human costs afflicted the other richest part of the slave South: the South Carolina rice district. Women had fewer children on the rice plantations than elsewhere, in part because of chronic malaria. The children they bore lived just half as long as those in other parts of the South; in one South Carolina county, more than 40 percent of children who reached five years of age died before they reached fifteen. Two-thirds of enslaved children in the rice districts did not live to the age of fifteen. William Dusinberre, *Them Dark Days: Slavery in the American Rice Swamps* (New York: Oxford University Press, 1996), 411–16.

47. David Hackett Fischer and James C. Kelly, *Bound Away: Virginia and the Westward Movement* (Charlottesville: University Press of Virginia, 2000), 137–40. Schermerhorn, *Money over Mastery*; Brenda E. Stevenson, *Life in Black and White: Family and Community in the Slave South* (New York: Oxford University Press, 1996).

48. Quoted in Lacy K. Ford, *Origins of Southern Radicalism: The South Carolina Upcountry, 1800–1860* (New York: Oxford University Press, 1988), 38. Ford paints a compelling picture of the upcountry.

49. John Hebron Moore, *The Emergence of the Cotton Kingdom in the Old Southwest: Mississippi, 1770–1860* (Baton Rouge: Louisiana State University Press, 1988).

50. Torget, *Seeds of Empire*; Randolph B. Campbell, *An Empire for Slavery: The Peculiar Institution in Texas, 1821–1865* (Baton Rouge: Louisiana State University Press, 1989); Barnes F. Lathrop, *Migration into East Texas, 1835–1860* (Austin: Texas State Historical Society, 1949).

51. This is the argument of Torget's excellent *Seeds of Empire*.

52. On railroads, see William G. Thomas, *The Iron Way: Railroads, the Civil War, and the Making of Modern America* (New Haven, CT: Yale University Press, 2011).

53. See David R. Goldfield, *Urban Growth in the Age of Sectionalism: Virginia, 1847–1861* (Baton Rouge: Louisiana State University Press, 1977); Schermerhorn, *Money over Mastery*.

54. Quoted in Ford, *Origins of Southern Radicalism*, 276.

55. See John C. Inscoe, ed., *Appalachians and Race: The Mountain South from Slavery to Segregation* (Lexington: University Press of Kentucky, 2001).

56. The following portrayal draws on a range of detailed and revealing studies I have tried to weave into the matrix of landscape and change in the maps of this book. See Oakes, *The Ruling Race*; Steven Hahn, *The Roots of Southern Populism: Yeoman Farmers and the Transformation of the Georgia Upcountry, 1850–1890* (New York: Oxford University Press, 1983); Bruce Collins, *White Society in the Antebellum South* (London: Longman's, 1985); J. William Harris, *Plain Folk and Gentry in a Slave Society: White Liberty and Black Slavery in Augusta's Hinterlands* (Middletown, CT: Wesleyan University Press, 1985); Orville Vernon Burton, *In My Father's House Are Many Mansions: Family and Community in Edgefield, South Carolina* (Chapel Hill: University of North Carolina Press, 1985); Gavin Wright, *Old South, New South: Revolutions in the Southern Economy since the Civil War* (New York: Basic Books, 1986); Joseph P. Reidy, *From Slavery to Agrarian Capitalism in the Cotton Plantation South: Central Georgia, 1800–1880* (Chapel Hill: University of North Carolina Press, 1992); Miller, "Plantation Labor Organization"; Charles C. Bolton, *Poor Whites of the Antebellum South: Tenants and Laborers in Central North Carolina and Northeast Mississippi* (Durham, NC: Duke University Press, 1994); Stephanie McCurry, *Masters of Small Worlds: Yeoman Households, Gender Relations, and the Political Culture of the Antebellum South Carolina Low Country* (New York: Oxford University Press, 1995); Samuel C. Hyde Jr., *Plain Folk of the South Revisited* (Baton Rouge: Louisiana State University Press, 1997); Morris, *Becoming Southern*; Timothy James Lockley, *Lines in the Sand: Race and Class in Lowcountry Georgia, 1750–1860* (Athens: University of Georgia Press, 2001); James David Miller, *South by Southwest: Planter Emigration and Identity in the Slave South* (Charlottesville: University of Virginia Press, 2002); Stephen A. West, *Yeoman to Redneck in the South Carolina Upcountry, 1850–1915* (Charlottesville: University of Virginia Press, 2008); Gary T. Edwards, "'Anything . . . That Would Pay': Yeoman Farmers and the Nascent Market Economy on the Antebellum Plantation Frontier," in *Southern Society and Its Transformations, 1790–1860*, ed. Susanna Delfino, Michele Gillespie, and Louis M. Kyriakoudes (Columbia: University of Missouri Press 2011), 102–29; David Brown, "A Vagabond's Tale: Poor Whites, Herrenvolk Democracy, and the Value of Whiteness in the Late Antebellum South," *Journal of Southern History* 79 (Nov. 2013), 799–840; Edward E. Baptist, *The Half Has Never Been Told: Slavery and the Making of American Capitalism* (New York: Basic Books, 2014); Bill Cecil-Fronsman, *Common Whites: Class and Culture in Antebellum North Carolina* (Lexington: University of Kentucky Press, 2015); Nancy Isenberg, *White Trash: The 400-Year Untold History of Class in America* (New York: Viking, 2016); Keri Leigh Merritt, *Masterless Men: Poor Whites and Slavery in the Antebellum South* (Cambridge: Cambridge University Press, 2017); Sydney Nathans, *Mind to Stay: White Plantation, Black Homeland* (Cambridge, MA: Harvard University Press, 2017); Tommy Craig Brown, *Deep in the Piney Woods: Southeastern Alabama from Statehood to the Civil War, 1800–1865* (Tuscaloosa: University of Alabama Press, 2018).

57. Don H. Doyle, *Faulkner's County: The Historical Roots of Yoknapatawpha* (Chapel Hill: University of North Carolina Press, 2001), 100. Doyle offers an equally penetrating study of a northern community in his *The Social Order of a Frontier Community: Jacksonville, Illinois, 1825–1870* (Urbana: University of Illinois Press, 1990). Also see John Mack Faragher, *Sugar Creek: Life on the Illinois Prairie* (New Haven, CT: Yale University Press, 1986). Following this shared formula, the newer states of the South kept pace with the growth of their counterparts above the Ohio River. In free population, Kentucky grew 178 percent between 1830 and 1860, while Ohio increased 149 percent. Alabama increased 176 percent and Indiana 294 percent. If enslaved people are included, the growth numbers are even closer for the Deep South, with Alabama growing 211 percent; Mississippi, 479 percent; Louisiana, 228 percent; and Arkansas, 1,335 percent. The North had its own squatters and speculators, its own agricultural poor and rich. Common areas were turned into private property in both regions. Settlers stayed in place no longer in the North than they did in the South, or vice versa.

58. On lower population density across the South and its consequences in comparison with the North, see William G. Thomas III and Edward L. Ayers, "The Differences Slavery Made: A Close Analysis of Two Communities," *American Historical Review* 108 (2003), at http://www2.vcdh.virginia.edu/AHR/.

59. William K. Scarborough, *Masters of the Big House: Elite Slaveholders of the Mid-Nineteenth-Century South* (Baton Rouge: Louisiana State University Press, 2003), 6–7.

60. Donald F. Schaefer, "Locational Choice in the Antebellum South," *Journal of Economic History* 49 (Mar. 1989): 145–65. He finds that "there is evidence that race (the proportion of whites in the population of a location) and the probability of choosing a location are positively associated for

nonslaveowning farmers. Second, locational choice and economic costs and benefits, as measured by the place characteristics, are strongly related for the nonslaveowning group." In other words, white farmers moved to places that made economic sense and where other white farmers lived.

61. These numbers come from a remarkable example of historical detective work. See Michael F. Doran, "Population Statistics of Nineteenth-Century Indian Territory," *Chronicles of Oklahoma* 53 (1975–76): 492–515.

62. See the excellent analysis in Daniel W. Crofts, *Reluctant Confederates: Upper South Unionists in the Secession Crisis* (Chapel Hill: University of North Carolina Press, 1989).

63. The study that best explains this connection is William L. Barney, *The Secessionist Impulse: Alabama and Mississippi in 1860* (Princeton, NJ: Princeton University Press, 1974), esp. 130–51. Barney ran tests for many variables to explain voting in those states and found that population growth rates explained those votes better than any other social indicator. Also see Collins, *White Society in the Antebellum South,* 97. Collins explains: "Only fresh farmlands, and the guarantee of future movement into them, would answer the future economic needs of so rootless, so young, and so determinedly agrarian a people. . . . For a denial of western expansion came, rightly or wrongly, to symbolize for Southerners a denial also of that geographical mobility which was a saving technique, a habit and almost a virtue in itself." While not focusing on population growth, Marc Egnal, in a useful survey of studies of voting on secession, argues that the state of origin of settlers shaped attitudes toward the Union, with migrants from the Upper South spreading unionism to states to their west and migrants from the Lower South spreading inclinations toward secession. See Egnal, "Rethinking the Secession of the Lower South: The Clash of Two Groups," *Civil War History* 50 (2004): 261–90.

2. THE RESTLESS SOUTH, 1860–1940

1. For a useful overview, see Yael A. Sternhell, *Routes of War: The World of Movement in the Confederate South* (Cambridge, MA: Harvard University Press, 2012).

2. See the enduring work of Mary Elizabeth Massey, *Refugee Life in the Confederacy* (Baton Rouge: Louisiana State University Press, 1964), and George C. Rable, *Civil Wars: Women and the Crisis of Southern Nationalism* (Urbana: University of Illinois Press, 1989). New perspectives appear in David Silkenat, *Driven from Home: North Carolina's Civil War Refugee Crisis* (Athens: University of Georgia Press, 2016); Stephanie E. Jones-Rogers, *They Were Her Property: White Women as Slave Owners in the American South* (New Haven, CT: Yale University Press, 2019); and W. Caleb McDaniel, *Sweet Taste of Liberty: A True Story of Slavery and Restitution in America* (New York: Oxford University Press, 2019).

3. Several excellent works help us understand the camps and their context. See Amy Murrell Taylor, *Embattled Freedom: Journeys through the Civil War's Slave Refugee Camps* (Chapel Hill: University of North Carolina Press, 2018); Chandra Manning, *Troubled Refuge: Struggling for Freedom in the Civil War* (New York: Alfred A. Knopf, 2016); and Jim Downs, *Sick from Freedom: African-American Illness and Suffering during the Civil War* (New York: Oxford University Press, 2012).

4. For a fascinating perspective on wartime contact between enslaved people and the U.S. Army, see the project overseen by Scott Nesbit, *Visualizing Emancipation,* Digital Scholarship Lab, University of Richmond, https://dsl.richmond.edu/emancipation/. For an attempt to see emancipation in a new way, see Edward L. Ayers and Scott Nesbit, "Seeing Emancipation: Scale and Freedom

in the American South," *Journal of the Civil War Era* 1 (Mar. 2011): 3–24. On Texas, see Julian Lim, *Porous Borders: Multiracial Migrations and the Law in the U.S.–Mexico Borderlands* (Chapel Hill: University of North Carolina Press, 2017).

5. On the Midwest, see Michael P. Johnson, "Out of Egypt: The Migration of Former Slaves to the Midwest during the 1860s in Comparative Perspective," in *Crossing Boundaries: Comparative History of Black People in Diaspora,* ed. Deborah Clark Hine and Jacqueline McLeod (Bloomington: Indiana University Press, 1999), 223-45 (quote, 228); and Leslie A. Schwalm, *Emancipation's Diaspora: Race and Reconstruction in the Upper Midwest* (Chapel Hill: University of North Carolina Press, 2009). On New England, see Janette Thomas Greenwood, *First Fruits of Freedom: The Migration of Former Slaves and Their Search for Equality in Worcester, Massachusetts, 1862–1900* (Chapel Hill: University of North Carolina Press, 2010); and Elizabeth H. Pleck, *Black Migration and Poverty in Boston, 1865–1900* (New York: Academic Press, 1979), 54–77.

6. See J. David Hacker, "A Census-Based Count of the Civil War Dead," *Civil War History* 57 (Dec. 2011): 307–48. A revealing state study appears in Hamilton Lombard, "The Demographic Impact of the Civil War in Virginia," Weldon Cooper Center for Public Service, University of Virginia, https://uvalibrary.maps.arcgis.com/apps/Cascade/index.html?appid=0d606d52ea0842308b399ff fbab8300c, accessed May 15, 2019.

7. Nancy Bercaw, *Gendered Freedoms: Race, Rights, and the Politics of Household in the Delta, 1861–1875* (Gainesville: University Press of Florida, 2003); Susan Eva O'Donovan, *Becoming Free in the Cotton South* (Cambridge, MA: Harvard University Press, 2007); Tera W. Hunter, *Bound in Wedlock: Slave and Free Black Marriage in the Nineteenth Century* (Cambridge, MA: Harvard University Press, 2017).

8. On competition for domestic work, see Thavolia Glymph, *Out of the House of Bondage: The Transformation of the Plantation Household* (Cambridge: Cambridge University Press, 2008), 157.

9. Quoted in Michael Wayne, *The Reshaping of Plantation Society: The Natchez District, 1860–1880* (Baton Rouge: Louisiana State University Press, 1983), 39.

10. Wayne, *Reshaping of Plantation Society,* 45. Some planters imported workers from China and Latin America, to little lasting effect.

11. Sven Beckert, *Empire of Cotton: A Global History* (New York: Alfred Knopf, 2014), 291–92.

12. I have detailed the events and transformations of the New South in *The Promise of the New South: Life after Reconstruction* (New York: Oxford University Press, 1992). For more on railroads, see R. Scott Huffard Jr., *Engines of Redemption: Railroads and the Reconstruction of Capitalism in the New South* (Chapel Hill: University of North Carolina Press, 2019).

13. Louis A. Ferleger and John D. Metz, *Cultivating Success in the South: Farm Households in the Postbellum Era* (Cambridge: Cambridge University Press, 2014); Wayne, *Reshaping of Plantation Society,* 45; Steven Hahn, *The Roots of Southern Populism: Yeoman Farmers and the Transformation of the Georgia Upcountry, 1850–1890* (New York: Oxford University Press, 1983).

14. Beckert, *Empire of Cotton,* 278, 311.

15. Erin Steward Mauldin, *Unredeemed Land: An Environmental History of Civil War and Emancipation in the Cotton South* (New York: Oxford University Press, 2018), 6–12.

16. See John C. Willis, *Forgotten Time: The Yazoo-Mississippi Delta after the Civil War* (Charlottesville: University Press of Virginia, 2000), 7–11; James C. Cobb, *The Most Southern Place on Earth: The Mississippi Delta and the Roots of Regional Identity* (New York: Oxford University Press, 1992);

Brian D. Page, "'In the Hands of the Lord': Migrants and Community Politics in the Late Nineteenth Century," in *An Unseen Light: Black Struggles for Freedom in Memphis, Tennessee,* ed. Aram Goudsouzian and Charles W. McKinney Jr. (Lexington: University Press of Kentucky, 2018), 13–38.

17. Nell Irvin Painter, *Exodusters* (New York: W. W. Norton, 1976); James H. Conrad, *Freedom Colonies: Independent Black Texans in the Time of Jim Crow* (Urbana: University of Illinois Press, 2005); Steven Hahn, *A Nation under Our Feet: Black Political Struggles in the Rural South from Slavery to the Great Migration* (Cambridge, MA: Harvard University Press, 2003). Ikuko Asaka points out, "As commonwealth settler societies steadily built themselves up into 'white men's countries,' the United States went through the final phase of western continental expansion without according African Americans equal access to its attendant material benefits or the symbolic status of the upwardly mobile frontier settler." *Tropical Freedom: Climate, Settler Colonialism, and Black Exclusion in the Age of Emancipation* (Durham, NC: Duke University Press, 2017), 24.

18. For powerful accounts of these struggles, see Mikaëla M. Adams, *Who Belongs?: Race, Resources, and Tribal Citizenship in the Native South* (New York: Oxford University Press, 2016); Gina Caison, *Red States: Indigeneity, Settler Colonialism, and Southern Studies* (Athens: University of Georgia Press, 2018); Rose Stremlau, *Sustaining the Cherokee Family: Kinship and the Allotment of an Indigenous Nation* (Chapel Hill: University of North Carolina Press, 2011); Katherine M. B. Osburn, *Choctaw Resurgence in Mississippi: Race, Class, and Nation Building in the Jim Crow South, 1830–1977* (Lincoln: University of Nebraska Press, 2014); and Christopher Arris Oakley, *New South Indians: Tribal Economics and the Eastern Band of Cherokee in the Twentieth Century* (Knoxville: University of Tennessee Press, 2018).

19. Michael J. Hightower, *1889: The Boomer Movement, the Land Run, and Early Oklahoma City* (Norman: University of Oklahoma Press, 2018); Michael F. Doran, "Population Statistics of Nineteenth-Century Indian Territory," *Chronicles of Oklahoma* 53 (1975–76): 492–515.

20. Kendra T. Field, "'No Such Thing as Stand Still': Migration and Geopolitics in African American History," *Journal of American History* 102 (Dec. 2015): 693–718; Field, *Growing Up with the Country: Family, Race, and Nation after the Civil War* (New Haven, CT: Yale University Press, 2018).

21. See Debra A. Reid and Evan P. Bennett, eds., *Beyond Forty Acres and a Mule: African American Landowning Families since Reconstruction* (Gainesville: University Press of Florida, 2012); and Robert C. Kenzer, *Enterprising Southerners: Black Economic Success in North Carolina, 1865–1915* (Charlottesville: University Press of Virginia, 1997).

22. Randolph B. Campbell, *Gone to Texas: A History of the Lone Star State* (New York: Oxford University Press, 2003), chaps. 9, 12.

23. See J. William Harris, *Deep Souths: Delta, Piedmont, and Sea Island Society in the Age of Segregation* (Baltimore: Johns Hopkins University Press, 2001), 120–31.

24. See Ayers, *Promise of the New South,* 156–59, with regressions on 501–3. The literature on lynching is enormous and growing, but the search for the determinants of lynching remain elusive—population change accounts for the patterns as fully as any other model. For a useful overview of the literature, see Amy Kate Bailey and Stewart E. Tolnay, *Lynched: The Victims of Southern Mob Violence* (Chapel Hill: University of North Carolina Press, 2015).

25. Gavin Wright, *Old South, New South: Revolutions in the Southern Economy since the Civil War* (New York: Basic Books, 1986), 65; George C. Wright, *Life behind a Veil: Blacks in Louisville, Kentucky, 1865–1930* (Baton Rouge: Louisiana State University Press, 1985), 43–44; Pleck, *Black Migration and Poverty in Boston,* 128-9.

26. Carter G. Woodson, *A Century of Negro Migration* (Washington, DC: Association for the Study of Negro Life and History, 1918), 161–65.

27. See Hightower, *1889.*

28. See Jason Carl Digman, "Which Way to the Promised Land? Changing Patterns of Southern Migration, 1865–1920" (PhD diss., University of Illinois, Chicago, 2001), 9.

29. Joseph A. Hill, "Interstate Migration," in *Supplementary Analysis and Derivative Tables: Twelfth census of the United States, 1900* (Washington, DC: U.S. Government Printing Office, 1906), 287–90.

30. The boll weevil's demographic consequences has produced a large literature, all of which challenges the common belief that the insect drove the first stages of the Great Migration. See James C. Giesen, *Boll Weevil Blues: Cotton, Myth, and Power in the American South* (Chicago: University of Chicago Press, 2015); Deirdre Bloome, James Feigenbaum, and Christopher Muller, "Tenancy, Marriage, and the Boll Weevil Infestation, 1892–1930," *Demography* 54 (2017): 1029–49; Fabian Lange, Alan L. Olmstead, and Paul W. Rhode, "The Impact of the Boll Weevil, 1892–1932," *Journal of Economic History* 69 (2009): 685–718; and Robert Higgs, "The Boll Weevil, the Cotton Economy, and Black Migration, 1910–1930," *Agricultural History* 50 (1976): 335–50. In general, these studies find that local and even individual actions interacted and counteracted one another so much that broad generalizations about the weevil's influence cannot be sustained.

31. See Jacquelyn Dowd Hall, James Leloudis, Robert Korstad, Mary Murphy, Lu Ann Jones, and Christopher B. Daly, *Like a Family: The Making of a Southern Cotton Mill World* (Chapel Hill: University of North Carolina Press, 1987), 106–11, 144 (quote); and David L. Carlton, *Mill and Town in South Carolina, 1880–1920* (Baton Rouge: Louisiana State University Press, 1982), 40, 132–33. For a useful account of the movement of a textile company from Massachusetts to Alabama and then succumbing to foreign competition, see Beth English, *A Common Thread: Labor, Politics, and Capital Mobility in the Textile Industry* (Athens: University of Georgia Press, 2006).

32. See Scott Reynolds Nelson, *Steel Drivin' Man: John Henry, the Untold Story of an American Legend* (New York: Oxford University Press, 2008).

33. See Ronald D. Eller, *Miners, Millhands, and Mountaineers: Industrialization of the Appalachian South, 1880–1930* (Knoxville: University of Tennessee Press, 1982); Robert S. Weise, *Grasping at Independence: Debt, Male Authority, and Mineral Rights in Appalachian Kentucky, 1850–1915* (Knoxville: University of Tennessee Press, 2001); and Richard A. Straw and H. Tyler Blethen, eds., *High Mountains Rising: Appalachia in Time and Place* (Urbana: University of Illinois Press, 2004).

34. There is, of course, a rich literature on the Great Migration. Of that work, I have found especially enlightening two collections of essays that crystallize a series of important studies from the 1980s: Joe William Trotter Jr., ed., *The Great Migration in Historical Perspective: New Dimensions of Race, Class, and Gender* (Bloomington: Indiana University Press, 1991), esp. the essays by Earl Lewis, Trotter, Peter Gottlieb, and Darlene Clark Hine; and Alferdteen Harrison, ed., *Black Exodus: The Great Migration from the American South* (Jackson: University Press of Mississippi, 1991), esp. the essays by Dernoral Harris, Carole Marks, James R. Grossman, and Neil R. McMillen. Helpful perspectives also appear in Daniel M. Johnson and Rex R. Campbell, *Black Migration in America: A Social Demographic History* (Durham, NC: Duke University Press, 1981); Neil Fligstein, *Going North: Migration of Blacks and Whites from the South, 1900–1950* (New York: Academic Press, 1981); Carole Marks, *Farewell—We're Good and Gone: The Great Black Migration* (Bloomington: Indiana University Press, 1989); and Neil R. McMillen, *Dark Journey: Black Mississippians in the Age of Jim Crow* (Urbana: University of Illinois Press, 1989). A beautiful account of the personal experiences

within generations-long migration, though it focuses more on the destination than the source of the migrations, is Isabel Wilkerson, *The Warmth of Other Suns: The Epic Story of America's Great Migration* (New York: Vintage, 2010). On World War I and the South more broadly, see Matthew L. Downs and M. Ryan Floyd, *The American South and the Great War, 1914–1924* (Baton Rouge: Louisiana State University Press, 2018).

35. R. H. Leavell quoted in U.S. Department of Labor, *Negro Migration in 1916–17*, reports by R. H. Leavell, T. R. Snavely, T. J. Woofter Jr, W. T. B. Williams, and Francis D. Tyson (Washington, DC: U.S. Government Printing Office, 1919), 20.

36. Harris, *Deep Souths*, 215–23 (quotes, 218, 219).

37. James H. Dillard, introduction to U.S. Department of Labor, *Negro Migration in 1916–17*, 9; Digman, "Which Way to the Promised Land?," 94–95.

38. William O. Scroggs, "Interstate Migration of the Negro Population," *Journal of Political Economy* 25 (1917): 1034–43.

39. James R. Grossman, *Land of Hope: Chicago, Black Southerners, and the Great Migration* (Chicago: University of Chicago Press, 1989), 259–65.

40. Darlene Clark Hine, "Black Migration to the Urban Midwest: The Gender Dimension, 1915–1945," in Trotter, *Great Migration in Historical Perspective*, 129–41.

41. Earl Lewis, "Expectations, Economic Opportunities, and Life in the Industrial Age: Black Migration to Norfolk, VA, 1910–1945," in Trotter, *Great Migration in Historical Perspective*, 22–45; and Lewis's exemplary *In Their Own Interests: Race, Class, and Power in Twentieth-Century Norfolk, Virginia* (Berkeley: University of California Press, 1991).

42. James N. Gregory, *The Southern Diaspora: How the Great Migrations of Black and White Southerners Transformed America* (Chapel Hill: University of North Carolina Press, 2005), 59–60, 83–89, 336; Chad Berry offers a sensitive analysis of white migrants from Appalachia in *Southern Migrants, Northern Exiles* (Urbana: University of Illinois Press, 2000). For a broad overview that links Black and white migrants, see Jacqueline Jones, *The Dispossessed: America's Underclass from the Civil War to the Present* (New York: Basic Books, 1992).

43. Thanks to the innovative work of James Gregory, based on the Integrated Public Use Microdata Series, we have much more precise numbers for twentieth-century American migration. Gregory offers these numbers (which are larger by 200,000 for white people and smaller by 70,000 people than previous numbers) in *Southern Diaspora*, 15; see also his methodological discussion on 329–58. The older numbers appear in Hope T. Eldridge and Dorothy Swain Thomas, *Population Redistribution and Economic Growth, United States, 1870–1950*, vol. 3, *Demographic Analyses and Interrelations* (Philadelphia: American Philosophical Society, 1964), 90, 99.

44. Giesen, *Boll Weevil Blues*, 141–68; Jack Temple Kirby, *Rural Worlds Lost: The American South, 1920–1960* (Baton Rouge: Louisiana State University Press, 1987), 144; Higgs, "Boll Weevil."

45. William A. Link, *Southern Crucible: The Making of an American Region* (New York: Oxford University Press, 2015), 433–37; Cobb, *Most Southern Place*, 129.

46. Thomas Graham, "The First Developers," in *The History of Florida*, ed. Michael Gannon (Gainesville: University Press of Florida, 1996), 276–95; William W. Rogers, "Fortune and Misfortune: The Paradoxical 1920s," ibid., 296–312.

47. George B. Tindall, *The Emergence of the New South, 1913–1945* (Baton Rouge: Louisiana State University Press, 1967), 76–78.

48. Gregory, *Southern Diaspora*, 26–28.

49. Tindal, *Emergence of the New South*, 354–67.

50. This account of the effects of the New Deal on the South draws from Tindall, *Emergence of the New South*, 391–430 (quotes, 409, 411–12); the numbers for Texas and Oklahoma come from ibid., 430. James Cobb portrays the role of the New Deal in *Most Southern Place*, 184–97, with details on tractors in the Delta on 188–89. Pete Daniel notes that Texas, Oklahoma, and the Mississippi Delta "mechanized first," and Arkansas planters soon followed. *Breaking the Land: The Transformation of Cotton, Tobacco, and Rice Cultures since 1880* (Urbana: University of Illinois Press, 1985), 175–79. The image of large machines demolishing an Oklahoma home was one of the haunting images of the film *The Grapes of Wrath* (1939).

51. Gilbert C. Fite, *Cotton Fields No More: Southern Agriculture, 1865–1980* (Lexington: University Press of Kentucky, 1984), 154–55.

52. Eller, *Miners, Millhands, and Mountaineers*, 239–40; Paul Salstrom, "The Great Depression," in Straw and Blethen, *High Mountains Rising*, 75–76.

53. Salstrom, "Great Depression," 79–80.

54. See James N. Gregory, *American Exodus: The Dust Bowl Migration and Okie Culture in California* (New York: Oxford University Press, 1989), 15–19, esp. map on 18.

3. ARRIVAL AND RETURN, 1940–2020

1. On the South and World War II, see Charles D. Chamberlain, *Victory at Home: Manpower and Race in the American South during World War II* (Athens: University of Georgia Press, 2003); Neil R. McMillen and Morton Sosna, eds., *Remaking Dixie: The Impact of World War II on the American South* (Jackson: University Press of Mississippi, 2007); Bruce J. Schulman, *From Cotton Belt to Sunbelt: Federal Policy, Economic Development, and the Transformation of the South, 1938–1980* (New York: Oxford University Press, 1991); Robert J. Norrell, *Dixie's War: The South and World War II* (Washington, DC: National Endowment for the Humanities, 1992); and Robert Lewis, "World War II Manufacturing and the Postwar Southern Economy," *Journal of Southern History* 73 (Nov. 2007): 837–66. Lewis writes: "The new economy, however, should not be viewed as emerging out of the cauldron of the war. Wartime changes have to be seen as part of a transitional period spanning the 1930s through to the 1960s. They were at best only one step in a much longer process of regional change in which the South slowly, hesitantly, and painfully moved from an agrarian and low-wage, nondurable economy to one centered on petrochemicals, aerospace, and tourism." Ibid., 866.

2. Dos Passos quoted in Schulman, *Cotton Belt to Sunbelt*, 88.

3. Chamberlain, *Victory at Home*, 17; Randolph B. Campbell, *Gone to Texas: A History of the Lone Star State* (New York: Oxford University Press, 2003), 396.

4. Monica R. Gisolfi, *The Takeover: Chicken Farming and the Roots of American Agribusiness* (Athens: University of Georgia Press, 2017), 33–34.

5. Gisolfi, *Takeover*, 2–25.

6. Perla M. Guerrero, *Nuevo South: Latinas/os, Asians, and the Remaking of Place* (Austin: University of Texas Press, 2017), 35–36; Angela Stuesse, *Scratching Out a Living: Latinos, Race, and Work in the Deep South* (Berkeley: University of California Press, 2016).

7. Harry D. Fornar, "The Big Change: Cotton to Soybeans," *Agricultural History* 53 (Jan. 1979): 245–53; Pete Daniel, *Breaking the Land: The Transformation of Cotton, Tobacco, and Rice Cultures since 1880* (Urbana: University of Illinois Press, 1985), 248–52; Gilbert C. Fite, *Cotton Fields No More: Southern Agriculture, 1865–1980* (Lexington: University of Kentucky Press, 1984), 194–200.

8. H. C. Nixon quoted in George B. Tindall, *The Emergence of the New South, 1913–1945* (Baton Rouge: Louisiana State University Press, 1967), 731.

9. Ronald D. Eller, *Uneven Ground: Appalachia since 1945* (Lexington: University Press of Kentucky, 2008); Chad Berry, *Southern Migrants, Northern Exiles* (Urbana: University of Illinois Press, 2000), 100–110.

10. James N. Gregory, *The Southern Diaspora: How the Great Migrations of Black and White Southerners Transformed America* (Chapel Hill: University of North Carolina Press, 2005), 14. Here and throughout, I have used Gregory's estimates for population change. He has revised estimates for the 1960s and 1970s in light of new work. See Gregory, "The Southern Diaspora (Black, White, and Latinx)", America's Great Migrations Project, University of Washington, https://depts .washington.edu/moving1/diaspora.shtml.

11. Gary Ross Mormino, *Land of Sunshine, State of Dreams: A Social History of Modern Florida* (Gainesville: University Press of Florida, 2005), 8–38.

12. See Isabel Wilkerson, *The Warmth of Other Suns: The Epic Story of America's Great Migration* (New York: Vintage, 2010).

13. See Charles M. Payne, *I've Got the Light of Freedom: The Organizing Tradition and the Mississippi Freedom Struggle* (Berkeley: University of California Press, 1995); John Dittmer, *Local People: The Struggle for Civil Rights in Mississippi* (Urbana: University of Illinois Press, 1994); Steven F. Lawson, "Long Origins of the Short Civil Rights Movement, 1954–1968," in *Freedom Rights: New Perspectives on the Civil Rights Movement,* ed. Danielle L. McGuire and John Dittmer (Lexington: University Press of Kentucky, 2011), 9–37.

14. Harvard Sitkoff, "African American Militancy in the World War II South: Another Perspective," in McMillen and Sosna, *Remaking Dixie,* 70–92.

15. Leah Platt Boustan, *Competition in the Promised Land: Black Migrants in Northern Cities and Labor Markets* (Princeton, NJ: Princeton University Press, 2017).

16. Gavin Wright makes this point persuasively in *Sharing the Prize: The Economics of the Civil Rights Revolution in the American South* (Cambridge, MA: Harvard University Press, 2013).

17. Quoted in Wright, *Sharing the Prize,* 24–25. For a useful overview of the interrelated changes in the region, see James C. Cobb, *The South and America since World War II* (New York: Oxford University Press, 2012).

18. Wright, *Sharing the Prize,* 142–43.

19. Wright, *Sharing the Prize,* 28–29.

20. See Boustan, *Competition in the Promised Land,* 154–56.

21. See Mikaëla M. Adams, *Who Belongs? Race, Resources, and Tribal Citizenship in the Native South* (New York: Oxford University Press, 2016). Adams traces the distinct experiences of six southeastern tribes: the Pamunkey Indian Tribe of Virginia, the Catawba Indian Nation of South Carolina, the Mississippi Band of Choctaw Indians, the Eastern Band of Cherokee Indians of North Carolina, the Seminole Tribe of Florida, and the Miccosukee Tribe of Indians of Florida. A valuable perspective also appears in Christopher Arris Oakley, *New South Indians: Tribal Economics and the Eastern Band of Cherokee in the Twentieth Century* (Knoxville: University of Tennessee Press, 2018). J. Douglas Smith, *Managing White Supremacy: Race, Politics, and Citizenship in Jim Crow Virginia* (Chapel Hill: University of North Carolina Press, 2002), details the struggles of Virginia's American Indians to defend themselves in the face of determined efforts to classify them as "colored." See, in particular, pp. 94–98.

22. Fite, *Cotton Fields No More,* 225–26.

23. For penetrating analyses of these patterns, see James C. Cobb, "Chasing Smokestacks: Lessons and Legacies," 316–31; and Peter A. Coclanis, "Failing to Excite: The Dixie Dynamo in the Global Economy," 332–53, in *New Voyages to Carolina: Reinterpreting North Carolina History,* ed. Larry E. Tise and Jeffrey J. Crow (Chapel Hill: University of North Carolina Press, 2017); and Pete Daniel, *Dispossession: Discrimination against African American Farmers in the Age of Civil Rights* (Chapel Hill: University of North Carolina Press, 2013).

24. For powerful overviews of these changes, see Jack Temple Kirby, *Rural Worlds Lost: The American South, 1920–1960* (Baton Rouge: Louisiana State University Press, 1987), and Pete Daniel, *Lost Revolutions: The South in the 1950s* (Chapel Hill: University of North Carolina Press, 2000).

25. Mark H. Rose and Raymond A. Mohl, *Interstate: Highway Politics and Policy since 1939,* 3rd ed. (Knoxville: University of Tennessee Press, 2012).

26. Gisolfi, *Takeover,* 41. For a powerful case study and details on "nuggets," see Bryant Simon, *The Hamlet Fire: A Tragic Story of Cheap Food, Cheap Government, and Cheap Lives* (New York: New Press, 2017), 94–95.

27. Gisolfi, *Takeover,* 63; Stuesse, *Scratching Out a Living.*

28. Raymond A. Mohl and Gary R. Mormino, "Boom, Bust, and Uncertainty: A Social History of Modern Florida," in *The History of Florida,* ed. Michael Gannon, rev. and expanded ed. (Gainesville: University Press of Florida, 2018), 497–528.

29. Raymond A. Mohl and George E. Pozzetta, "Immigration and Ethnicity in Florida History," in Gannon, *History of Florida,* 470–96.

30. Julie M. Weise, *Corazón de Dixie: Mexicanos in the U.S. South since 1910* (Chapel Hill: University of North Carolina Press, 2015).

31. Campbell, *Gone to Texas,* 456; "Immigrants in Texas," Fact Sheet, American Immigration Council, https://www.americanimmigrationcouncil.org/research/immigrants-in-texas; James David Nichols, *The Limits of Liberty: Mobility and the Making of the Eastern U.S.-Mexico Border* (Lincoln: University of Nebraska Press, 2018); Ana Raquel Minian, *Undocumented Lives: The Untold Story of Mexican Migration* (Cambridge, MA: Harvard University Press, 2018).

32. Hannah Gill, *The Latino Migration Experience in North Carolina: New Roots in the Old North State* (Chapel Hill: University of North Carolina Press, 2010).

33. Douglas S. Massey, ed., *New Faces in New Places: The Changing Geography of American Immigration* (New York: Russell Sage Foundation, 2008).

34. Cameron D. Lippard and Charles A. Gallagher, eds., *Being Brown in Dixie: Race, Ethnicity, and Latino Immigration in the New South* (Boulder, CO: FirstForum, 2011).

35. Perla Guerrero offers a powerful portrait of these changes in *Nuevo South.*

36. Perla Guerrero makes this point effectively in *Nuevo South,* 17.

37. See David M. Reimers, "Asian Immigrants in the South," in *Globalization and the American South,* ed. James C. Cobb and William Stueck (Athens: University of Georgia Press, 2005), 100–134; and Jigna Desai and Khyati Y. Joshi, *Asian Americans in Dixie* (Urbana: University of Illinois Press, 2013).

38. Desai and Joshi, *Asian Americans in Dixie,* 19–20.

39. See David R. Goldfield, *Cotton Fields and Skyscrapers: Southern City and Region, 1607–1980* (Baton Rouge: Louisiana State University Press, 1982).

40. Mormino, *Land of Sunshine,* 32.

41. Mormino, *Land of Sunshine*, 129–32.

42. Andrew C. Baker, *Bulldozer Revolutions: A Rural History of the Metropolitan South* (Athens: University of Georgia Press, 2018), 4.

43. Baker, *Bulldozer Revolutions;* "The Double Standard at Work: European Corporate Investment and Workers' Rights in the American South," AFL-CIO, Oct. 2019, https://aflcio.org/sites/default/files/2019-10/EuroSouth_Oct2019_FINAL.pdf.

44. Andrew Wiese, *Places of Their Own: African American Suburbanization in the Twentieth Century* (Chicago: University of Chicago Press, 2004), 165–74.

45. William H. Frey, *Diversity Explosion: How New Racial Demographics Are Remaking America* (Washington, DC: Brookings Institution Press, 2014), 125; Cobb, *South and America since World War II.*

46. "After Nearly 100 Years, Great Migration Begins Reversal," *USA Today*, updated Mar. 8, 2015, https://www.usatoday.com/story/news/nation/2015/02/02/census-great-migration-reversal/218 18127/.

47. For a detailed overview of these remarkable changes, see Frey, *Diversity Explosion.*

48. Tina Morris, Paula L. Vines, and Elizabeth M. Hoeffel, *The American Indian and Alaska Native Population: 2010*, 2010 Census Briefs, U.S. Census Bureau, Jan. 2012, https://www.census.gov/content/dam/Census/library/publications/2012/dec/c2010br-10.pdf; Roberta Estes, "Indians and the Census, 1790–2010," *Native Heritage Project* (blog), May 14, 2013, https://nativeheritage project.com/2013/05/14/indians-and-the-census-1790-2010/.

49. For the political dynamics of southern suburbs, see Matthew D. Lassiter, *The Silent Majority: Suburban Politics in the Sunbelt South* (Princeton, NJ: Princeton University Press, 2006), and Matthew D. Lassiter and Joseph Crespino, eds., *The Myth of Southern Exceptionalism* (New York: Oxford University Press, 2010).

50. See Avidit Acharya, Matthew Blackwell, and Maya Sen, *Deep Roots: How Slavery Still Shapes Southern Politics* (Princeton, NJ: Princeton University Press, 2018), 209. The authors argue that the strongest indicator of white conservatism remains the earlier presence of slavery and its dislocating aftermath, what they call "behavioral path dependence." Another recent survey, Angie Maxwell and Todd Shields, *The Long Southern Strategy: How Chasing White Voters in the South Changed American Politics* (New York: Oxford University Press, 2019), argues that Republican strategists since the 1960s had to "mirror" southern white culture.

51. The indispensable source as the crisis unfolded, and the basis for the map displayed here, was the Coronavirus Resource Center at Johns Hopkins University, available at http://coronavirus.jhu.edu/us-map.

52. Olivia Paschal, "Here's What's Driving the Rural South's COVID-19 Outbreaks," https://www.facingsouth.org/2020/05/here%27s-what%27s-driving-rural-souths-covid-19-outbreaks.

53. Texas and Florida, with long histories of immigration from Latin America, saw nearly half of their statewide infections in people of that ethnicity, while North Carolina and Virginia, states with more recent arrivals of Latin American ancestry, saw proportions almost as high, patterns followed by Arkansas, Georgia, Kentucky, and South Carolina. Black people in every southern state other than Virginia contracted the virus at rates higher than their share of the population, with ratios particularly high in Alabama and Mississippi.

See the COVID Racial Data Tracker project at https://covidtracking.com/race. On the rates of death, see the report from the Centers for Disease Control and Prevention, https://www.cdc.gov/mmwr/volumes/69/wr/mm6928e1.htm?s_cid=mm6928e1_w.

54. See the maps in Audra D. S. Burch, Weiyi Cai, Gabriel Gianordoli, Morrigan McCarthy, and Jugal K. Patel, "How Black Lives Matter Reached Every Corner of America," *New York Times*, June 13, 2020, https://www.nytimes.com/interactive/2020/06/13/us/george-floyd-protests-cities-photos.html.

APPENDIX: THE METHOD OF MAPPING MIGRATIONS

1. A "union" is a spatial analytical process that combines two or more layers into one single feature.

2. This formula appears in the documentation for Chris Prener and C. Revord, "Areal: An R Package for Areal Weighted Interpolation," *Journal of Open Source Software* 37 (2019): 1221, https://slu-opengis.github.io/areal/articles/areal-weighted-interpolation.html. It is used with kind permission.

3. Elisabeth S Nelson, "Using Selective Attention Theory to Design Bivariate Point Symbols." *Cartographic Perspectives* 32 (1999): 6–28.

SOURCES FOR MAPS

Most of the maps for this book were created by Justin Madron and designed by Nathaniel Ayers from the data sources listed below. Other maps, separately listed, were adapted from previous publications, for which we are grateful.

SOILS

Soil Survey Staff, Web Soil Survey, Natural Resources Conservation Service, U.S. Department of Agriculture, https://websoilsurvey.nrcs.usda.gov/, accessed Dec. 16, 2019.

POPULATION CHANGE

John Long et al., "Atlas of Historical County Boundaries," Dr. William M. Scholl Center for American History and Culture, Newberry Library, https://publications .newberry.org/ahcbp/.

Steven Manson, Jonathan Schroeder, David Van Riper, and Steven Ruggles, IPUMS National Historical Geographic Information System: Version 14.0 (Database), University of Minnesota, 2019, http://doi.org/10.18128/D050.V14.0.

RAILROADS

Railroads and the Making of Modern America, University of Nebraska, Lincoln, 2006–17, http://railroads.unl.edu/resources/.

VOTING

MIT Election Data and Science Lab, 2018, "County Presidential Election Returns 2000–2016," https://doi.org/10.7910/DVN/VOQCHQ, Harvard Dataverse, V6, UNF:6:ZZe1xuZ5H214NUiSRcRf8Q== [fileUNF].

DOMESTIC MIGRATION

"Estimates of the Components of Resident Population Change: April 1, 2010, to July 1, 2018," U.S. Census Bureau, Population Division, https://factfinder.census. gov/faces/tableservices/jsf/pages/productview.xhtml?src=bkmk.

Release Dates: For the United States, regions, divisions, states, and Puerto Rico Commonwealth, December 2018. For counties, metropolitan statistical areas, micropolitan statistical areas, metropolitan divisions, and combined statistical areas, April 2019. See "County Population Totals and Components of Change: 2010–2018," U.S. Census Bureau, https://www.census.gov/data/tables/time-series/demo/popest/2010s-counties-total.html.

HEALTH DATA

Behavioral Risk Factor Surveillance System, National Center for Chronic Disease Prevention and Health Promotion, Centers for Disease Control and Prevention, last update, Nov. 5, 2019, https://www.cdc.gov/brfss/.

POVERTY

American Community Survey Data, U.S. Census Bureau, https://www.census.gov/programs-surveys/acs/data.html.

SPECIFIC MAPS AND FIGURES

Indigenous Peoples, Communication and Trade Routes, and Spanish Territory

Helen Hornbeck Tanner, "The Land and Water Communication Systems of the Southeastern Indians," in *Powhatan's Mantle: Indians in the Colonial Southeast*, ed. Gregory A. Waselkov, Peter H. Wood, and M. Thomas Hatley, rev. ed. (Lincoln: University of Nebraska Press, 2006), 27–42, map on 29.

Cessions of Indigenous Lands Between 1814 and 1835

Thomas D. Clark and John D. W. Guice, *Frontiers in Conflict: The Old Southwest, 1795–1830* (Albuquerque: University of New Mexico Press, 1989), 239.

Figure 1.1. Prices for Enslaved People

Samuel H. Williamson and Louis P. Cain, "Measuring Slavery in 2016 Dollars," MeasuringWorth.com, https://www.measuringworth.com/slavery.php#footstar.

Louisiana Sugar Parishes, 1860

Richard Follett, *Sugar Masters: Planters and Slaves in Louisiana's Cane World, 1820–1860* (Baton Rouge: Louisiana State University Press, 2005), frontispiece. Adapted with permission of the author.

Percentage of Foreign-Born Population, 1860

"Foreign-Born Population, 1850–2010," American Panorama, Digital Scholarship Lab, University of Richmond, http://dsl.richmond.edu/panorama/foreignborn.

Election of 1860

"United States Presidential Election Results by County (1860)," Wikimedia Commons, July 5, 2013.

Minnesota Population Center, National Historical Geographic Information System: Version 2.0 (database), University of Minnesota, 2011, http://www.nhgis.org.

Emancipation, 1861–1865

Visualizing Emancipation, Digital Scholarship Lab, University of Richmond, http://dsl.richmond.edu/emancipation/.

Eastern Refugee Camps and Western Refugee Camps

Adapted from Chandra Manning, *Troubled Refuge: Struggling for Freedom in the Civil War* (New York: Alfred A. Knopf, 2016), 42–43, 98. Used with permission of the author.

Percentage of People Living in Small Towns, 1880 and 1900

Adapted from Edward L. Ayers, *The Promise of the New South: Life after Reconstruction* (New York: Oxford University Press, 1992), 18–19.

Spread of the Boll Weevil

W. D. Hunter and B. R. Coad, *The Boll-Weevil Problem*, U.S. Department of Agriculture Farmers' Bulletin 1239 (Washington, DC: USDA, 1923), 8.

The Interstate Highway System

Nathaniel Baum-Snow, "Do Highways Cause Suburbanization?," *Quarterly Journal of Economics* 122 (2007): 775–805.

Clayton Nall, "Replication Data for: 'The Political Consequences of Spatial Policies: How Interstate Highways Facilitated Geographic Polarization,'" Harvard Dataverse, V1, https://dataverse.harvard.edu/dataset.xhtml?persistentId=doi:10.7910/DVN/29641. Data matched with NHPN Data using a near analysis to transfer mile-marker openings to more detailed interstate data.

Confirmed Cases of COVID-19 by Population, Spring 2020

Coronavirus COVID-19 Global Cases by the Center for Systems Science and Engineering (CSSE) at Johns Hopkins University; the Red Cross; the Census American Community Survey; the Bureau of Labor and Statistics.

INDEX